Cavalry Fighter Pilot . . . and Three Wars

Cavalry Trooper to Fighter Pilot . . . and Three Wars

by
Colonel Jack W. Hayes

Sunflower University Press®
1531 Yuma • P. O. Box 1009 • Manhattan, Kansas 66505-1009 USA

Cover: "*Cavalry Sabre*," the North American F-86 Sabre of World War II Cavalry officer, bomber and fighter pilot Colonel Jack W. Hayes attempting to intercept a Russian MiG-15 flown by Soviet ace Casey Jones. The engagement occurred over the Yalu River on the Sino-North Korean border, February 1952.

The painting by David Pentland was selected to appear in the 1997 Guild of Aviation Artists Exhibition in London.

ISBN 0-89745-213-5

Edited by Amie Goins

Layout by Lori L. Daniel

To
Margee Lou

Contents

Jack Hayes in his P-51 Mustang, September 1944, at Leiston Army Air Base, England, awaiting the "start engine" signal for bomber escort.

The Fighter Pilot

*S*AY WHAT YOU *will about him: arrogant, cocky, boisterous, and a fun-loving fool to boot — he has earned his place in the sun! Across the span of sixty-some years he has given this country, and its allies, some of the proudest moments and most cherished military traditions.*

But fame is short-lived and little the world remembers. Almost forgotten are the 1,400 fighter pilots who stood alone against the might of Hitler's Germany during the dark summer of 1940 and in the words of Sir Winston Churchill gave England "Its finest hour." Gone from the hardstands of England, Europe, and Africa are the P-51s, which along with -47s and -38s terrorized the finest fighter squadrons the Luftwaffe had. Dimly remembered — the fighter pilots that gave Americans some of their few proud moments in the skies over Korea, how fresh in recall are the air commandos who valiantly struck with their aging "Skyraiders" in the rain- and blood-soaked valley called "A Shau." And how long will be remembered the "Thuds" over "Route Pack Six" and the flak-filled skies over Hanoi.

So here's a "nickel on the grass" to you, my friend, for all your spirit, enthusiasm, sacrifice, and courage — but most of all your friendship. Yours is a dying breed and when you are gone, the world will be a lesser place.

Source Unknown

Chuck Yeager and the experimental aircraft that broke the sound barrier, *Glamorous Glennis*.

Foreword

$\mathcal{Y}$ HAVE KNOWN Jack Hayes, personally and by reputation, since I returned to the 357th Fighter Group after D-Day, June 6, 1944, after being shot down.

Jack was on his eternal quest for more fighter experience. Our paths crossed often: in March 1968, I relieved him of command of the 4th Tactical Fighter Wing in South Korea during the *Pueblo* incident. I was in the F-4 Pilot's School when the deployment was directed and was ordered to complete transition before reporting to Kunsan, South Korea. We met again when the Lockheed F-104 Starfighter Training terminated at Luke AFB, Arizona. I still remember his look when I told him that NASA was going to *pay me* to fly the "Beauty" F-104 as part of the Space Program!

Jack's book is interesting, humorous, and an insight into the actualities of combat flying. The World War II "go-to-hell" attitude he describes was slow to die!

Chuck Yeager
Cedar Ridge, California

To Jack Hayes
With respect and admiration
to a great fighter pilot.
Bob Hoover

Bob Hoover.

A Note to the Reader

I HAVE KNOWN Jack Hayes since he commanded a fighter squadron converting from the P-80 Shooting Star, the second operational jet in our Air Force, to the swept-wing F-86 Sabre Jet, the first airplane capable of going supersonic in a steep dive. At the time, 1950, I was an experimental test pilot for the North American Aviation Company.

Jack had a well-established reputation as a responsible fighter squadron and fighter group commander, whose leadership qualities were well recognized. He flew eight different types of combat aircraft in three wars, shot up his share of targets, and was injured twice. I was sent to bases under Jack's command on several occasions to demonstrate the F-86 Sabre Jet and F-100 Super Sabre. After his retirement we performed at many airshows together.

Cavalry Trooper to Fighter Pilot . . . and Three Wars is a great description of the life of a fighter pilot — serious, humorous, as appropriate.

We are fortunate that Jack decided to put his memories, history, and accomplishments into a book for all of us to share. He brings a different approach to the history of air warfare.

Bob Hoover
Palos Verdes Estates, California

Chapter 1

Citizens Military Training Camp

$\mathcal{Y}$OU HAVE TO understand the life, economics, and politics of America in the 1930s to appreciate the almost impossible odds facing those realists who believed that the days of peace and honey were about to "turn dark brown," as we fighter pilots would put it! Days of "America First" isolationism, Depression, and the world's hero, Charles Lindbergh, worshipping at the feet of the Third Reich. You can't be more wrong than that! Maybe flying across the Atlantic by yourself for 34 or so hours really doesn't qualify a guy in the field of international affairs! Certainly not *that* Ace!

Lindbergh waved the swastika and supported the Axis until we got the bejeezus kicked out of us in the Pacific! Once he figured out who the "Bad Guys" were,

> . . . the days of peace and honey were about to "turn dark brown," as we fighter pilots would put it!

however, he contributed immeasurably to the P-38 Lightning long-range cruise performance and was reputed to have clobbered a Rising Star Japanese fighter or two. But he never regained the status he could have had, at least among the gents kicking ass with his former idols.

Our Depression President, Franklin D. Roosevelt, handled this. In the late '30s and early '40s, he showed slick sleight-of-hand in sneaking things like fighters, transports, all sorts of weapons — even by-God *destroyers* — to England and Russia! Now that's sneaky, especially with stuff that size!

So the folks who suspected that the olive branches might be up to their pits in termites, knew they had to take some — *any* — kind of action to keep from joining the list of "histories," like *Rise and Fall of the Roman Empire*.

From kindergarten, I have faced severe career limitations because of losing battles with scholastics. Odd, because I was an avid reader all my life, sort of an Abe Lincoln type, except for the candlelight and developing a brilliant mind.

Despite my close familiarity with the deepest literature, I barely slid through junior high, then graduated from an Augustinian High School because: 1. I played football; 2. I was a fair altar boy, despite kneeling, bowing, and standing in the wrong order; and 3. My mother threatened to sue the diocese and the Vatican if her boy didn't wear that funny hat with his classmates.

I skidded through San Diego State College, Omega Xi Fraternity, from 1936 to 1940, when I barely had enough credits to qualify for United States Army Air Corps flying cadet pilot training. The way I was building up "credits" — or better, "debits" — saved my rear. I might not have graduated until 1960 — or would have been eligible for Social Security, whichever came first!

Since my first days of attaining reading skills, which were well above the norm (amazing, considering my troubles with math, biology, history, and especially penmanship; my handwriting is still compared to that of an inebriated physician, endowed with less than the normal assignment of pills), I was enchanted with military history. I considered Attila the Hun a real tiger; recognized that Hannibal started the panzer concept with all those elephants; and still think that Custer was a victim of poor officiating!

In order to provide a minimal source of partially trained officer and enlisted cadre upon which to base an expanded Department of the Army, eight existing Regular Army posts across the nation were designated "Citizens Military Training Camps." The Citizens Military Training Camps (CMTC) were legislated by far-seeing and dedicated military/civilian figures of the early and mid-1930s who recognized the beginning storm clouds and the requirement for added military strength.

The CMTCs provided 30-day summer training sessions for civilian volunteers labeled "candidates." Enrollees received travel expenses, uniforms, food, and lodging (tents). With completion of four camps and some additional weekend training, commissions as second lieutenant, U.S. Army Reserve, were bestowed, requiring annual retraining to remain on the active lists.

I enlisted in the CMTC at 15 years old, falsified by two years, but not a criminal departure from the truth since the Army was scrounging for applicants and the only one who suffered was me. I found it tough keeping pace with guys two to seven years older, who were further advanced physically and mentally. And their experience in sexual activities and the bull sessions revealed an unknown world to this rookie!

Three high school classmates joined with me; they were at the proper age, for whatever that's worth, between our sophomore and junior years.

We were sent to the Presidio of Monterey, California, which offered training in three Army branches. The first year was in the Infantry, for Basic Training. The candidate could then "march on," or select Cavalry or Field Artillery, both horse-powered and still active, now designated "Mechanized," "Air Mobile," and other glitzy titles.

I volunteered for Cavalry in the last two years of training, which was as far as I went. Prompting this selection were the emotions and rationale that evoked my desire for the pursuit/fighter branches when I entered Air Corps pilot training — a desire that intensified throughout my flying career. The dash, flair, flamboyance, and individualism of the Cavalry trooper were reflected in the fighter pilots of World War I, World War II, Korea, and Vietnam.

First Year — Infantry
My fellow soldiers and I had led what could be called sheltered lives.

We did do a little smoking and throwing up, however; and for a long time, we thought that they went together! We had obeyed our folks, which beat getting bad things done to you, and learned that there were things a young man could do with his hand, or fist, which were lots of fun, unless God or an Angel caught you — and then you might find the hand, or fist, starting at your elbow! I thought I could overcome this by keeping my hands in my side pockets, but found the area much too warm, and so I walked around with my hands on my hips. You can imagine the guys that attracted!

Despite being the rawest of recruits, it was amazing that we encountered little of the harsh treatment met by those of World War II and of the boot camps of today. This was no doubt because at the time the Army was encouraging career interest, as Citizens Military Training Camps and Reserve Officer Training Corps (ROTC) were the only sources of officer material.

We had trepidations about the United States Army instructors who were to mold our military careers, as they were reputed to be derelicts, criminals (who had been given a choice at sentencing, X number of years at hard labor, or enlistment in the Army!), or failures from the rigors of civilian life. But those I met in CMTC and Army Air Corps pre-war days fit none of those categories. They were different, and showed self-respect and dignity in the face of arrogance and demeaning attitudes from civilians and their signs, "Dogs and soldiers not allowed."

Although attitudes toward trainees were less demeaning in my day, the training would be familiar to any rookie of this century: the Manual of Arms (shifting a rifle from all kinds of odd positions to whatever stance the driller expected the drillee and rifle to end up at). The relevance to combat was constantly described — and just as constantly escaped me — and close order drill (marching forever!), familiarity with weapons, and qualification firing.

There were many memorable hours sitting on the ground or in bleachers, listening to monotone reading from Army manuals on intriguing subjects like Field Sanitation, Manual of Courts-Martial, Location and Construction of Latrines (johns, toilets) in the field, the Infantryman on the Offense, the Infantryman on the Defense. We guessed that the Infantryman never retreated, because we never heard about that.

We progressed on to squad, platoon, and company deployment and tactics. And *the* attention-getter — the risk, avoidance, and *treatment* of venereal diseases. Because risk and avoidance don't work, you gotta treat! Training films were a rarity, so we were spared those VD shockers, though there were dissertations from hard-bitten Docs who had been the route and could nauseate and terrorize as well as the best, or worst, film. When listeners barely clear the seated area before upchuck, that's graphic!

The only exception to my protected early days was that Dad started me off on exhibition and tournament boxing at the age of 12! I advanced from "freebies" to 25¢ a bout, and finally, $2.50 per — not much net gain after the corner man was paid and reimbursed for any healing or coagulate medicines applied. I tried taking care of myself once or twice, but I dropped the water bottle and no one would hand it back up to me. I caught my foot in the bucket and tangled up in the stool legs, once each, both times answering the between-rounds bell! The corner man was welcomed.

Mother always gave Dad hell for my pugilistic efforts, which didn't change things, and she was always around for cleaning, bed-making, and TLC. Her efforts, plus my being two years under minimum age, resulted in a shaky start for my military career.

Not only was I unsettled by living in a tent, which was supposed to be spotless *all* the by-God time, but I slept on a cot, which wasn't so bad, except that when it wasn't being slept in, it was to be a thing of impeccability! I found myself sadly wanting in both these prescribed virtues.

With the first training camp inspection, I was found so sadly lacking in the intricacies of the 45° angle and other niceties of the military sack that the inspector suggested that my efforts be preserved as the classic "before" example. Our Regular Army platoon sergeant, temporarily a private (because he had had some difficulties with the booze and had made caustic reference to the ability and ancestry of folks senior to him), volunteered that he could teach me the intricacies of military bed-making, including not wetting thereon!

At the next inspection there was amazement at the improvement — due mainly because the Ole Sarge/private had explained that he would personally kick the bejeezus out of me all the way to the main gate if I didn't shape up.

After taps, I spent hours making and remaking that damned cot. I borrowed blankets from tentmates and slept on the cement floor for the two nights prior to the inspection.

No matter what the appearance of the cot, the final test was the height reached by a quarter bounced off the top blanket. Due to my efforts, the coin dropped on my cot gave a pleasing twang and required some search of the area to recover.

Even though I was found qualified in making soldier beds, it was obvious that there had to be major changes in my nighttime habits, and thus I worked out entry and egress procedures with minimal disturbance to the desired bed appearance. There were also changes necessary in sleep habits and patterns: no variation from the on-back position and *never* leave the bed until reveille! There was much discomfort after ingesting sauerkraut and wieners, potato salad and beans, etc., and even with induced frequency and depth of breathing, pain was increased with my "*never* leave the bed" admonition.

My memorable tentmate, Ed, probably at maximum enrollment age, was built like a tree and epitomized the saying, "he could fight a grizzly bear with a switch." He took interest in my well-being, contributed to my bed-making education, and otherwise assisted more rapid attainment of maturity.

The Ole Sarge, who had initially contributed to my orientation with bed-making proficiency, teamed up with Ed and furnished tips and special instruction on the rifle range so that I was in the shoot-off for the National Rifle Championships. I didn't really have a chance, but I know that the Sarge got me the Outstanding Battalion Rifleman Award. And I couldn't even make a bed!

Ed found out that I had been boxing in exhibitions and at stag nights and had entered me in the camp tourney, where I was eliminated in the first stage.

Under the tutelage of Ed and the Sarge, I managed to get two workouts, not that any more would have affected the results, but if they hadn't been in my corner I would have been out as soon as my opponent appeared!

In my sub-minor leagues of boxing I had never seen a resin box (two feet square, two-inch high sides, filled with a fine powder that made boxing shoes adhere to the canvas mat flooring), and so I entered the ring and went to my corner.

The "Pro" — and he was one — danced over to the aforesaid box, shuffled his feet in the resin, and put the dirty glares on me. I smiled and waved a friendly glove, resulting in outraged cuffings by my seconds behind the ropes. I had obviously committed a breach in the rules of pugilistic conduct. But this was nothing, I knew, compared to what I was about to experience.

I did feel that I should correct any misconceptions regarding my professionalism, and so I danced over to the resin box, not too successfully, as I tripped on one side and damned near went through the ropes! I regained my composure and thought I looked pretty sharp as I did my shuffle act.

Years later, a fellow soldier and friend who had witnessed the "fight," called to say that he had just seen Jerry Lewis and found his antics the closest he could imagine to mine in the resin box! I recall that everyone ringside, including my corner, were having the gasps and sneezes!

I lasted the three rounds, certain that it was only because Ed and the Sarge had carefully explained to the Pro the bad things that would happen to him, like broken limbs and face rearrangement, if he took me out right away. I wished that they hadn't; it just prolonged the agony.

I went back to the tent, bloody and battered, but with the right eye open enough for me to make qualification shooting the next day. And those two tough characters swore that the referee said I showed real promise for a great boxing future. I never lived up to those words, even with many more fights. I did win one fight the next year, and two the following, but only to "Quarter-Finals." I didn't have a great future, but I guess I did show improvement.

Over the years, when people became aware of my nine years and 52 bouts of boxing, I was always asked about the win/loss record, which I avoided with the "Aw shucks" of false modesty. And with the years, I now reply, "Both eyes were recently operated on to remove eyebrow scar tissue. Does that answer the question?"

Sadly, Big Ed had entered the Army Air Corps, received his pilot rating in 1939, and was killed in action in the Philippines. I never saw the Ole Sarge again, but I'll be forever grateful for their friendship and the time they devoted to helping an immature kid who was in over his head. I never met any better men, and they are forever paramount in my deepest memories.

On to the Cavalry!

My first experience in the Cavalry was an introduction to the unique attitude, appearance, philosophy, and swagger of the trooper. With experience, I found the exact duplication in the fighter pilot and considered myself the luckiest of men to have qualified in both branches of the military.

I was overjoyed to find that the only ground maneuvers were marching to the mess hall, and to and from the stables, although there were days (most) when the trudge from the horse habitat to quarters was agony. "Dashing troopers" were waddling along in whatever posture that would minimize inner-thigh contact!

The first day I learned how to properly blanket, saddle, bridle, and groom my steed. It was a real shock to discover how many parts there are on a horse that gotta be cleaned — or rather, groomed. There are some very private areas, and you only hoped that you hadn't offended your mount, or you could expect activation of certain sewage disposal agencies at the most inappropriate times. The Vets insisted that animals had no control over such functions, but they were medicine men, not groomers!

Of all the Cavalry memories, none is as vivid as your first mount. Mine was "High Hat," and I could never visualize a closer relationship between man and animal — although I have heard some pretty lurid tales involving shepherds and their flocks!

There was general trooper anxiety, which was well founded, when we heard the command, "Feet out of stirrups, Ho!" (We troopers always talked that way, "Ho.") Compliance with the order, however, caused severe punishment to the rider's lower quarters, and mounts suffered from the unsynchronized bouncing of the inept oafs astride, whose sole concern was retaining the agonizing saddle position.

This exercise was to teach the function of thigh pressure in transmitting orders and developing feel, anticipation, and reaction to the horse's movements so that horse and rider moved as one — a goal rarely attained. The exercise had started on the second day of training and became every day's routine. This justified the Infantryman's labeling of us as "blister-butts!"

On a particularly memorable day, as we were practicing troop line-abreast formation at the walk, trot, and gallop (with feet out of stirrups), High Hat and I stood next to a mare in heat — a delicate description of a female condition often obscenely described in the pithy words of the cadre. We were executing the line-abreast turn when the "Call of the Wild" overcame the disciplines instilled in my steed. He dropped back and out of line, thence accelerating enough to assume the procreation position.

To answer the obvious question, why didn't I exercise control and keep

High Hat in ranks: because the only time that I was ever really in control was during grooming at day's end, and then only because I was pleasuring him.

My amorous mount's approaches were greeted by violent kicks, and I have no idea whether the reaction was motivated by a desire for retention of virginal status, headache, personality conflict, or other of the many reasons for female rejection of male advances! (All of which I, too had encountered during my bachelorhood.)

Meanwhile, the trooper astride the young mare was fighting to avoid losing his seat and landing among the surrounding pounding hooves while loudly, and obscenely, decrying my ability and lack of guts, with harsh comments on my ancestry!

But his resentment was short-lived because, at the first kick, High Hat chose discretion over *amour* and planted his front hooves in the dirt. I should have been propelled over his head, but I had developed sufficient proficiency to somewhat retain my seat, so I was stopped with my crotch implanted on the pommel! The resultant agony can only be appreciated by one who has encountered it. For those not so unfortunate, the only description is imagining a knife thrust upward through the groin and into the abdomen, slowly twisting all the way! Fairly close — inadequate, but close.

Thankfully, the pain was short-lived, being terminated by unconsciousness, which still seemed a long time coming. At the highest degree of agony, I pleaded, "Lord, whatever ya got for the pain, please lay it on me!" The Boss must have been on frequency, because things dimmed to dark, and I felt myself sliding off the saddle, but didn't give a damn. The aftereffects, an extremely delicate condition and sensories, required changes in walking, sitting, and sleeping positions.

I was lying in the dust, High Hat standing over me with a nonchalant, bored equine expression, and some contempt. Surrounding me were four of the mounted Regular Army cadre, with broad grins, like "Welcome to the Cavalry, trooper." As more of the world came into sight, a beautiful blonde lady appeared.

She stopped her car and approached the fence near where I was still suffering. I realized that good was about to happen when she addressed the senior non-commissioned officer (non-com) with "Sergeant, if one of your troopers is hurt, I would be glad to drive him to the Dispensary."

I came back to the real world when the Sarge replied, "Thank you,

Ma'am, but troopers always return mounted, unless totally disabled. Ain't that right trooper?" This was addressed to me, and I figured I qualified as "disabled."

To eliminate any doubt, I lapsed into simulated unconsciousness, maybe coma, but realized that the performance was wasted when I was lifted to my feet, propped against High Hat, left foot placed into the stirrup and boosted into the saddle. (How I would have loved for him to have been his usual self and dance away, allowing my collapse, and just maybe, a ride with the Angel. But the nag picked that time to be the model Cavalry mount.)

Suddenly came the realization that, in my semi-comatose condition, I was going to hit that saddle, dead weight, receiving all the force on some personal parts, which had received severe damage. I grabbed the pommel frantically, and held myself up until I could find the right stirrup and avoid another catastrophe. On the five-mile ride to the stables, I kept my weight on the stirrups.

Forever vague is the march to quarters, but I recall that I passed up chow and hit the sack. I wasn't up to the sarcasm and vulgar nicknames being bestowed on me by my fellow troopers. Welcome to the Cavalry! I figured that combat couldn't be worse than the day's events. And I resolved in the future to determine the gender of mounts on either side of me.

As part of B Troop, U.S. Army 12th Cavalry, we went on maneuvers from the Presidio of Monterey in open country to the east, at the trot and gallop, in varying formations. We were in parade formations, however, rather than tactical, since the two Reserve lieutenants and the captain, the troop commander, were less than skilled equestrians and were primarily concerned with maintaining the mounted position in order to complete another month of active duty without personal injury.

To minimize casualties, sabers were not issued and carbines were received, less ammunition. Training was only realistic when officers were attending the endless meetings, which seemed to go with the commissioned status, and the non-coms were in charge. We moved in line-abreast formations, at the gallop, through woods and open fields — shades of the "Light Brigade" and the typical Cavalry charge! But we never trained in the charge, nor in jumping. It seemed that you either learned the technique or plowed up the soil with your face!

As for our maneuvers, we arrived at the bivouac and conditions were rough — sand, mesquite, and sagebrush. We were indoctrinated into the *primary* Cavalry precept: no personal cares are taken until your mount is fed, watered, groomed, and picketed. If there had been strenuous riding, mounts were first cooled by an hour of slow walk, under a blanket.

Troopers were paired, to combine our shelter-halves for a pup tent. The shelter-halves contained the trooper's personal possessions for the sortie, and were rolled and lashed behind the saddle. After the first night, it was amazing how many articles were deemed excess and scattered along the next day's route of march — not left behind, because the bivouac area was to be spotless! Some of the articles were of a very personal, and sexual nature. How could there be an opportunity for *amour* on maneuvers?

With the sounding of "Taps," we realized that it was impossible to sleep comfortably any place but in bed — where you're supposed to sleep! However, "Boots and Saddles" sounded about 3:00 a.m. anyway. It was pitch black when we were trying to locate our saddles and other gear and finding our trusty steeds.

It was bad enough that I had to stumble over cacti, sagebrush, and deposits that accumulate wherever horses congregate, but I was loaded with saddle, bed roll, horse blanket, pad, and bridle! Luckily, we were not ordered to mount until first light. We sat in front of our individual steeds, maintaining a firm grip on the reins; they of course, were in a very high state of anticipation, as evidenced by the damaged shoulder muscle or biceps of a trooper who lapsed into a doze!

With dawn, we charged into pursuit of "the enemy," galloping hither and yon, in mounted and dismounted combat. Once we had dispatched any threats, we went back to camp to do the good things to the horses, and to eat breakfast.

All this may suggest that Citizens Military Training Camps contributed little to the revision and updating of military tactics and doctrine, but we were instructed to make some observations. B Troop, and I suppose others, were to test, evaluate, and comment on a long-standing procedure. In dismounted combat, should the horse-holder continue to be responsible for four mounts (one-half a squad) or eight mounts (the entire squad)? The smaller number had been in practice since pre-Custer, but it occurred to someone that assigning four mounts per holder subtracted from combat two troopers, or one-fourth of a squad.

Some adherents of the status quo held that the trooper really wasn't unavailable for combat; he could hold two reins in his teeth, wrap one around each arm, and still fire his carbine or pistol! It was conceded that the saber couldn't be effectively wielded, but maybe that could be worked on.

The eight horses per holder was favored since there would be one more trooper available in each squad, increasing combat strength for the troop and regiment. Obviously, the proponents of this approach were unbloodied, untried, and narrow-minded staff officers, or plain idiots! Maybe both. The toughest and most experienced Cavalryman would shudder at the thought of one man controlling eight unruly and single-minded mounts, even on the parade ground. In the combat environment, amid shot and shell, the poor bastard would be drawn, quartered, and stomped into the earth if he even tried to maintain control!

This was considered a complex and multi-faceted problem by the Cavalry planners — which tells you something about how busy those guys were — and you can bet that the dog-faced trooper was not consulted, which was typical of war planners and developers of strategy and tactics.

Some thinkers on the last Cavalry days suggested that the smaller ratio of horses to horse-holders, and decreased trooper availability, may have contributed to the demise of Custer. But the General got his bell rung at Little Bighorn all by himself — mainly by not heeding advice from others, especially those at the fighting level!

I think I can predict how the combat Cavalryman would have addressed the problem of securing X number of high-strung horses in the roar and chaos of combat. Stated simply, "Trees or brush available, tie 'em. If the area is a desert or prairie, drive spikes and tie 'em. One trooper, any size unit, to ensure security of lines." A simple and practical approach, but irrelevant now. Except it is hoped that sometime, the working and fighting men will contribute to and establish how they will fight the battles and wars!

Chapter 2

Flying Cadet: Pilot Training

*A*T THE TIME OF U.S. Army Air Corps expansion, the Training Command consisted of eight Primary Flying Schools: Civilian, which was under contract; Basic Flying and Headquarters at Randolph Field; Advanced Flying and Graduation at Kelly Field and Brooks Field — the latter three at San Antonio, Texas. In little more than a year there were three Major Flying Commands — Eastern, Midwest, and Pacific — and uncounted flying fields!

The Ryan School of Aeronautics at Lindbergh Field in San Diego, California, was awarded a contract with the U.S. Army for Primary Ground and Flight Training. Trainers were the Ryan PT-16, -20, and -22, with open cockpits, metal construction, two versions with radial and inline

I . . . reported to Ryan for flying physical exam, knowing that the failure rate was 50 percent.

Jack Hayes as a newly assigned Primary Training flying cadet, April 1940, at Lindbergh Field, home of Ryan Aeronautical Company, which produced the PT-16 (PT-20) and the *Spirit of Saint Louis.*

engines. Ryan purchased a new motel and converted it into cadet quarters with mess hall, offices, rec room, and supply room — plush, especially when compared with what came later.

I enlisted in the Army and reported to Ryan for flying physical exam, knowing that the failure rate was 50 percent. I pestered the Doc by constantly asking, "How am I doin'?" and when I passed the eye exam he said I had it made. I then relaxed somewhat, but I hadn't faced the "Finger Wave," or being carried around the room on two fingers while being exhorted to cough. This almost made me drop out of the program, but I figured, "What the hell, if it's not any worse and the Doc don't try and kiss me, I'll hang in there."

I became a familiar figure to the cadets and Army/Ryan personnel as the guy hanging on the fence and watching, longingly, all the activities. Dad put up the dough for a couple of flights in the civilian Ryan trainer and a ground course in navigation. The flight lessons introduced me to "flying time builders," young pilots who had scrounged flight time for instructor's certificates and were teaching, for pay, to build time for the airlines, ferrying airplanes, or anything in civil aviation.

My flights were really only sight-seeing; instruction consisted of, "Pull back to go up, NOT THAT FAR BACK, JEEZUS!"

Jack Hayes (second from right), with other unidentified flying cadets in front of the barracks at Lindbergh Field, California. The cadet quarters were in a new motel that had been taken over by Ryan under a government contract.

"Now we turn left, then right. To go down, we throttle back and lower the nose." I had not the vaguest notion of the names of the controls with which we were doing all these things! All our activities were close to Lindbergh Field to be sure that we could smoke back in, not a second over the allotted time. This was an education.

I expected imminent call-up, so I dropped out of the 1939-1940 school year at San Diego State. April came, and a new class of cadets reported into Ryan, *sans* Hayes. My introduction to the clout of "Congressional interest" came when Dad called in a couple of tabs from a San Diego Senator. The next day, a telegram arrived ordering me to report to the U.S. Army Detachment at Lindbergh Field for pilot training in Class 40-H.

The class was originally designated 41-A, the first to graduate in 1941. Training was shortened from 11 months to 9, with no decrease in flying or ground training time. My class was still being processed, so no time was lost. The upper class sensed that some strings had been pulled for me, the late-joiner, which made for a severe "indoctrination!"

The first difficulties came with the start of flying — a bad omen, since flying's the name of the game! I was assigned to an old instructor, a taciturn Swede from Alaska, who was convinced that every man was meant to fly and it was just a matter of bringing out those God-given talents. The wording "every man" was crucial; in those days, "Women's Movements" would be construed as relating to bodily functions! Even a suggestion of female fliers would have induced tremors, shock, and hyperventilation in our manly teacher.

My problem of total ignorance of the rudiments of flight was aggravated by the experience of the other cadets assigned to this instructor; they had completed the Civilian Pilot Training program — comparable, I suppose, to Hitler's Glider Clubs, although I don't think the CPT violated the Versailles Treaty.

CPT training meant that they had logged the minimum flying time required for a Private Pilot's Certificate in civil aviation. So, these three veterans of flight swaggered up to our mentor, followed by me, klutz Hayes, tripping over chocks and trying to conceal a tremendous amount of silk, a result of my carrying the parachute by the release handle — or rip cord, as we pilots call it. And it gets worse!

The initial conversation between the instructor and the three Intrepid Airmen, hereafter referred to as "aces," went something like this:

Instructor: "I see that you have considerable flying experience, so I will schedule two short flights with each and then clear you for solo."

This was greeted by the aces with "Aw gosh, shucks" expressions, with heads modestly lowered and toes scuffing on the pavement.

He then turned to me, and I had a dire premonition that things might not be too rosy.

"You, Nayes."

"Hayes."

"Whatever. Listen to the instructions I give the other cadets before and after each flight, familiarize yourself with the airplane, and be ready for dual on the third day."

This was a fine plan, except that instructions were in a language totally foreign to me and cadets were not allowed in an airplane that had not been assigned. I stumbled after the instructor and aces trying to pick up the lingo but was told to get out of the way, so I spent most of my time chasing my hat across the ramp, to peals of laughter from the aces and others. And thus, I learned about prop-wash!

Finally, my first flight came, along with the realization that I, a fledgling pilot, had bunches of problems. Expecting a description of airplane controls and functions, I got instead, "Start up, take off, and go to Auxiliary Field number two," except it came out, "Starp, toff, go aux fil two."

Having no idea of how to start, taxi (which he omitted, but I was fairly sure it came before "toff"), plus a blank on what or where the hell "aux fil two" was, I dared to request to begin with the basics.

With disgust came the reply, "Sayerlon, elvator, rudrs, ta bank-clim-div en turn. Stik ta trn-clim-div, rudrs tern. Throtl to go stp. Flps to go dn fas. Mekanik start en wego. Quessions? Wego."

"Mekanik" started us up and I was relieved later to find that he suffered only contusions when I jumped the chocks and leveled him with the wing. By God, you say "wego" to Cadet "Haze," and WEGO!

We were airborne, in what could best be described as a joint maneuver, and, recognizing that he was up to his rear in "doodoo," the instructor flew to the auxiliary field and demonstrated what traffic pattern, landing, and takeoff were all about. Twice!

I have no idea how many times I hurled us through the air and assaulted the ground, but I found that the instructor's concept of teaching was to overpower me at crucial times in the takeoff and land functions, screaming incomprehensible commands on the intercom, or holding the speaker outside in the windstream. The resulting agony caused my overpowering desire to kill the cretin, after which the U.S. Army would be graphically told what to do with the Flying Cadet Program.

The instructor realized from the outset that there was a major problem in molding me into an aviator, and I'm sure that he expressed those misgivings early to those in authority. Also, I'm sure that "Congressional interest" deflected the falling ax. One of the status symbols required that, on the ground, goggles would be worn around the neck until first solo, and I was finally the only cadet so attired, the rest having soloed or washed out!

After more takeoffs and landings than the average cadet had on graduation, the instructor threw caution, and me, to the winds for the required solo ups and downs. Classmates on the auxiliary field told me that he locked himself in the outhouse with instructions that he was not to be bothered until I crashed or taxied in after the third landing!

We then had dual flights, attempting to develop my proficiency in more advanced maneuvers, without much success. In my defense, these attempts involved minimum teaching from the instructor, *e.g.* Ground Reference Maneuvers: describing proscribed ground tracks by compensating for wind, maintaining constant altitude and airspeed.

The instructor's command was, "Gonna do tur bou poin" (turn about a point). Then came a 360° turn in each direction, around an unspecified point on the ground, with no explanations, followed by a shake on the stick, and "Yudo." I had not the slightest idea where the airplane went, not knowing were it was supposed to go. A dismal shake of the head came from the front cockpit, and we went on to the next challenge, with the same instructional technique and student performance.

As I approached the proscribed dual flying time, for the entire course, and only one more solo flight, which I understand caused the instructor severe mental stress, I realized that desperate action was in order. I requested audience with the detachment commander, a captain. He and the commandant of cadets listened to my request for evaluation and a different instructor. The commandant got up, picked up his parachute and said, "Come on, Hayes, let's go have some fun."

Fun? Flying's fun? Boy, was it! Less than 20 hours flying time and we looped, Immelmanned, spun, slow, and snap-rolled, until he grinned back at me and said, "Let's go home, you're wearing me out."

He turned out to be one of the most important people in my life. The commandant assigned me to a different instructor, but most important, he taught me the joy of flying. There were more challenges along the way, happily met and conquered. I finished in the top 10 percent of my class, so he must have seen something.

After graduation, I was sent in July 1940 to Randolph Field in San Antonio, Texas, for Basic Flight Training. At the railroad station outside the main gate, we were all met and harassed by upper-classmen. Dressed in civvies with two suitcases per man, we double-timed the 3/4-mile to the cadet barracks. Inside the flight line, we passed close enough to see the new airplanes, which caused feelings of inadequacy, and by the married officers' quarters, which seemed even farther out of reach than the airplanes.

Processing was well organized and efficient, even with the "hurry up and wait" — I suppose an unavoidable part of the military way. Then we were measured for uniforms and flying gear, to be available in a few days. We soon found out that "fatigues" were appropriately named; in the next week we "enjoyed" close order drill, the Manual of Arms, and hazing. The latter is described as "Indoctrination, discipline, and character enhancement," and more, but it's *hazing* and does a good job of getting the attention of the hazee, leaving no doubt of his status in the new life.

The first days consisted of: drill, drill, drill, posture exercises, double-time everywhere, meals at attention with eyes straight ahead, while reciting required memorizations. Then, the rifle and all its foibles, intricacies, and weight. Oh, God, the weight! But after a week, we put on a pretty damn good battalion parade — in fatigues, no visitors — but not bad.

But the flying was *heaven*, along with the amazement of two separate flying programs on opposite sides of the field, with four flights per side. It all operated on grass, with radio control only for checking in and out — and lousy radio control, at that. Traffic patterns were indicated by a huge "T" on each hangar side, illustrating what the folks running the show thought might be a nice way to take off and land, in case anyone couldn't tell by watching the way everyone else was going and coming.

Patterns varied from parallel to the line of hangars, north or south, to 45° increments, including takeoffs and landing directly toward or over the hangar line, where there was a chance to watch the officers' ladies sunbathing. It was amazing there were no collisions, but we did lots of ground loops and nose-ups.

My instructor operated on the theory that *he* made it this far, *ergo* anybody could. He did a minimum of teaching: mainly "I show, you do." I guess he figured that if no one in the airplane got hurt in the "do," progress was satisfactory and off to the next lesson. Four of us were assigned to Lieutenant Easy-Going, and we soloed in minimum time, which reduced the time he had to spend on dual instruction.

We progressed through the program and check flights, although we never felt prepared, even for the final, 40-hour check ride. The local business community was tuned in to the system: San Antonio car dealers lined up for a mile outside the main gate, and the only requisite for purchase and ownership of an exotic vehicle was an affirmative reply to the query, "Passed your 40-hour check?" They knew there were few wash-outs after Basic Training.

Randolph Field, San Antonio, Texas, in 1939. The four large buildings forming a "U" were the cadet barracks and administration. In the center is the mess hall and cadet headquarters; the large building at the base of the "U" is the Flying Training Command Headquarters. The swimming pool and recreation areas are at the left, but were still under construction at that time.

Those who earned wings after the early 1940s did not experience one facet of Ground School: Morse Code. A principal means of radio communications, all aircraft were equipped with short-range, high-frequency radios. Codes were sent by the left hand, with a headset for reception. This required considerable dexterity by us southpaws: write messages on the right knee with the left hand, and discard the pencil (usually on the floor) to send the code — all while flying the airplane with the right hand! A definite challenge flying in formation, especially at night. Once the ability to send and receive 30 words a minute was achieved, we were excused from daily class, but still were required to pass a weekly test. Morse Code was never used by any of us, but who knew in those days? The future was unknown, and training programs were established on the basis of very limited experience.

The first Open Post came after three weeks of indoctrination, blood, sweat, and tears, with most of the wash-outs through the gate. Civilian clothes were authorized, even encouraged, and we headed off to the big city and the Gunter Hotel Cadet Club. I had my introduction to Cuba Libras (no more horrible hangover can be imagined) and "cadet widows" — not a very nice handle to hang on those lovely ladies, although I understand that their "kill rate," if percentage of cadets leaving bachelorhood can be so denoted, was much higher than wash-out rate and losses in aerial combat!

On to upperclass status, and we had it made, although a few more of us dropped by the wayside. After a couple of weekends of Open Post, "San Antone" was losing some glamour and I decided on rest and relaxation in the barracks. Until a classmate named Fritz, an All-American halfback, approached me on a Saturday with, "Hey you. You boxed a lots, hey? How 'bout us hitting the big city tonight?"

I should have questioned what boxing had to do with social events, but I was so flattered at being chosen by a celebrity that I responded eagerly in the affirmative. It did occur to me that Fritz always seemed to start the weeks with lumps and bruises around the face, but too late. Off we went in Fritz's car, past the Gunter and Cadet Club, headed for an area unfamiliar, but recognizable as Hispanic.

I was not concerned, as I have always enjoyed Mexican/Spanish food and the señoritas, but any expectations regarding the joys of cultural exchange vanished when my new-found friend, unable to find parking, drove up on the sidewalk before a disreputable looking place. The locals

Randolph Field, August 1940. The Class 40-H is starting night flying in the North American BT-9 trainer.

North American BT-9, the first Basic trainer.

wore Levis, mustaches, serapes, and long knives for cleaning fingernails. And these were the kids on the front porch!

I recognized the recurrence of alligators when Fritz trotted up to the swinging doors, turned to me and said, "Now for some real fun, eh, you?" He kicked open the doors, pulling me behind him into a dimly lit, smoke-filled room, as the novels go, and belted out, "Me and my buddy can lick any greasers in the house!" I'm his "buddy," and he didn't even know my name!

My vague recollections are that my maximum engagements were two at a time, and I noted that Fritz was doing very well; sliding and bouncing around me were well-tanned types with Latin American features, most bleeding profusely. There were periods of darkness, and I'll never know how we got home. I dimly recall visiting the Army First Aid Station in the city, where most clientele, I understand, were interested in prevention of venereal diseases.

I missed church call next day, as I was one big mass of pain and was certain that I had used up any "tickets to heaven" I had coming. The day was made when Fritz, my friend and comrade-at-arms, bounced into my room announcing to all our glorious feats of valor, how I had more bandages than him, and his plans for next weekend! I might have gone, but he still didn't know my name! I used that as my first excuse, and held on even when he promised to study all next week and know my name by Saturday. We remained good friends, but I felt that I had lost stature with him after that. But better stature than life!

Another memorable upperclassman incident occurred when I was appointed Cadet First Sergeant, D Company. My chief responsibility was maintaining discipline and order, though this was not conducive to popularity. A cadet captain, a company commander named Etchemendy, had been with me at Ryan, and I thought he had been overdoing the rules of discipline, appearance, and conduct for the lower class, constantly demanding of me improvement in those areas.

Mid-week, prior to first Open Post for the lower class, "Etch" called me into his office and very seriously told me about rumors that some lower-classmen were eagerly awaiting the opportunity to lay hands on my body and make major rearrangements of the facial characteristics of me, their "Sarge!" I thought about working out in the gym, but . . . get in shape for a *whole class*? They had some big and tough boys!

I had decided not to stay on post for the weekend, but I had trouble bumming a ride to town. I heard things like, "I'm not getting caught in a fracas between Jack and the lower class."

I finally paid a civilian gardener to drop me at the Gunter, but he made me jump off while the car was still moving. I stayed close to the wall of the lobby, used stairs rather than the elevator, and sat in the bar with my back to a corner. I didn't dance, wouldn't go to the John without company, and slept in the lobby — the hotel was sold out and there was no ride available back to Randolph.

I dreaded the coming weekends until some kindly lower-class guys tipped me off that the whole thing was Etch's prank! He made damn sure that we were never alone until being transferred to Kelly Field, but I have to agree that it was a good one!

In looking back, I also recall the "Uniform of the Day" system at Randolph Field, which utilized various banners on the flagpole at Battalion Headquarters. Changeable weather gave the flagpole and cadets quite a workout: cool morning meant blues and greatcoat, thundershowers prior to noon mess and it was rain gear, heat wave by mid-afternoon meant summer gear. We got to relax during the half-day of flying, because there was only one type of flying gear!

Advanced Flying School, Kelly Field

We finally made it to Advanced Flying School in October 1940. The increased class size could not be accommodated at Kelly, so some of our class lived and trained at Brooks Field, on the other side of San Antonio. Class records were maintained at Kelly, and meetings and graduation were also held there.

We got relaxed handling and living conditions since we were probably going to make it — though a few more did drop out, for a final elimination rate of more than 37 percent. We only had formations for reveille, mess call, and retreat. Life was a change from the Randolph Field plush quarters to six-man tents, but they did have cement floors!

The flight line consisted of the North American BC-1 (Basic Combat), the first monoplane advanced-basic combat trainer, and the North American AT-6, the advanced trainer that would become famous in World War II, with retractable gear, constant speed prop, and the usual first impression, "Oh God, I'll never be able to fly *that!*"

Here we had a higher ratio of cadets to instructors, since less dual flying was required: two or three duals before solo, then cadets teamed up for instrument practice, and solo formation flights after dual sign-off. Instructors always led flights of three and sections of six.

Cross-country flights were solo, with instructors at a checkpoint to monitor progress and notify Kelly in case of a missing student. The traffic patterns were similar to our earlier training: parallel to hangar line, 45° increment changes resulting in the majority of landings and takeoffs over hangars, including three- and six-ship formations. There were lots of thrills, but no major mishaps. More radio control was attempted, but the high amount of traffic resulted in the following information: who went out, who came back, and who's missing — "we think!"

This "ace" was humbled on the long cross-country, which turned out to be a lot *longer* than planned. I have forgotten the where-to-where on each leg, but it's not important, since I obviously really screwed up at least one leg. I do remember, however, that it was all to have been in the state of Texas, and my landing at Fort Sill, Oklahoma, for gas tells you something!

The most important lesson learned — and the hardest to remember — was that when the "Where am I's?" strike, ignore the "maybes, could be here's," and other panicked reactions, and hold the planned heading. Eventually you'll find you're on course, or at least a lot closer than you thought. It's amazing, but that mistake can be made even by those with more experience, as I found out. An old saying goes, "If you can say you've never been lost, you're either a liar, it's gonna happen to you tomorrow, or you weren't lost — just temporarily unsure of your location!"

I have no idea how I got to Fort Sill, but all of a sudden, there it was. I had to find out the "where am I's?" from the NCO who met me and pumped the gas, of which considerable was needed. I pawed through the maps, drew a course back to Kelly, and after profusely thanking my greeter (who had a knowing look like he'd been this route before), leaped off for home base. I estimated time en route to be one hour and 45 minutes, but don't think the figure was given much validity — if I couldn't find my way through the skies, how could I possibly figure out how long it would take to get anywhere?

I was smart enough to contact the Kelly Tower at maximum range, canceling the massive search formations about to take off. It was obvious that the tower guys weren't enthusiastic about my return to the living; they were on overtime — which was not a part of the Army pay system — due to my screw-up. I almost pointed out that they would have spent lots more time with the tower strapped to their rears if I hadn't made it, but I noticed that the morale improved greatly when I was informed that I would report to my stage commander, the big guy right next to the REAL BIG GUY.

The details of that meeting are left to the imagination, but I think I was saved by the proximity of graduation, the awesome dollar amount spent on me to date, the fact that my boss had been saved from an unpleasant session with his bosses, and the reams of paperwork that had been avoided by me not joining the deceased.

Formation flying was one of the greatest thrills, and I even did some formation aerobatics with less than 200 hours of flying time! The aerobatics were illegal, by the way. My instructor, a frustrated fighter pilot who wished he was with The Flying Tigers, recognized my aerobatic interest and we used some of the dual-instrument flights for practice on the fun things. (He had not been instructed in that stuff, either.) I learned the rudiments, and then figured out what could be applied to formation flying: Chandelles, Lazy Eights, steep turns, building up to loops and rolls.

A classmate, also a Tiger type, was assigned to the same instructor. He was sharp on formation flying and, I happened to know, had done some solo aerobatics, and he became the third point in our "V." Our solo practice at Randoph had explored loops, Immelmanns, and barrel, slow, and snap rolls, and could have been spotted by other solo studs or instructors and reported.

We counted on the fact that an observer would have problems identifying us. Getting close enough to read our plane numbers and having no idea what or where the next maneuver would be, he could find himself head-on to us, or find us overtaking him rapidly from the tail position (six o'clock) — or worse, be at the wrong end of a vertical climb or dive, with minimum time for evasive action and no idea what direction the evasive action should take!

We lucked out and were never caught, although there were mutterings at Kelly about T-6s seen doing mighty odd things. We were smart enough to play around during maximum flying activity, especially solo, thereby complicating our identification.

As we "Three Musketeers" probed — or stumbled — through the intricacies of formation aerobatics, it was agreed that there would have to be unanimous judgment that the lead plane was smooth and coordinated, in order to avoid collisions.

There *were* times when we returned to the flight line with inexplicable dents and scratches on the airplanes. Once the lead's canopy was scratched, which required sincere avowal to our pale-faced, palsied lead that we would increase separation distances.

Those damages we had were repaired under strict secrecy — and at considerable outlay of our personal funds in the purchase of booze to ensure that secrecy. It helped that non-coms appreciate departures from the norm, within reason, and that the lieutenant engineering officers never questioned certain unscheduled metal work. One of the non-coms respectfully explained the officers' silence: "They couldn't pour piss out of a boot if it had a spigot in the toe and instructions on the heel!"

With agreement that we would limit formation maneuvers to loops and barrel rolls, with minor modifications, we launched, formed the V, and flew off to the outer limit of the practice area, as far as possible, to play around and make it home before fuel became vapor!

The experience was indescribable. We were learning the discipline to ignore any views except the precise angles in the vertical, longitudinal, and horizontal axes, always aware of the ever-changing and crossing pictures of earth to sky to earth.

We called it off just before graduation — there had been too much talk about formations seen doing odd things and some maintenance mutterings about fuel consumption and oil-streaked windshields and fuselages. We couldn't buy booze for *all* the troops!

It finally occurred to us that the flight line was aware of, and exulted in, what we were doing. With "Ops" strictly limited within "regulations and standard operating procedures," the men enjoyed us breaking those boundaries and going way beyond them, without endangering any but ourselves.

Chapter 3

First Assignments

ON DECEMBER 20, 1940, graduation was held in the Kelly Field theater. We had brand-new officers' uniforms, complete with Sam Browne belts for sword or saber, though I never knew which, since it was never issued. I like to believe it was the saber — the Cavalry weapon! Military outfitters in San Antonio operated on the same guidelines as the car dealers; pass the 40-hour check ride and you're eligible for the first fitting. They were the finest uniforms any of us had, except for the few who made general and could afford the custom-made.

We had a large class so it was a fairly brief ceremony, with some emotional wing hangings — pinning on of the wings — by mothers or girlfriends, and some bitter feelings if both were present! With no family, girl, or

Who knew that these young and dedicated officers would be generally ticked off at their first assignments, . . .

other friends there, I wallowed in self-pity, paid my buck to the first soldier to salute me, and had my first dinner at the Officers Club after smashing myself in the face with several drinks. Then it was back to the cadet tent to sweat my upcoming orders.

Bunches of new "officers and gentlemen" headed for nuptials at the Randolph Chapel. The brides were hometown girls or local ladies. The pomp and ceremony was abbreviated to crossed swords, rice, and tears. The clergy ran shifts and there was some suspicion that they went heavy on the sacramental wine between ceremonies! It was understandable, with only 20 minutes allowed per rite, changing trappings for different faiths, sweeping up rice and drunks, ministering to parents, and rounding up swords from the last wedding, usually found in the hands of tipsy ushers playing "Three Musketeers."

Who knew that these young and dedicated officers would be generally ticked off at their first assignments, some in combat under a year, and that more than half of the marriages would end in divorce or widowhood?

There was no activity for a few days, except checking the bulletin board for assignment information. We were still authorized to wear civilian clothing, which was nice because it was tiresome ducking around corners and into doorways to avoid mass saluting of enlisted men; the GIs arranged themselves into six-foot intervals, requiring robot-like officer salutes. It was a comedy, and we countered by going single file and wearing out the other guys' saluting arms.

Finally, we were ordered to assemble at the base theater for assignments: the first orders were to pursuit groups (who later became fighters), a dream assignment for most of us. Then came bombardment, attack, reconnaissance, and — ugh! — Randolph Field and basic flight instructor. The latter list included a Hayes, of which there were two in the class, and I sounded off, "Initials?" I was relieved to hear that they weren't mine. But that feeling was short-lived; the next announcement was clear: "Randolph Field. Hayes." I was to be a flight instructor.

It was little known that 30 or so of our classmates were released from active duty and reported to Pan American Airways as potential airline pilots. Some of our leaders recognized that the need for overseas ferry routes was of the greatest urgency and PAN AM was deemed the most qualified, but needed pilots. Most of these classmates retired as senior captains.

I checked in at Randolph Field and was assigned bachelor officer's quarters (BOQ): living room, bedroom, and bath, in permanent buildings surrounding the bachelor mess. The structure had been built in the '30s, and it was the best I would see until fighter group duty on the West Coast in 1946. I confined myself to the BOQ area, since I was not comfortable around senior types — first lieutenants and up. Also, base regulations required a Class A uniform or tuxedo in the evening at the main officers' mess and the base theater! Obviously, the changes in expansion had not reached these ivory towers.

With evening time on my hands and being dedicated to an Army Air Corps career, I completed a correspondence course in mess management. It had no effect on my professional progress, but I sure as hell knew how to feed an Infantry company!

With the rapid Air Corps expansion, there wasn't time to develop a formal course for flight instructors, so we had 24 hours' flying time, at least 80 landings from the back seat, and no ground school. We had a couple of flights with an instructor who had graduated just ahead of us and then "buddy rides" with other rookies.

On a selective basis, I experimented some more with aerobatics. Unfortunately, most of our vintage had not been exposed and wanted no part of the fun things. I found two others of a like bent, and we scared the hell out of each other, but also got proficient in spin recoveries, high-speed stalls, and other maneuvers still unidentified. We practiced in a "secret area," which meant the roughest terrain available, with no place for forced landings, so we would be the only ones there.

But there was still enough of a sense of responsibility that we brushed up on the basic maneuvers while to and from our secret practice areas, so I was fairly ready for the first class of cadets.

I think I handled my first — and only — class at Randolph without much trouble. Happily, I found one stud, a Captain Ace, who loved the dipsy-dos, and we had a ball! I learned some good lessons, among them: flight time and experience are not accurate gauges of ability, and *always* learn from the other guy, no matter what his background.

I reported to my flight commander, my first contact with a West Pointer. He had an attitude I recognized in later contacts with the joy boys of Strategic Air Command (SAC) — jutting jaws and steely gray eyes! It was one of the Gawd damnedest chewing-outs of my career, and I was just reporting in!

The assistant flight commander gave my check ride, and passed me, but with this guidance: "Be on time, in proper uniform, stay out of the commander's way, and don't ask questions." Now that's a real junior officer retention pitch!

I guess I didn't screw up too much, at first. Ole Stone Face spoke with inspiring passages like, "Good morning/night. How are you?"

It was soon obvious that my aviation proficiency barely exceeded that of most of my students, a potential problem which I solved by stating in a direct and honest manner: "I'm almost as virginal as you guys, so let's work together to get you through. Remember, I got the loaded gun, and if you can't work with me, you're outta here!" This was one of my more inspirational messages.

I didn't finish my first class. Seems my "gung ho" attitude backfired and bit *me* in the rear. One fabulous west Texas morning during the third week of training, we awoke to a 500-foot ceiling, silky-smooth air, and visibility to forever. One of my early military principles was "If nobody said you can't, then you can." (This principle lasted about as long as my tour at Randolph!) Flying hadn't been cancelled that day, so we flew.

I grabbed the first stud scheduled, signed out, and we were off. I missed the message evident in the absence of flight-line activity and later realized the attention aroused by the launch of a single North American BT-9 trainer of the "Hayes Air Force." I didn't, and still don't, feel that there was a problem: three radio antennae formed a triangle between Randolph, Kelly, and the city outlining our practice area. I simply figured they would penetrate the clouds, and they did.

We climbed through the clouds, using the penetration procedures of those days of minimal instrument flying experience: under clouds, airspeed to the max, or red line. Full power, pull the stick back, and hope you break out of the clouds before stalling and spinning out! It worked again, and we broke through to dazzling sunshine and smooth air, with the three antennae still outlining the practice area and providing a fix for letdown into the Randolph traffic pattern.

After a good hour's practice, we smoked on down between the towers and landed. I debriefed the cadet and went to the instructors' room, where a glacial atmosphere suggested that I might have a problem. Our august flight commander spewed forth a tirade, never mentioning my name, "It has come to my attention that one of my instructors, with a student, penetrated the clouds and *flew above the overcast!*"

My reaction was unvoiced: there was a happy ending, so why the sweat? But it didn't take long for the answer; when names were posted for transfer to the newly activated basic training base, "Hayes" was first on the list — and was repeated, to be sure.

Before I departed Randolph Field, there was another contribution to my military experience. On the duty roster one day appeared the following: "Officer of the Day, Jack W. Hayes, Jr., Second Lieutenant, United States Army Air Corps, Reserve." That's a spine tingler.

I pored over all available material at base Headquarters and library on the history, duties, and responsibilities of the OD. Some of the duties seemed appropriate: "Conduct reveille and retreat formations, post and relieve all guard stations, be responsible for overall discipline and order of the command."

I had to question the applicability of some material to present times, like, "At least once in tour of duty inspect for proper care and forage of unit mounts. With unit veterinary officer, inspect mounts of commanding officer and other senior officers, for health and condition."

Changing of Officer of the Day required outgoing and incoming "looies" reporting to the adjutant with, "Sir, I have nothing to report and request relief as Officer of the Day."

New second John (lieutenant): "Sir, I am familiar with all instructions and duties of the Officer of the Day and assume all responsibilities." If the Adjutant, a non-flier, is in a benevolent mood, or hung over, the transfer is approved and it goes to the outer office for transfer of arm band and sidearm.

With experience came understanding of the real reason for an OD, *i.e.*, someone junior to hang the can on if bad things happen during off-duty hours, and I was sorely tempted to deviate from the stereotypical comments of the outgoing OD with statements like, "and wish to report the following incidents: base commander's vehicle ticketed for being parked on his lawn, with damage to lawn and shrubbery.

"OD was called to the Officers Club: fight between Captains Smith and Wilson over local belle. Damage to club property is substantial and estimated costs are being submitted. The officers involved are suspended from flying status, pending evaluation by flight surgeon. Object of their affections left the club escorted by a young lieutenant and she expressed no interest in welfare of the combatants.

"Other incidents which don't warrant immediate attention of the Adjutant will be covered in separate reports from base fire department, Military Police, and local police and fire agencies."

I can just see the reactions, but I never found the guts — probably just as well!

Finally, my first OD tour at Randolph, and it was humbling: the retiring OD and I went to the outer office where I donned the "OD" arm band and web belt with .45-caliber sidearm. No one had suggested to me that the weapon was to be worn in a particular way, but I remembered how the old-time Westerners looked, so I adjusted the belt so that the holster hung midway from hip to knee, and swaggered down the Headquarters steps.

Approaching me up the steps came a captain (a captain at that time had at least 15 years of service), and I threw him a snappy salute. Without returning the salute, he blasted me. "Lieutenant, who in the goddamn hell do you think you are, Buffalo Bill?"

He proceeded to cinch up the belt, so that it was horizontal to the ground again, imposing severe restrictions on my respiratory and circulatory systems!

And so in the summer of 1941 it was on to San Angelo Army Air Field, Texas, which was later renamed Goodfellow Field after a local hero of World War I. I stopped at a service station to don the uniform, and was confronted by newspaper headlines, "AIR BASE BAPTIZED IN BLOOD!"

The previous day had been the day to transfer the San Angelo Field from Army engineers to Air Corps, with Army brass and local bigwigs in attendance, and ceremonies to be climaxed with large formation fly-by.

Formation lead, for some unknown reason, was flying at airspeed below normal cruise, misjudged a turn to review leg, and pulled into a steep turn. He should have positioned the final turn farther from the field, allowing easy "S" turns for line-up, and maintaining comfortable airspeed.

In a screw-up like this, "Tail End Charlie," or "Green Sixteen," pay the piper! The leader's turn steepens progressively, down the formation, accompanied by decreasing airspeed, leaving the last guys close to stall and running out of flying speed.

There is no way that any jock worth his salt will break out of formation, especially on a big show with lots of folks. (I'm not justifying that attitude,

The bachelor officers quarters (BOQ) at Goodfellow Field, San Angelo, Texas.

only explaining it.) So, about a mile from the field, tail-end Charlie crossed over the edge and spun in from 500 feet.

I soon found that military/civilian relations varied with the age of the military facility. The oldest had the poorest regard by surrounding locals; those stations constructed since the 1940s had great relations and mutual respect with the local citizens. In making the military feel welcome and a part of the community, I rate the people of San Angelo, Texas, among the top four or five! They immediately threw open homes, churches, service clubs, and recreational facilities to all Army personnel. Ranchers entertained at barbecues. I know that several of those stationed there returned after the war and made their homes in San Angelo.

I was assigned three cadet "studs," just starting the first phase of basic training. We flew North American BT-14s at first, then switched to the BT-13 and -15 Valiants, which earned the appropriate nickname "Vultee Vibrator." Inconsistent spin recovery was a problem as long as I was at Goodfellow. We had several bail-outs, dual and solo. In a two- or three-turn spin, rotation could sometimes continue after control inputs as many as four more turns before recovering.

A bunch of jocks felt that this exceeded their contract with Uncle Sam and "gave the airplane back to the contractor," as the saying goes. I always recovered, but admit that I climbed to "nosebleed" altitude before spin

A North American BT-14 in the clouds over Randolph Field, Texas.

entry. It was never determined why a particular airplane would have three lousy write-ups on spin recovery, then perform beautifully for the next ten or more flights. But it did keep flying interesting!

Duty was relaxed and leisurely until the fall of 1941 — three- to four-hour flight time days and a five-day week. I enjoyed the challenge and learning of teaching and am proud that I only eliminated one stud in seven classes. I was his third instructor and believe that he had decided against the "Wild Blue Yonder." No one could screw up the way he did, and this was verified when he came to me before leaving and allowed that he was a "born Infantryman!"

Pearl Harbor came December 7, 1941, and with it seven-hour flight time days, including night flying.

The monotony of instructing was broken by flights to the West Coast, ferrying Vultees to Goodfellow, for an average of ten hours' flying time. Our flight commander had heard, or read in *War Aces* (a World War II flight combat book), about formation landing procedures for 9 to 18 airplanes: two Luftberry circles — a defensive maneuver developed by and named after the German ace — with 500-foot altitude separation. After each 360° turn, a lower aircraft peeled off and entered the landing traffic pattern, replaced in his circle by someone higher.

But it was never clear how the guy peeling off, or his replacement, was to be designated, which resulted in a rat race! I wondered how it looked from the ground and found out when I taxied in and discovered the ground troops convulsed with laughter. Thereafter, whenever we landed at a field that had been graced with our display, work stopped and the word was out: "The Keystone Kops are back!"

We were the only ones in the Air Corps doing the maneuver and we never could convince the flight CO to change. I understand that he was killed during World War II in a mid-air collision during formation join-up.

Besides the enjoyment of instructing, my interests were increasing flying time and broadening experience, so I flew cross-country almost every weekend and volunteered for any official flights. On one ferry trip, I took ten days of leave and got some flights in the Lockheed P-38 Lightning. What an airplane! With other cross-country flights and classmates passing through, I managed to talk my way into flights in the P-39 Airacobra, P-40 Warhawk, and even the B-18 bomber.

I had my first close contact with a fatal aircraft accident while stationed at San Angelo. A crash was reported five miles from the base, and I was sent by jeep to secure the area. A solo student had spun in at a fairly flat angle with his engine displaced at 90°, just forward of the instrument panel. Several ranchers and hands were grouped some distance from the wreckage, and I wished I could join them.

The pilot had thrown his arm up at impact and was leaning forward with his arm and glare shield imbedded in his face. I couldn't find a pulse, so I draped a tarp over the body, momentarily exposing his face. Somehow, I didn't vomit, but some of the onlookers couldn't hack it. My first introduction to life in the raw.

Goodfellow Field can't be passed over without crediting the lessons and impressions gained there, 16 valuable months. It was at Goodfellow that I verified what a French general once said: "Any army is only as good as its non-commissioned officers corps." Our training squadron's engineering officer, a good friend who was well qualified for the job, took two weeks' leave and recommended me as fill-in. Me, the seeker for left-handed screwdrivers, right-handed hammers, reverse drive screws, *ad infinitum*.

On my first duty day as squadron engineering officer, I was trying to sneak into the office, snapping to a stiff brace when startled by a bellowed "Attention" from a flight chief, master sergeant. I finally realized that I probably didn't have to assume the posture, being the only officer in the room.

The non-coms could have painted me as the dunce I was, but instead asked things like, "Would the Lieutenant sign the forms 392, 489B, as indicated by paper clips?" And "If the Lieutenant approves, would he initial the fuel requisitions?"

The base commander, Charley Palmer, was an old-timer who was close to retirement, and was a good customer at the Officers Club bar. Charley was never out of line nor missed any duty, but I wondered why he always had a junior pilot with him on his weekend cross-country flights. I found out and learned why they were called "seeing-eye pilots" when advised that I would have the duty for a trip to College Station, Texas, for an Aggie football game.

I wondered why the proposed takeoff time was way in excess of time en route, but was soon edified. My leader had a crumpled area map, no course lines, and I was not consulted until well into the flight, at which time we were heading in the wrong direction.

I had been following our path, within a county or so, and finally realized that the boss would not resist my stick and rudder pressures toward a desired heading. In fact, he expected them. I finally found a river, which I suspected might go by our destination, and off we went. Damned if we didn't find the field, landed, and taxied in, exactly one minute early! The ranchers and rich folk chuckled and greeted us with "By God, Charley, when you say 11:45, you mean it."

The next day was no sweat! I flew him home with the world's greatest hangover — his. I don't think his feet touched the ground from the hotel to his quarters. Monday morning came, and he was the first one in Headquarters, and the last one out. A real old soldier.

If it hasn't yet, it will soon be noted that I seemed to meet with more than my share of misadventure, and the question will arise as to why I didn't seek another occupation. Simple: I loved flying more than anything in life, except for Margee Lou!

Which leads to my demonstration of night flare landing. Aircraft procured through the late 1930s were equipped with parachute flares and release mechanisms, which were to be used strictly as a last resort — pitch black, lost, and up to the navel in the "gotta get downs!"

No tactical doctrine or written procedures were available, but we listened to the Old Eagles (who never volunteered for the demo, which should have told me something) and developed this scenario: "Upon determining best landing area and wind direction" (I never knew how this was done when you can't see the goddamned ground!), "fly upwind at 800 feet over desired landing point" (see comment above), "release flare, and into left hand, descending turn."

Now, the flare life was two minutes, which just happens to be the time required for a 360° normal rate turn, so you had to honk that baby around and land prior to flare "death" (burn-out).

In early World War II training and combat, it was found essential that crew members, mainly pilots, be protected from bright light for a substantial period prior to takeoff and during night flight. So our Air Corps pilot, flying in pitch black, activated the landing flare, with the multi-candle power exposure, knowing it would go back to black by landing time. All this in an unknown area, altitude, and terrain!

I always wanted to learn something new, so I volunteered for the demo. Results were as to be expected: a grass field, black, flare died, and I ran out of vision, airspeed, altitude, and ideas, all at once! Amazingly, the BT-14 was undamaged, but the embryo "second John Instructor," who begged to ride along "and learn," developed a speech impediment and never uttered a word to me again!

After Pearl Harbor Day, I submitted requests for transfer to any tactical unit, with no response, so I volunteered for every quota levied on the base — even gliders, and that's desperate! Finally, I got a personal audience with the commander who allowed that if I was so damned eager, I would be on the next levy. I prayed for fighters, but a B-17 bomber quota came. I left for Sebring, Florida, in June 1942.

Chapter 4

B-17 Training

AT SEBRING, FLORIDA, I encountered my first B-17 Flying Fortress — a monster! (The B-17 would fit under one wing of transports and bombers of the 1950s and on). From June 1 to July 17, heat and humidity were the same — 100 degrees and 100 percent. Buildings were new and rough, one-storied (except for the barracks), and my class got a top floor.

The first week was all ground school and note-taking, impossible because the paper soon became saturated with sweat. I had to study with my texts at arms' length, because of perspiration drippage. Meals were miserable and sleep impossible. We drew fresh sheets daily, but they were soon saturated; we hung mattresses over outside stairways hoping for some dry-out, but they were usually wetter from afternoon thunderstorms. I had the greatest

. . . I encountered my first B-17 Flying Fortress – a monster!

sympathy for those fighting in the Pacific — they had even worse discomfort and were getting shot at, too!

We spent half the day flying: 150 hours in 40 days. I flew as pilot, copilot, or just passenger. There were four students and an instructor on each flight. We had to wear gloves on the flight line and in flight, or we could expect severe burns from touching metal. This was my first realization that "war is hell!"

Among the morale crunchers were the training programs for aircraft check-out, unit training, and continuing combat proficiency. Rather than analysis of general and specific requirements to develop flight/ground training and numbers of hours/missions, the approach was to estimate, by wild-assed guess (WAG) an impressive total of flying/ground hours, and add to or maybe double it, just to be sure. From this came a "training program" to meet these magic figures, without guidance or priorities. And what the hell, toss in a few more hours.

The millions of hours wasted could have only gone unquestioned in the panic, confusion, and ignorance that accompanied World War II. After flight proficiency was attained, more training squares were filled by "boring holes," which essentially meant carrying depth charges on anti-submarine missions with no bombardier or navigator aboard! The jocks did not have the foggiest idea how to point the charges at a sub (assuming that's what it was), how to distinguish between friend or foe, or how to ensure explosion of the charge if it happened to get close to the enemy. There were also lengthy "Navigation Training Missions," without one of those worthies in the neighborhood.

Ground training was even worse. When appropriate material had been covered, we dug out whatever could be found to meet the magic number of hours. Lessons in "Military Law" would fill in any hours required and it helped keep us scared. "Role of the Military in American Government" was obviously interesting and motivating, especially to the 18-year-old crew member! Finally, we covered the old standby, "Venereal Disease: Recognition, Avoidance, and Cure." "Cure" was always included, indicating lack of confidence in "avoidance!"

The guy ram-rodding the B-17 program was an airline captain who inspired us in his greeting with, "One thing you will learn here is that there is no danger in flying through thunderstorms, if you know how to fly."

He was always checking area weather for thunderbumps and, finding one, would schedule the first available B-17 and look for volunteers. Us flying folks would immediately climb out windows, crawl under things, and lock toilet doors.

Now and then he would catch a brand-new "second John" and off they'd go. It seems that there were no debriefings on record from these co-pilots; the word was that they were either AWOL, assigned to the hospital "boob ward," or awaiting processing of "Request for Release from Flying Status" papers. I heard later that the captain was killed in 1943, flying in a thunderstorm!

I received orders in June 1942 to Geiger Field in Spokane, Washington — the Headquarters for organizing, equipping, and training bombardment groups for combat.

I was still a second looie with 19 months of commissioned service, but I was surrounded by boys with higher rank and less service. There were no problems until the "rendering of the salute by junior officers to those senior in rank" was gleefully brought to my attention by those "senior in rank." They even suggested that I walk on their left, two paces to the rear!

This situation resulted in a few rhubarbs, most behind the barracks, but one in front of the Officers Club. The latter brought the MPs into the picture, and got the attention of the brass. Actually, I was glad, because I was fast running out of teeth and knuckles. There was some talk of courts-martial, but the problem was resolved by these words of wisdom: "Gentlemen, understand something — rank among lieutenants is like virtue among ladies of ill repute!"

I was assigned to the newly activated 96th Bombardment Group (H) — for *Heavy*, as in B-17s! — given command of a ten-man combat crew, and moved to Boise, Idaho, for outfitting and training. There was not an approved training program so we bored holes in the ozone and flew parts runs to Cheyenne and Memphis, 9 hours and 20 minutes out, 9 hours and 45 minutes back. I logged 146 hours flight time the first month!

The 96th Bombardment Group was then transferred back to Rapid City, South Dakota, for the next phase of training. It was still a fairly relaxed way of life until the approved training program arrived, when it really hit the fan. But before that, I was sent to a nearby base to pick up a Douglas A-20 Havoc light attack bomber for target towing. There was no manual or instructions, but I met a pilot who had a friend who had flown them.

Between us, we located essentials like throttles, prop controls, landing gear, and flap handles, and figured out how to start the two engines, and I was off! The manual was waiting for me at Rapid City, so I felt smart enough to start check-outs.

Nothing short of a direct order would have me towing targets — I would take my chances with enemy fire overseas, but exposing myself to rookie gunners while still in the U.S. of A. had no appeal. But to get more flying time in the A-20 — a beauty — I convinced Ops that pilots checking out should observe touch-and-go landings from the nose section, thus getting me 12 more hours of flying time. A few pilots lost interest in becoming qualified; some experienced "fear of flying" temporarily. I confess to having experimented and found that barrel and aileron rolls and loops could be done in airplanes with more than one engine. This may have accounted for some of the loss of interest!

To illustrate our naiveté in aerial gunnery, gunners fired at banners towed parallel, on the same or reciprocal headings. This bore no resemblance to fighter combat tactics, but did present problems in estimating angle-off and deflection. Without the ability to determine individual accuracy, effectiveness of this training could not be determined.

Even more questionable were the gunners firing on ground targets, day and night, from B-17s at low level and high speed. Most of the pilots had a ball, while the rest of the crew, including some of the gunners, were engaged in upchuck! But training blocks were filled, maximum flying time was attained, and gasoline and ammunition were expended.

After a few of these flights, with minimum ground time, the stench was so bad that crew members were throwing up on pre-flight. Finally, the aircraft were grounded after two ground gunnery flights for clean-up. The next problem was that the maintenance guys argued, rightly, that they were technicians, not porters. The solution was to use prisoners with high-pressure hoses, but they had to be issued portable oxygen masks and gloves. No one could have anticipated these problems, so we became adept at stomping out such fires as they flared up.

We were shipped off again in late 1942, this time to Walla Walla, Washington, and the 24-hour training program. Crews were assigned to one of three training groups, or sections. The schedule went as follows: flying and/or ground training for eight hours; play, recreate, or whatever suited, for eight hours; sleep eight hours. And you better, by God, be doing whatever your schedule called for!

Recognizing that there could be a problem in getting through the "play" period, the Officers Club bar was on a 24-hour schedule. But even I couldn't face a dry martini at 8:00 a.m.! Lots of B-17s were left in the hills around Walla Walla, most due to the inadequate instrument and radio approach and letdown procedures, but it's certain that some crews had what we now call "jet lag."

And to be sure that combat crews were in top physical condition, pilots were directed to lead their crews in 30 minutes of calisthenics on the ramp after each flight! If there hadn't been a war on, that bit of genius would have received the treatment it deserved!

Soon it was time to practice moving again. We were off to Pocatello, Idaho — the same training, just a different place. But we had a nice break, because six crews were picked to go to Albuquerque, New Mexico, to fly for a war effort movie called *Bombardier*. A typical World War II product, it would be laughed off the screen in later days and we got "booed" when it was shown in England. Maintenance worked all night, but couldn't get all six ships ready to go to Albuquerque at the same time. The group CO, a real "iron ass," said the whole formation would go at once, even if it took forever, and it damned near did!

Finally we launched at dusk, and I was leading the second "V" stacked under the lead three. A low pass over the field almost drove us into the ground, until I casually mentioned to the junior birdman who was leading that, if we lived through it, I intended to do all sorts of bad things to his face! We were flying at an altitude estimated to clear most of the mountains on course, in pitch black dark, and "Ole Fearless Up Front" ordered, "Assume en route formation and check in."

None of us had had any B-17 night formation experience and had never heard of "en route formation!" Check in? With what? We did work out altitude assignments, but not too effectively, since we all fought propwash — the turbulence created by following other aircraft — the whole trip. It was a real laugher when we were supposed to join up for peel-off and landing. Our "mass attack" on Albuquerque caused the tower guys to evacuate when six B-17s rained down from all directions.

During the ten days of filming, we stayed in the hotel with the movie folks, all expenses paid, within reason. We tried to slip some drinks by the exchequer type, with no joy until we worked out a deal with the waitresses to pad meal chits with drinks. He never questioned a 35-cent hamburger costing $3.50.

Six B-17s, flying for the movie *Bombardier*, on the ramp at Albuquerque, New Mexico. Jack Hayes's airplane and crew are the first in line.

Jack Hayes with Marge Stewart, starlet in the movie *Bombardier*, at Albuquerque, New Mexico.

Most filming was of taxiing, takeoffs, and landings, but there were a few aerial formation "takes," as we movie types call them! The leads were Anne Shirley, Pat O'Brien, and John Ryan.

But the real star, and a doll, was a beautiful bit player named Marge (the first of two Marges in my life). She furnished sex appeal and fabulous "propwash" shots. I was to meet her again in England at the close of the war.

Following our short movie careers, we went back to Pocatello for the same training and supply runs. I was promoted to assistant group Operations officer and had to leave my crew. I would never forget them and the wonderful memories.

I went to Pyote, Texas, a real jewel, for more preparation for overseas. But I did fly one more time with my old crew — an endurance flight with bomb-bay tanks lasting 23 hours. This was my first experience with pilot fatigue. I leveled off for landing at around 50 feet, and it was a real tooth-rattler! I'm sure the crew was glad to see me become a staff type.

Around this time, I passed the 2,000-hour flight-time mark. I flew back to Goodfellow Field to visit old friends, most of whom stayed there, or elsewhere in training command, during the war. While there, I found that while I was escorting a group of B-17s on a mission, one of my Goodfellow friends was shot down by flak and marked KIA — killed in action.

Finally, the group went to Salina, Kansas, for final inspections of equipment and flight checks for pilot qualification. I blew the instrument take-off, but passed. They wouldn't flunk anyone that close to deployment!

One evening at the Officers Club, I was in an altercation with another captain concerning homesteading rights on a young lady. The discussion resulted in a clinch. We rolled down the stairs to the ballroom, stopping at the feet of the group commander. We jumped up, brushed each other off, and said, "Friendly argument, Sir." He gave no response — none was expected — and we were gone!

I did become enamored of another local lass, and exchanged all kinds of vows and teary farewells. (Come to think of it, I never saw *her* crying!) I got a "Dear Jack" letter shortly after arriving in England — I guess it just wasn't meant to be.

Finally, I was off to England and the wars via Presque Isle, Maine, Gander, Canada, and Prestwick, Scotland. The flight lasted 20 hours and 50 minutes, single ships, 10-minute separation. The navigators were easily recognized — they were the cadavers who only left their beds to eat or fly.

We arrived in England on April 27, 1943, and I flew my first mission on May 14.

Chapter 5

B-17 Bomber Combat

NY DISCUSSION OF the air war in Europe must also contain the battle of concepts in the U.S. Army Air Corps — bomber *vs.* fighter. Those believers in the precision bombing and invulnerability of the heavy bomber — from junior officer to chief of staff — were convinced that war could be won by strategic bombing without fighter support, and using Army troops for mopping up, establishing prisoner of war (POW) camps, and occupation of enemy territory!

The aircraft production program was, initially, heavily devoted to the B-17 Flying Fortress and B-24 Liberator bombers. Concession was given to some production of twin-engine bombers, to assist the Army in the final stages of the war.

Not until the . . . massive losses . . . did the reluctant call go out for fighter escort and increased fighter aircraft production.

Boeing B-17 Flying Fortresses pulling contrails in June 1943. The bombers could not fly without fighter escort, because the visibility of the contrails made the B-17 an easy target for German fighters.

The fighter aircraft devotee, who was dubbed "fly-boy," was ignored in the establishment of strategic policy. None, or very few, were awarded senior rank, even after World War II.

The German Luftwaffe and the British Royal Air Force had learned that only night bombing was possible for the "heavies" — the B-17s and B-24s — but their experience, and the advice of the RAF, were ignored.

Not until the early missions of 1943 and the massive losses later (like 120 B-17s lost on two separate missions), did the reluctant call go out for fighter escort and increased fighter aircraft production. Even then, bomber commanders attempted to dictate the tactics and utilization of fighter escort! This only stopped when the group and command leaders threatened resignation.

The bomber element prevailed postwar, and in September 1947 the United States Air Force was finally designated as a separate command. Strategic Air Command (SAC) and its bombers were in complete domination, not only relegating the fighter to an insignificant role, but "picking the pockets" of the other two major services, Army and Navy, to make SAC even more dominant! This "tunnel vision" lasted until the fall of the Russian Republic, the "Evil Empire."

The Fighter Command was only saved from oblivion by the Korean "police action" and the Vietnam War. In Korea, World War II P-51 Mustangs flew for most of the conflict. In Vietnam, the Douglas A-1 Skyraider — a Navy fighter used in Korea — and the McDonnell F-4 Phantom — a Navy jet fighter — were the primary fighter forces of the USAF. The Republic F-105 Thunderchief, the only USAF-procured fighter (a multi-million-dollar product), was equipped for long-range, *strategic* bombing, but was used in the tactical mission and averaged losses of one squadron a month!

I predict that before the next century the USAF will be dissolved and their missions and weapons assigned to the Army and Navy, or retained as "Space Command" — a designation longed for by Air Force academia!

Our first English base had been constructed specifically for the U.S. Army Air Forces, but was nothing like the early World War II, former RAF fields which some American units had occupied. We were housed in

corrugated steel Nissen huts that were coal-heated. With coal in short supply, the men invented some most ingenious schemes for raids on the central coal depot.

On all bases the ground facilities were spread out, in addition to the aircraft being dispersed, and transportation was a continual problem. Bi-
cycles helped, but they had limited use during rainy seasons, which
seemed to be nine months of the year.

It is recorded that the American soldier maintained high morale in the
face of all discomforts, and the Army Air Corps trooper in Europe never
demonstrated less than the finest attitudes, fierce unit loyalty, and pride in
the accomplishments of his pilot, or crew, and airplane. There was a deep
sorrow and sense of loss when "his" failed to return. Ground crews sometimes refused to leave the hardstand, even long after they knew fuel ex-
haustion time had passed.

With eventual acceptance of reality, others granted that crew privacy as
they gathered and disposed of equipment belonging to their aircraft, and
turned over combat crew items entrusted to their care to the personal
affairs officer. Items were supposed to have been turned in after mission
briefing, but some combat guys felt that it was a reverse hex on luck if you
left something with the last one you saw — someone on the ground crew
— before flight: "I'll be back to pick up what I left with you."

This idea was one of the thin threads that helped us to accept, or maybe
ignore, the fact that some of those taking off would not return. The "It
won't happen to me" attitude helped us face combat and losses day after
day. It has been suggested that the only outlook to get through combat
was, "I'm gonna' die, the only question is when!" But most combat veterans — land, sea, or air — will say that fatalism is rare, and that with the
loss of hope comes the inability to face danger. Well, look who's sounding like a shrink!

Our first group combat mission was a comedy of errors reflecting lack
of experience. Ground echelon, via ship and train, arrived shortly after the
aircraft and crews. There was ground instruction on formation and combat
procedures, and crews flew familiarization flights over the UK.

On three consecutive days, crews were briefed, pre-flighted, and
boarded their Fortresses, only to be cancelled. This was tough on fliers and
ground troops. Crews were sweating out "the first one," and maintenance
personnel were reconfiguring airplanes. For an unknown reason, when a
mission was scrubbed, the planners changed bomb loads, and/or fuze set-

tings, and sometimes even fuel loads — all for the same target! Finally, the 96th Bombardment Group launched, and therein lies a story!

The lieutenant colonel group commander led, with a Headquarters brigadier general observing. The group Operations officer flew as deputy lead, and I was the assistant, which meant being responsible for ground coordination and unscrewing screw-ups. I had no problems with coordination, but it was later suggested, forcefully, that I really fouled up!

The Fightin' 96th was airborne, and I was heading for the sack, when the RAF officer in charge of the control tower (or "Flying Control") flagged me down: "Lead is aborting and requests that he be parked next to standby aircraft, to expedite relaunch."

Standby?! In my defense (which was worthless at the time), a "standby" aircraft had not been designated. The shortness of the mission negated returning to the base and getting off in time to rejoin our group before target time. Obviously, a standby would have been effective in the event of ground abort, but this was never brought up. Rest assured that thereafter, there were standbys and substitute aircraft all around the place, until the days of "maximum effort" made even satisfying the field order requirements problematic.

Anyway, here comes the lead, roaring toward the field at full power and pulling vapor trails, indicating that his airspeed was above red line. His B-17 racked up into a 90° bank turn to a downwind leg, with landing gear and flaps lowered well above the maximum allowable speed. He came too fast into his landing and turned off the runway so hot that the tires should have peeled off! He pulled into the hardstand next to a B-17 that might have been the standby. The tower was unable to advise the location of the replacement aircraft for reasons discussed above, and I understand that when lead was so informed, his reaction shattered windows!

I kept my jeep out of sight until the lead had parked, then I pulled into the adjacent hardstand and watched from under the jeep the fascinating events that transpired. Before the engines had stopped, the waist door slammed open, scattering ground men and knocking the general, who meant to be the first man out, all the way into the tail gun position. The boss apologized, briefly, and then let go with, "Where in the goddamn hell is the substitute airplane?"

With this, everyone suddenly developed intense interests in important things like the condition of tires, proper number of rivets in metal surfaces, and anything else that would get them out of the way of what promised to

be a large-scale explosion and royal chewing out! Everyone, that is, except
the public relations people who had been sent from London to photograph
and interview our leader after the group's first strike at the Hun. Sadly,
they were unaware that the target would probably be farther away than a
40-minute round trip. To their subsequent grief, a "first balloon" — head-
line maker — and a picture-taker were all over the Old Man as he snarled
and clawed his way out the door.

This was the only time I have seen someone suffer severe shock without physical injury! They staggered away, supporting each other, grateful
that the interviewer wasn't digesting his notepad and the photographer's
camera wasn't protruding from his rear end — both of which had been
graphically announced as the commander's intentions if they weren't
immediately out of sight.

And there was another grievous error by an onlooker: still searching for
the substitute B-17, the boss called for someone from the base support
group. In his desperation and rage, he had forgotten that the support group
was responsible for housekeeping, basic supplies, feeding the troops, and
stuff like that — certainly not involved in designating spare airplanes,
which this next character would have done well to remember.

To his eternal regret, but responding to a chance to contribute to the war
effort, a slight, meek "first looie" stepped up and asked how he could help.
The following conversation, slightly sanitized, ensued:

"Where in the goddamn hell is the standby airplane?"

"Sir, I don't know where in the goddamn hell it is."

"Why don't you know?"

"Sir, I don't know why."

"Aren't you the goddamn maintenance officer?"

"No, Sir, I'm not the goddamn maintenance officer."

"Then who in the goddamn hell are you?"

"Sir, I don't know who I am!"

Rumor has it that this sad character still roams the fields around Snet-
terton Heath, trying to find someone who can tell him just who in the hell
he is!

The question became moot when the roar of engines indicated an
approaching formation, and coming into view was the 96th Bomb Group
(H), in magnificent formation. But elapsed flight time told the sad story —
group abort! Seems the deputy lead (we *did* have one of them) encountered all kinds of trouble, including radios out, and when he tried to abort,

he couldn't shake the group! By God, he was the deputy and where he went, they followed!

An inauspicious start, yes, but our group finished with one of the greatest combat records in the Eighth Air Force. Although it led in losses, it should be noted that the 96th Bomb Group was one of the earliest in combat; at first the missions were long and unescorted — and a large number of losses occurred in Russia from German bombers, on the first shuttle mission.

My first mission is a memory that will never diminish in clarity, though perhaps in accuracy, with the passing years. Our target was in France — either an industrial complex or airfield, but not a very long one. We had a Spitfire escort as far as the coast, in-bound, and they picked us up there on the way out. I was in the copilot seat, deputy lead, on the Old Man's right wing.

I got my first look at flak, which had been described as "moderate and inaccurate" — a classification reached by counting bursts per second, number of hits in the formation, and computed by some "chairborne warrior" who would never be exposed. It was a fascinating sight at first, but with experience came terror and a sense of disbelief, and then gratitude every time you got through it!

Even the enemy fighters were fascinating in grace and maneuverability; they were not really recognized as a threat, then. The other pilot naively said, "Look, they're blinking their landing lights at us." Then came the realization that we were being *fired* at, when we saw pieces coming off us and other aircraft, which brought forth . . . "Holy Shit!"

Things improved with the P-47 Thunderbolt, P-38 Lightning, and P-51 Mustang escorts farther and farther into the European continent, though there were still heavy bomber losses. Even in the last missions of the war, some were going down. I feel strongly that these losses would have been reduced if the bomber brass had listened to the suggestions of the fighter leaders.

These fighter escorts — our "Little Friends" — did a tremendous job! Observing them increased my determination to join their fold, and I worked toward that end, without detracting from my performance with the bombers — the "Big Friends." I was lucky to have an understanding commander in the 96th Bomb Group, and I went with him when we were assigned to a combat wing, and a higher command.

While in bombers, I disregarded a fundamental precept of flying, which

Above and opposite page: B-17 combat formations in mid-1944 showing lead, high, and low squadrons (the latter usually received the heaviest fighter attack). The formations required exceptional pilot technique for high and low squadron leaders to maintain position without scattering the formations.

says that "Flying proficiency is directly proportional to frequency and recency of flight, regardless of experience, total flight time, and types of aircraft." I considered myself quite capable of flying from the pilot's seat and resented the practice of task force, division, and group leaders occupying the copilot seat, even standing between seats with the designation of "command pilot." Not only did I feel this was an affront, but it opened the door for the unqualified to ride along on a sortie or two, stay out of the way, and be decorated.

It is to my discredit that I did not understand that: 1. The leader had to concentrate on communications and command decisions; 2. Coping with the mechanics of flying would reduce his command effectiveness; and 3. In the event of battle damage, the crew deserved the highest proficiency in the guy who would have to get them home — or, at least control the wounded beast long enough for crew bail-out!

With shameful arrogance, I prevailed on the group and squadron commanders to allow me to fly from the pilot's seat on the crew leading the

high squadron, their pilot being temporarily grounded. Without any idea
of his flying ability, I have no doubt that he was *really* appreciated, after
my fiasco!

Simply stated, I was to lead two flights of three, above and down sun
from the lead, on a 10½-hour flight to southern France. The length of the
flight should have been recognized as a physical challenge, but except for
dressing properly, I didn't do anything right the whole day.

We departed the field in a perfect high squadron position — I have no
idea why — and things went "ape shape" from there on. We changed

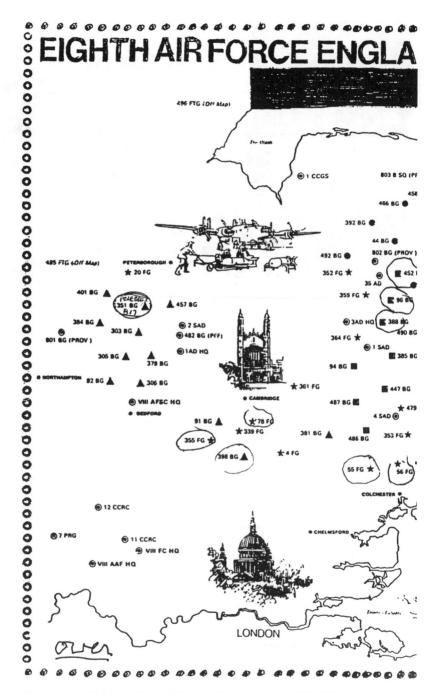

Map showing Eighth Air Force fighter and bomber bases, 1942-1945.

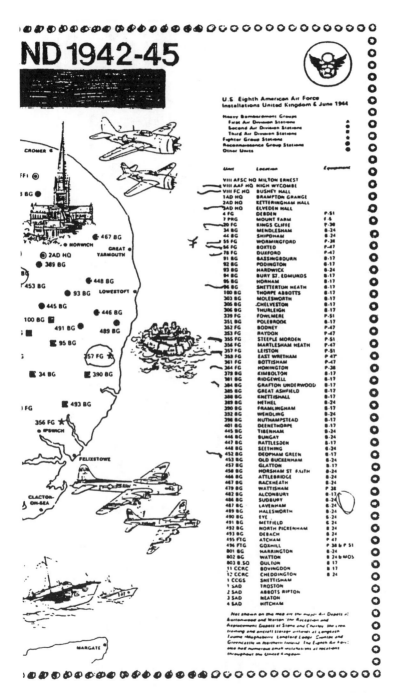

ND 1942-45

U.S. Eighth American Air Force
Installations United Kingdom 6 June 1944

Heavy Bombardment Groups
  First Air Division Stations
  Second Air Division Stations
  Third Air Division Stations
Fighter Group Stations
Reconnaissance Group Stations
Other Units

Unit	Location	Equipment
VIII AFSC HQ	MILTON ERNEST	
VIII AAF HQ	HIGH WYCOMBE	
VIII FC HQ	BUSHEY HALL	
1AD HQ	BRAMPTON GRANGE	
2AD HQ	KETTERINGHAM HALL	
3AD HQ	ELVEDEN HALL	
4 FG	DEBDEN	P-51
7 PRG	MOUNT FARM	F-5
20 FG	KINGS CLIFFE	P-38
34 BG	MENDLESHAM	B-24
44 BG	SHIPDHAM	B-24
55 FG	WORMINGFORD	P-38
56 FG	BOXTED	P-47
78 FG	DUXFORD	P-47
91 BG	BASSINGBOURN	B-17
92 BG	PODINGTON	B-17
93 BG	HARDWICK	B-24
94 BG	BURY ST. EDMUNDS	B-17
95 BG	HORHAM	B-17
96 BG	SNETTERTON HEATH	B-17
100 BG	THORPE ABBOTS	B-17
303 BG	MOLESWORTH	B-17
305 BG	CHELVESTON	B-17
306 BG	THURLEIGH	B-17
339 FG	FOWLMERE	P-51
351 BG	POLEBROOK	B-17
352 FG	BODNEY	P-47
353 FG	RAYDON	P-47
355 FG	STEEPLE MORDEN	P-51
356 FG	MARTLESHAM HEATH	P-47
357 FG	LEISTON	P-51
359 FG	EAST WRETHAM	P-47
361 FG	BOTTISHAM	P-47
364 FG	HONINGTON	P-38
379 BG	KIMBOLTON	B-17
381 BG	RIDGEWELL	B-17
384 BG	GRAFTON UNDERWOOD	B-17
385 BG	GREAT ASHFIELD	B-17
388 BG	KNETTISHALL	B-17
389 BG	HETHEL	B-24
390 BG	FRAMLINGHAM	B-17
392 BG	WENDLING	B-24
398 BG	NUTHAMPSTEAD	B-17
401 BG	DEENETHORPE	B-17
445 BG	TIBENHAM	B-24
446 BG	BUNGAY	B-24
447 BG	RATTLESDEN	B-17
448 BG	SEETHING	B-24
452 BG	DEOPHAM GREEN	B-17
453 BG	OLD BUCKENHAM	B-24
457 BG	GLATTON	B-17
458 BG	HORSHAM ST. FAITH	B-24
466 BG	ATTLEBRIDGE	B-24
467 BG	RACKHEATH	B-24
479 BG	WATTISHAM	P-38
482 BG	ALCONBURY	B-17
486 BG	SUDBURY	B-24
487 BG	LAVENHAM	B-24
489 BG	HALESWORTH	B-24
490 BG	EYE	B-24
491 BG	METFIELD	B-24
492 BG	NORTH PICKENHAM	B-24
493 BG	DEBACH	B-24
495 FTG	ATCHAM	P-47
496 FTG	GOXHILL	P-38 & P-51
801 BG	HARRINGTON	B-24
802 BG	WATTON	B-24 & MOS
803 B.SQ	OULTON	B-17
11 CCRC	BOVINGDON	B-17
12 CCRC	CHEDDINGTON	B-24
1 CCGS	SNETTISHAM	
1 SAD	TROSTON	
2 SAD	ABBOTS RIPTON	
3 SAD	NEATON	
4 SAD	HITCHAM	

Not shown on the map are the major Air Depots at
Burtonwood and Warton for Reception and
Replacement Depots at Stone and Chorley; the area
training and aircraft storage airfields at Langfoth
Towne Maghaberrie Langford Lodge, Cwmbe and
Greencastle in Northern Ireland. The Eighth Air Force
also had numerous small installations at locations
throughout the United Kingdom.

Map labels: CROMER, FF1, 3 BG, 467 BG, NORWICH, GREAT YARMOUTH, 2AD HQ, 389 BG, 448 BG, 453 BG, 93 BG, LOWESTOFT, 445 BG, 446 BG, 100 BG, 491 BG, 489 BG, 95 BG, 357 FG, 34 BG, 390 BG, 493 BG, 356 FG, IPSWICH, FELIXSTOWE, CLACTON-ON-SEA, MARGATE

Eighth Air Force Historical Society

Painting by Frank E. Beresford of the task force that bombed Regensburg, crossing the Alps to North Africa.   Eighth Air Force Historical Society

power settings, adjusted airspeeds, and "S'ed" to maintain position, requiring anticipation and a delicate touch on the controls. I was over-controlling, pumping throttles, and was so far behind the airplane that it was like I wasn't even there — and a bunch of those bomber types wished to Christ that I wasn't!

After some time of exertion and terror, trying to stay with (or avoid collision with) me their leader, the wingmen headed for positions vacated by aborts. Where none were available, they tagged on wherever they could on lead or low squadrons — but not, by God, on the high one!

The pictures of massive bomber formations over Europe, while awesome, could not depict the airmanship, ability, and effort required to maintain force integrity in the face of flak and fighter attacks. Also, maneuvers were restricted by, and dependent on, positions of other formations, including bomb-fall clearance from above and below. There were several cases of lost or badly damaged bombers when "friendly" bombs removed essential aircraft components in passing.

And so a greatly deflated and humble "Pussy Cat," as opposed to a "Tiger," I reported to debriefing. I heard one of the pilots bending the squadron CO's ear about the horrors experienced trying to stay with the yo-yo leading the squadron. He spotted me and shut up, but I told him to let it all out. I then turned to the squadron CO and said, "Next time some chairborne warrior wants the left seat, send him to me and I'll handle the problem." What a way to relearn something I already knew!

Later on, as I gained fighter experience, it became evident that many aborted bomber missions could have been salvaged with proficiency in weather formation flying, plus an understanding of those types of weather that could not be handled in formation. Command policy dictated mission cancellation, or diversion to alternate targets, when target cloud tops were above briefed bombing altitudes. And some strike forces turned back because of en route conditions, with their target area wide open.

Early in the B-17 build-up, experience in formation weather flying would have demonstrated that visual contact could have been maintained, in most conditions. Operating procedures would be revised for more time separation between large formations, as an example, and there would have been an increase in combat-effectiveness percentages.

Of the many fighter weather penetrations I flew, there was only one formation breakup. A flight of four F-100s were redeploying from Japan to the U.S. On letdown into Hickham AFB in Hawaii, the clouds looked black, and were! The flight separated as had been briefed, reformed under the klag (overcast), and landed.

But as for my B-17 combat, a memorable mission was the shuttle to North Africa after bombing Regensburg. The rest of the Eighth Air Force was to strike Schweinfurt and return to England. The key to success was strict adherence to task force timing, so that German fighters launched against us would be refueling and rearming when the Schweinfurt formations penetrated. Also, their withdrawal was to be covered by every available U.S. and RAF fighter, rendezvousing at the longest range ever attempted.

Weather, the nemesis of the Eighth Air Force, delayed takeoff of the shuttle force to the last possible moment that would still allow daylight landing in North Africa. Even then, bombers were lost in formup due to mid-air collisions in the poor visibility.

The Schweinfurt task force takeoffs were delayed even more, and their mission should have been cancelled, because the delay allowed Luftwaffe fighters time to reservice and attack on penetration and withdrawal. This was the first mission to lose 60 bombers, and it was said that ground tracks were clearly defined by burning wrecks, from both sides!

I often wonder if all combat folks have a mission, or two, when they weren't really sure that they took all the right actions, gave all the proper orders, and acted with valor and bravery. There's a monkey on my back — the only one I'll acknowledge: I was leading the Eighth Bomber Command deep into Germany, on one of the most beautiful days imaginable. I turned from initial point onto the bomb run in flak you could walk on, so thick we were in turbulence from the explosions. Just prior to rollout, we received a direct hit on the pilot's side, blowing out the left side and the top windows, and part of the windshield. Glass was flying and instrument panel lights were blinking, including the "Bomb Release" lights.

I took over, rolled out of the turn, held the pilot off the wheel, and saw that he was conscious. I called on the intercom, "Did the bombs drop?" With that, the formation bombs were released, while I was yelling, "NO, NO, NO!"

The nose section had also taken flak, and in the confusion, the bomb aimer said he thought that both pilots were hurt and that I had said, "Drop bombs." I supported him, and noted that I should have continued the run without comment.

Ever since, there's been a little man on my shoulder who will ask, until I go to the Big Hangar in the sky (or wherever), "What did you really say?"

And there's also a nightmare wherein I sneak up to the pearly gates and Saint Pete, the Number Two man, gives me, "Yer outta here!"

There were breaks and relaxations from the rigors and demands of combat — tours of ancient churches and castles, museums, art galleries, and other cultural pursuits.

Three of us on our first visit to London took in *Panama Hattie*, starring Bebe Daniels, with the orchestra conducted by her husband, Ben Lyons. After the first act, we laid considerable cash on the usherette with a note to go backstage reading: "Three Yank combat pilots on first trip to the Big L. Could you suggest a place to meet ladies?"

Back came a note, "Bring this backstage after the show. Would love to meet you and can introduce some ladies. Bebe."

Unbelievable! Bebe and her husband were two of the most gracious people I would ever meet. They gave us the warmest welcome, and the finest American booze, usually only seen in possession of the flight surgeon for after-combat belts. Most important, five lovely ladies of the chorus, including the Premier Danseuse — the premier solo dancer, Diane Gardiner — to whom I immediately laid claim.

That romance could fill several chapters, but modesty and sense of honor forbid such revelations. Besides, she married a navigator after I went to fighters!

On that first night, the eight of us were off on a three-day blast, the two spares peeling off early after being engaged by "Friendlies."

Another fond memory is of a voluptuous black-haired, dark-eyed Army nurse. She was frank and outspoken, no ties, and gave a big "No Way" at any mention of wedlock, which I liked. Once, she made three-day reservations for us at a charming bungalow in central England. I flew the group P-47 up, and the landing gear wouldn't retract. I wasn't about to let that interfere with my carnal pursuits, so that's the way I went! The RAF base tower officer met me and mentioned, "We noted that your undercarriage was down when we first spotted you."

My clever response was, "Yes, we have to drop the gear way out to slow down."

He looked at the big, round, multi-drag engine of the P-47 Jug and responded with the equivalent of today's "Yeah, right!"

Dancer Diane Gardiner.

Over breakfast on the morning of the third day, my lovely lady asked if I knew how much she appreciated me, and why. When I modestly responded in the negative, she made me choke on my coffee and spoiled the whole trip with, "I'm doing my best to get pregnant so I can get out of the Army."

It was obvious to me that the P-47 landing gear wasn't the only thing that wasn't going to get up that day. After arranging her early train departure, me and the Jug struggled back home, with nothing working.

I finally wangled orders to Fighter Command and was almost out the gate, when there was a change. General George S. Patton was about to make a breakout from southern France and head northeast into the heart of Germany. Eighth Air Force bombers were to provide saturation bombing ahead of friendly lines, immediately prior to his offensive. The Eighth and Ninth Air Force fighters were on close air support and armed reconnaissance for targets of opportunity.

Air Force accuracy had been somewhat less than auspicious, so it was decided that there would be *one* controller for the initial attack and breakout. Once there was a breakout, fighter pilots would serve as forward air controllers (FACs) and act as advisors for the leading combat units, up to division level.

The controller would be assigned a radar-equipped, air-to-ground mobile control facility, who was to be *me!* This was Bomber Command's revenge for my being a "turncoat" and attempting to switch to fighters.

I picked up three equipment trucks and a bus load of technicians in central France and drove to Patton's Headquarters to the south, a two-day trip. I used the time, in my lead jeep, listening to a captain and lieutenant explain how the mysterious stuff in the trucks worked — just the principles, because no one had any idea how it was supposed to be used in controlling air strikes.

With my realization that I was totally unqualified for the mission came the chilling thought that there would be hundreds, even thousands, of casualties if I screwed up, which was becoming ever more of a sure thing. How to get out of it? I decided to press on, call Bomber Command from Patton's Headquarters, and then hurl myself on my sword!

The second day out, a few miles from the "blood and guts" place of business, we were stopped in a narrow ravine by our guys — who were heavily armed, I noted. The slopes on both sides were populated by more GIs, all with very large weapons and all pointed at us. (I discovered later that English-speaking SS troops had been dropped behind Allied lines with the mission of killing senior officers.)

A looie approached me with his carbine muzzle centered on my chest, which I thought was unnecessary, and started asking questions about the last World Series. I had no interest in baseball, and I noticed some nervous trigger fingers as I blew the oral exam. Luckily, my jeep driver was a Dodgers fan and we were allowed to pass.

Patton's Army area was clearly identifiable — spit-and-polish troopers and "gung ho" attitudes and morale. After seeing to my detachment's housing and messing, I policed myself up for the evening briefing. My first look at the legendary leader came when I was introduced as "Army Air Corps director of bomber and fighter support."

Patton barked, "Think you fly-boys can hit your goddamn asses?"

How to reply to that? The best I could come up with was, "Sir, we're going to give it our best."

I'll never forget those eyes on me when he added, "You better."

It turned out that I didn't have to meet the challenge. That night Patton was called to a Supreme Command meeting, and two days later he started movement of his Army to the north in relief of Bastogne and the Bulge.

There will never be an end to the debates regarding the contribution of the Eighth Air Force to victory in Europe. It's difficult to see how a war can be analyzed to the degree that definitive percentages of contribution can be attributed to individual services and branches. With deep respect for ground and sea forces, I find victory inconceivable without air superiority.

Be that as it may, I can't express enough admiration for those young pilots and aircrews that faced overwhelming odds and high losses, day after day, until the job was done. Courage beyond description!

My fighter experiences contributed to this admiration — the view from a bomber cockpit is limited, although very personal! But flying a fighter down the bomber stream, looking for your assigned group to escort, and watching the bombers fall, with never a waver, was an unbelievable sight. My heart went out to them and I felt a humble pride at having been one of that gallant force.

Chapter 6

Fighter Combat

FTER 27 MISSIONS in the B-17, I had wrangled the transfer to Fighter Command, which almost cost me my life and career! I got in trouble for going directly to the two-star division commander who was sympathetic to anyone wanting more combat — especially in fighters, being of that breed himself. The reaction was much better than I expected, or deserved, but after all, General Old had approved (or closed his eyes) when I was flying combat in P-38s, P-47s, and P-51s while under his command in the 96th Bombardment Group.

My real gratitude was to the 357th Fighter Group Commander, Colonel Irv Dregne, and his folks who accepted — or maybe just tolerated — me, and helped me

. . . the 357th Fighter Group Commander, Colonel Irv Dregne, . . . helped me become a card-carrying member of the fraternity of fighter pilots.

become a card-carrying member of the fraternity of fighter pilots. Friend-ships from the Dregnes included Andy Evans, who was a POW in the Kor-ean conflict and retired as a general; Bob Foy, one of the greatest, who was killed as a passenger in a modified B-25 after the war; and too many more to mention.

Whatever the fighter airplane, most jocks welcomed you and did all they could to help you transition to a new plane and a radically new way of life — provided you showed a desire to learn and recognized your rookie status in the business. Otherwise, you got the cold treatment and were shown the door.

This wasn't my first experience in the fighter business. I had the initial check-out in the P-38 Lightning, three flights, while ferrying to California. After the 96th Bombardment Group settled into combat and practice mis-sions, I had found a flying cadet classmate in the 364th Fighter Group at Honington, England, and got more time in the beautiful Lightning, includ-ing formation and tactics.

I flew P-38 combat in late 1943 and early '44, and the high point was seeing Tony Levier's spectacular demo flights. Tony was the chief test pilot for Lockheed, and his shows increased confidence and respect for the P-38 immeasurably. He repeatedly cautioned against trying the shiny things he did at low level without bunches of practice up high. Fighter pilots being what they are, we "splashed" a few until orders came out for-bidding any low-level aerobatics. The jocks did ease back down to near ground level, but were smarter about their showy gyrations.

At a high-level commander's conference, where I was only a "horse-holder," I met a P-38 group CO who was sympathetic to my fighter longings and gave me more combat missions in the P-38. I flew a wing position on the second of four cover missions over the beaches of Nor-mandy on D-Day, June 6, 1944. Indescribable!

There will never be a sound like that of a group taxi-out and runup of the Lightnings. It only took one flight to understand the phrase "P-38 pilots have the biggest legs in the Air Corps." There was no hydrau-lic reservoir, so pressure had to be maintained by constantly pumping the brake pedals. It was always a while after a flight before my legs stopped trembling, although some shakes could have been due to nerves!

The beautiful P-38 bird was sold short in the European Theater of Oper-ations. Its initial troubles were that it was easily identified at maximum distance, and it suffered engine failures and frozen pilots at high altitudes. These problems would have been minimized, even before external fuel tanks arrived, by using the Lightning in medium- to low-altitude penetrations, and by arriving at German bases ahead of bombers and as fighters taxied for takeoff. Squadrons could strafe and then take position below and level to the bomber stream, intercepting Luftwaffe fighters climbing to bomber altitudes.

Fighter range would be extended since Lightnings would not take off until bombers were almost across the English Channel. The group and squadron formations would be formed on course rather than in orbit, with normal cruise airspeeds until bomber rendezvous, then to maximum range speeds, S-ing to stay with assigned bombers. With the number of P-38 groups, attacks could be in continuous waves or simultaneous penetrations, depending on enemy fighter reaction and en route/target weather. P-51s and P-47s could provide en route, target, and withdrawal support from high altitudes.

Fine tactics, except that the bomber leaders, and probably all their folks, demanded that fighter forces be in sight at all times! Obviously, this curtailed the types of support available to fighter leaders; pre-penetration sweeps, high cover, wide abeam, and low altitude were eliminated, severely reducing fighter effectiveness. Even when high fighter kills, contacts, and engagements were reported (fighters must have been doing *something* right!), there were still bomber losses to enemy fighters, with the following reason often given: "Fighter support minimal, inadequate, or none." *Sheesh*!

With my arrival in Fighter Command came these orders: "Effective upon receipt, all escorting fighters will attach flights of four, in close formation with each three-ship bomber section, and will maintain formation *until under attack*, resuming close formation when enemy fighters repelled, until relieved." (Or when friendly fighters got shot down!) It's hard to believe, but the ludicrous order was not cancelled until the commander of the Eighth Fighter Command, and every fighter group commander, demanded transfer.

I had managed more fighter experience when the 96th Bombardment Group was assigned a war-weary P-47 "Jug" Thunderbolt in early 1944, to assist in formation join-ups and assemblies. By then, I had moved up to the Combat Bomb Wing with General Old as his chief of staff. We had operational responsibility for three bombardment groups. Like most Headquarters, we were over-manned and over-ranked for the responsibilities and authority. This suited me fine, because I had time to spare and lots of excuses for travel.

I made the Jug my personal baby, found a frustrated crew chief and armament tech who had been in Jug squadrons until they were hospitalized, for reasons which I did not question. Then they were assigned to a personnel pool, and then, logically, assigned to our B-17 group! I was their savior and took them with me when I went to fighters.

I made friends with some fighter wing Operations personnel and, for a few bottles of good booze, got scheduled time on the ground gunnery range. There were questions directed to the range control officer, like "Why do two flights have to orbit while one goddamned Jug takes his own frappin' time?"

I understand that their answer was that it was a general about to take over Fighter Command, and that all complaints would be passed on to him, including name, rank, and serial numbers. They tell me it worked every time.

I felt better qualified and later got some Jug combat with the 56th and 78th groups. The P-47 Thunderbolt showed why it had a low loss rate on ground attack missions, compared to the P-51 Mustang. I had a couple of top cylinders shot off on a sweep, flew back 80 miles, and landed on a pierced steel strip outside of Paris — one week after Liberation, by the way. My flight called, said that they would make a report, and I probably wouldn't have to wait for repairs. However, I called my boss and told him that I felt responsible for return of the airplane.

It didn't occur to him that I was probably the first Yankee fighter pilot to hit Paree since the Liberation bashes started. What gratitude was bestowed by the great French folks! I couldn't pay for a drink, meal, or anything! *Vive la France!* It became obvious that I had over-stayed my leave when a red-hot wire arrived informing me that I would be home in 24 hours or face court-martial. There were some unpleasant moments after I returned, but I think my stories were so entrancing that all was forgiven. Besides, my orders to Fighter Command had arrived.

I was assigned to the 357th Fighter Group at Leiston in September 1944 as group Operations officer, flying P-51s. The North American P-51 Mustang was the first fighter with enough range to escort bombers to Germany and Poland and return to England — or proceed to Russia or North Africa on shuttle missions. (Incidentally, the "P" stood for "pursuit," a carryover term from World War I. Post-World War II fighters were designated "F," for "fighter.")

I was unqualified for my new post, but with my rank, it was the only place I could be assigned without screwing up the chain of command. Bob Foy, one of the best fighter pilots and a great friend, carried me while I learned the business. I worked my way up from Green 16, the number four wingman in the last flight of the last squadron, to element, flight, and squadron leads, and led the group on some of the last missions of the war.

On one of my first flight leads, we had orders to complete a "Rhubarb," a fighter sweep against airfields, to hit any military units or ground transportation. From 5,000 feet, I spotted a Luftwaffe fighter base at our three o'clock, and nonchalantly strolled on by, as if saying, "We didn't see you and wouldn't do anything if we had."

We stayed on the same heading until we thought we were well out of radar contact, and found a railroad on the map that went directly from our position to the east side of the field. We hit the deck and followed the tracks, popped up to strafe, and found that we hadn't fooled the gun guys!

Even before I started firing on a German JU-88, the flak came boiling up, just as I got hits and an explosion, and the element lead called, "Number Four's gone."

I looked back and saw a ball of fire hit the ground, and told everyone, "Hit the deck, let's get outta here!" I was so low, I came back with grass stains on the prop and foliage in the scoop.

Number Three gave out more bad news: "There goes Number Two." I saw him go in, inverted and on fire.

As we finally reached the far edge of the field, a 57- or 88-millimeter shell exploded just to my left, blowing out most of the canopy and the left side of the windshield. Metal and glass fragments flew in my face and eyes.

I had to go home at 20,000 feet to avoid flak and nearly froze. I spent a long time on the Sawbone's table while they extracted the extra "hardware." The doctor said it was nice that I came back in temperatures that helped the blood congeal, or I might have become too unhealthy to make it. He always looked on the positive side.

Disturbing to me then, and later, was the fact that I couldn't remember the faces of those two young men who had just given their lives. It's so impersonal. I went by the orderly room to get their families' addresses, wrote what I could, and spent time looking at their pictures. What were they like; what could they have been and done? But such thoughts have to be dispelled if you're going to continue in combat.

That was the roughest mission of all the ground attacks, though any time we hit German airfields, there was a very high "pucker factor," right up to the last missions of the war.

During the accelerated orientation with the 357th Fighter Group and my progress up the ladder of performance and responsibility, it became obvious that rank was given its due in the air, if the individual met fighter pilot operational standards. Otherwise, pointed and usually obscene suggestions were made regarding corrective action to be taken by the "rookie," before abandonment to the fighter pilot's limbo. The fact that the speaker was unidentified did not diminish the impact.

There were important lessons, like never, *never* transmit without squadron, flight, and numerical designation, especially in a panic situation requiring dropping external tanks, and/or a hard break left or right. These messages meant "under attack" or "Lots of bad guys around and we'd better do something."

If the jock didn't say who he was and who he was talking to, everyone around had to assume it was meant for him, and then you have 48 or more fighters honkin' it around in a maximum performance turn, punching tanks off, with the boys downstream fighting to miss a hassle of external tanks!

Obviously, releasing tanks that still contained fuel reduced escort, or area support, time for the Big Friends — the bombers — plus additional time was lost in reforming. This caused considerable displeasure on the part of the brass and bomber Joes, and many questions were raised regarding the ability of fighter pilots to master the intricacies of "goddamned simple radio communications."

Another lesson: There comes a time in a mission when a flight leader has to find something requiring his total concentration, thus rendering him unable to acknowledge the call, "Flight lead, take yer flight down and check for flak." This is in the vicinity of a Kraut airfield, where they always put the first team of anti-aircraft shooters!

You have to understand that "checking for flak" is as unnecessary as practicing bleeding! What the bold leader wants you to do is take your flight down to the hornet's nest and get the hornets all stirred up, while he picks out the area of least hornet activity for his run.

With experience, a flight leader could anticipate the call and come up with, "Permission to check the Bogies at three o'clock." The Bogies' position, of course, being directly away from the airfield. Or, "Number Two, I have high/low pressure in my oil/fuel/oxygen/hydraulics," or maybe, "high/low temperature in . . . ," adding "Pull up and check me over," if applicable.

As a last resort, you give no response to the first calls, then say, "Red Leader, are you calling? You're garbled."

The rest of your flight crew is properly disciplined and has no more desire than you to go flak hunting, and so they will help with the charade. Everyone else in the squadron knows what's happening and wishes that Red Leader would give up, assign spacing and attack directions, and "have a go at it."

If the "radio trouble" is going to work, it is best to donate booze to the communications troops, because you can be sure that you and your bird will be met at the base by bunches of trouble-shooters, and there had better be valid troubles.

On one mission, I was leading an element in Bob Foy's flight, a sweep at 4,000 feet, the altitude that the low and middle-sized guns think is keen! The stuff (flak) was boiling up and Bob was studying his map and scanning the terrain. His wingman, on his first mission, felt it his duty to keep the lead aware of all the hostile action going on around us and blurted several transmissions: "Red Lead, flak at three o'clock and six, flak at nine and twelve o'clock. Flak everywhere."

Bob is cruising along, and gently banks to better see the ground. Finally, in plaintive tones the wingman says, "Red Leader, they're shooting at us!"

Red Lead replied, "That's OK, son. They're supposed to!"

Another time, I was leading a squadron behind Bob's group lead and everyone was pretty well splitup chasing German Messerschmitt 109s and Focke Wulf 190s through weather. Bob allowed on the radio that he might be shot-up, was coming up on Dummer Lake, and his flight was low on fuel.

I headed that way and broke out of clouds east of Dummer, found Bob climbing and trailing vapor, meaning that he was losing coolant and wasn't going to make it home. I sent the rest of our two flights home and told them to contact RAF Air Rescue, give them our course, and let them know that there would soon be a "nylon letdown."

As I pulled up on Bob's left wing at 19,000 feet, coolant was streaming from his radiator and he was busy unstrapping for bail-out. The RAF air-sea rescue launches were under us as always, and as we reached a position between the first and second boats, flames belched from the Mustang's exhaust stacks and the prop froze.

Bob said, "See you at home, Jack. Tell the vultures to leave my stuff alone." (It was a tradition for "friends" to take parts of your belongings that they claimed had been willed to them.)

Off came the canopy, the Mustang half-rolled, and out went Robert. It was a good chute; I circled once, got the OK sign, and headed home. It's what happened thereafter that makes the tale unique. Bob was floating down, knew that he would be picked up, and thought, "I wonder if my lighter will work in this wind?" He pulled out a pack and lit up with no sweat.

It happened that the closest launch had press and photo Joes on board, and they got great shots of the Yank enjoying a cigarette on the way down, flicking the butt away just prior to his splash!

Bob hardly got wet before he was picked up and then had a ball at the RAF base. The story and pictures were in all the papers and when he was flown home the next day, with a king-sized hangover, he had telegrams from all the big tobacco companies offering him the world.

Most enticing, and from one of the biggest outfits, read something like, "Our representative is authorized to offer any size cashier's check if you will certify that you were smoking Brand X cigarette in pictures of your recent bail-out and safe recovery."

This was followed by lots of legalese, and we were happily debating what they meant by "any size cashier's check" when the Army Judge Advocate called and laid on the squelch. Soldiers were not allowed to sponsor commercial products!

Then there came the rocket-powered German ME-163 Komet fighters, passing through bomber formations, vertical, firing on the way up and back down, causing damage on both passes. But we were really sweating out the twin-jet ME-262 since they could spend considerable time going after the bombers. Despite their superior speed, we could out-turn and keep them away from the bomber stream, if they were spotted in time.

One day, I was leading a squadron escorting B-17 Fortresses in lousy weather. To keep them in sight, I had to stay directly over the stream, S-ing constantly. It was impossible to maintain squadron formation, so I positioned a flight below and one on each flank, and prayed. Bomber contrails and the weather made visibility zilch from the initial point to "bombs away," so I circled my flight over the rally point.

I picked up the bombers coming out of the flak and dropped down to a thousand feet above, calling other flights to see if they were with us. Got a "Coming up behind you," and I glanced back and saw what I thought were P-51s with external tanks on, until the next message came: "Red Lead, we've lost you!"

Looking to my right, I was eyeball to eyeball with an ME-262 driver, one in a wave of eight, all firing at the bombers! They went by us and I saw two more waves driving in. I called, "Drop tanks, break right," and watched the following -262s wing-over and go down.

Even before our hard break, two B-17s exploded and three caught fire and pulled out of formation, some props feathered, and chutes opening. It was an unforgettable experience!

I had split-S'd after the Jerries (German soldiers so-called because their helmets resembled a British chamber pot — a jerry!) and took a steep dive, trying to close. Coming into view at the top of my canopy, and dropping directly into my line of flight, was a parachuting bomber crewman. I didn't see how the prop could miss him, but I jammed the stick forward, and was partially blinded by dirt, cigarette butts, and assorted trash that had been disturbed by the negative stick forces.

His feet barely missed the canopy, and the tail, I assume. Indelibly engraved in my memory is a picture of that young man climbing the shroud lines, hand-over-hand, looking at me with "saucer-sized eyes!" I really believe that I would recognize him today, even in a casual encounter.

I hadn't realized the extent of navigational errors in the bomber stream until faced with the problems they gave the escort fighters in accomplishing rendezvous at the prescribed time and location. And there were two navigators in the group lead aircraft!

As a matter of information, the escort fighters did not take off until the bombers were at least mid-Channel. This was a great luxury to me, listening to the bombers droning overhead on formup, rolling over for some more sleep, and then having a leisurely breakfast before briefing.

And so, rendezvousing typically went something like this: fighter lead checks in with fighter control, "feet are wet" — meaning, obviously, that landfall is next — and receives intercept information. Thence to bomber lead, who transmitted in reference to Ops order flight plan times, and usually reported, "on time, on course."

Then 30 minutes or so prior to rendezvous time, comes the message, "Little Friends, Big Friends here. We seem to be X minutes early/late," or "X miles north/south/east/west of course!"

So fighter lead, with only a map in his lap and no navigation aids except ground checkpoints (when visible), makes a quick WAG (wild-assed guess) at a new heading and airspeed, knowing who will be blamed for a late rendezvous!

It was easy to spot the mission leaders at any fighter group. Group and squadron commanders, Ops officers, and senior flight commanders were identifiable from bloodshot and squinty eyes from straining to find the Big Friends. Some had nervous tics, others talked to invisible persons, and the bad cases were on the milk drinks at the O Club.

Also inexplicable was being fired on by gunner(s) as a fighter moved in to check for battle damage, at the request of the bomber pilot. After evasive action, we would tell the Big Friend that "Yer on yer own," but positioned the flight to react to any attack, while out of sight of the bomber crew. I enjoyed the mental picture of the crew kickin' the bejeezus out of the trigger-happy ones.

Of all memories, most vivid and poignant are the valor of the German fighter pilots facing overwhelming defeat and utter futility of further resistance. Russians were only miles to the east, and Allies close on the Western Front.

On the next to last mission of the European War, as we swept ahead of the bomber stream, ME-262s took off from Prague and continued to take off in spite of falling wing tanks and attacking Mustangs. We claimed eight destroyed, plus several probables and damaged.

On the last Eighth Air Force mission, the -262s were up, as were eight FW-190s, and even a twin-engine fighter! All but a few jets were shot down.

I make no excuses for the Germans in the war. I do feel, however, that recognition should be given to, and admiration bestowed on the dedicated, selfless, and valiant Luftwaffe pilots who exemplified the "Fighter Pilot's Code!"

If you like playing historical "what ifs," here are a few: What if Hitler had invaded England rather than attacking Russia; what if the Germans had the "A" bomb as programmed; or what if the ME-262 and ME-163 had met the planned production schedules?

Chapter 7

Occupation of Germany

ITH V-E DAY ON MAY 8, 1945, came the realization that I had made it, and a great feeling of satisfaction and accomplishment. At the same time, there was a letdown and a "where do we go from here?" feeling. Surprisingly, there weren't bunches of knock-down, drag-out parties, just "When do I go home?"

The military developed a points system for determining priority of return to the U.S. and discharge from service. Numerical values were established for all aspects of military service: *i.e.*, total service, months overseas, combat duty time, rank/rating, wounds, decorations, and some other criteria that I have forgotten. If there was any injustice, it would have been found in the wide variance between combat theaters on the definition of "combat," promo-

With V-E Day . . . there was a letdown and a "where do we go from here?" feeling.

tion and awards policies, and what constituted combat "wounds." And yet, though there may have been some on the short end of the stick, it was generally agreed that the system was fair and expedited demobilization. Many of us felt that it was too rapid: before postwar problems had been discovered and the bad/good guys identified, an overwhelming bargaining power had been lost with the defeat of the greatest military power in history.

Commanders' main efforts were in keeping everyone busy, while relaxing the demands and pressures of combat. Tons of equipment had to be inventoried and prepared for disposition, and most was deemed surplus to future requirements. Massive amounts were destroyed, dumped in oceans, or sold by bid or auction. The toughest was the heartbreak of watching fighters, some brand new, being demolished by dynamite, bulldozers separating the remnants by metal types, to be sold as scrap!

The 357th Fighter Group was to return to the Zone of Interior (ZI) — the continental United States — and an uncertain future. I was casting around for a way to get to the Pacific War when the fighter wing commander called to see if I would be interested in taking command of the 55th Fighter Group, which was scheduled to deploy directly to the Pacific from England. Did I jump on that one!

It seems that the group CO was shot down on one of the last missions, a colonel was assigned and "bought the farm" on a night flight, and I was selected. I was curious as to why the deputy group commander — a lieutenant colonel who had been with the group since its organization in the States — hadn't been given the command, but not curious enough to keep from grabbing the job.

I was dreading the goodbyes to my ground crew. My crew chief, in his thirties or forties (it's hard to tell when you're 24!), was certainly beyond draft age, so he was a volunteer. The assistant crew chief was a big, young, and rangy Midwest boy, a perfect match for the Ole Sarge. An armament technician filled out the crew — an Italian lad from Brooklyn, who was always at the end of the runway to see if tape had been shot off the gun barrels, which meant that there had been a fight, or at least we shot somebody!

I always referred to *my* P-51, *Love of Mine* (from the Tommy Dorsey/ Frank Sinatra ballad), as ours, and had the feeling that the crew chief was just loaning that Mustang to me. So, I felt lots of guilt when I came back with dents, scratches, and holes. Many times, he worked throughout the

Jack Hayes's first fighter, a P-51 Mustang named *Love of Mine*, parked on the hardstand at Leiston Army Air Base, England, September/October 1944.

Love of Mine parked on hardstand at Leiston Army Air Base, December 1944, after a return from escorting B-17s to Berlin. Jack Hayes's crew, left to right: Assistant Crew Chief, Crew Chief, Hayes, and Armorer.

January 1945, re-
turning alone in
Love of Mine after
a dogfight in the
clouds. The naviga-
tor of a B-17 took
this shot and auto-
graphed the photo
for Jack Hayes.

night, fine-tuning everything, with arthritis so bad that he had to stop every 30 minutes to warm himself in the crew chief's shack.

I flew every mission I could, but I did miss a few when I felt I needed training in some area, or when the boss suggested that it would be nice if I now and then made motions like an Operations officer, since that was my title! Not only was *Love of Mine* always available, she looked like she had just come off the factory floor.

There may be a way to express gratitude to people like that, but I couldn't find it. At our last meeting, they were uncomfortable with my stammering, until I announced that they were authorized to go with me to my new command, and to the Pacific! When I left, they were leaning on each other, with guffaws and pounding backs.

Next, *Love of Mine* and I went to Wormingford, England, and the 55th Fighter Group — tremendous people and fabulous experiences. I was met by staff and commanders, and went to my office to sign my first "Assumption of Command" general order. A briefing had been prepared on the group status: "awaiting orders for move to Pacific and disposition of equipment and personnel."

I scheduled a staff meeting and a tour of the base for the next day, and went to my new quarters. This was my first taste of command privileges, and I decided it was a nice way to live. The boss had a bedroom, bath, and living room with fireplace. The deputy CO and service group CO had private bedrooms and shared a bath.

No sooner had I parked my car at the new abode, than I was met by a chaplain. I was fairly certain that word of my piety, sanctity, and other good things had not preceded me — although there was no reason why it shouldn't have — so I had some misgivings about his visit (well-warranted, as it turned out).

The man of the cloth expressed distress that he had met with failure in his crusade for purity and clean living on the base. It was imperative that I be aware that "Ladies were spending nights, and sometimes *days*, in officer and enlisted quarters!"

I muttered that I would look into it — which was cowardly, since I had no intention of changing something that had been going on since there were armies!

Enjoying the smug looks from the men at how I had placated the Rev, I was unpacking and sipping on a libation, when there came the sound of a motorcycle outside — where the road to enlisted quarters happened to pass — and I heard an MP shout, "You, Soldier, you can't take her to yer billets. The new group commander says 'No babes!'"

I was out the front door asking the MP whose orders he was quoting, and he replied, "The chaplain's, Sir."

There ensued a short discussion with the MP, which went something like: "Who's runnin' this goddamned air base?"

My reaction triggered a "Way to go, Boss," from the soldier of amorous bent, a big grin and salute from the MP, and I realized that I'd been had! But I refused to reopen the matter and had no moral pangs. After all, *I* wasn't doing that sort of thing, was I?

With uncertain days in the Pacific ahead, I decided that a good way for the troops to meet the Old Man would be to lay on a group mission to display, for the last time, a part of the greatest fighter force ever assembled.

We launched 64 Mustangs — 16 flights of four squadrons. It was an unbelievable sight. I led them on mock strafing attacks on six fighter outfits that I had flown with, rattled some Big Friend domiciles, and even dusted off a Headquarters or two.

Then, we held a mass fly-by over Wormingford, and a spine-tingler at the exuberance of the ground guys who were all around the runways and taxiways. The big show was really over! I handled phone calls late into the evening, military and civilian, dignitaries and low ranking. Some were very irate, but almost without exception, the conclusions were, "Thanks for the memories. Good show!"

Having been on the base for only two nights when I launched the mass gaggle, I wasn't sure that I could find the taxiway, but I sure found *Love of Mine* and her new crew chief, Technical Sergeant "Doak" Easton, who always crewed the group CO's airplane.

Not only was Doak outstanding, *Love of Mine* was even more so! There had been loving care previously bestowed on my steed, but in two days the gleam was brighter, the canopy displayed larger names, and there were five swastikas for my one air and four ground kills.

Incidentally, I picked *Love of Mine* as a name not only because of the song's heritage, but I found it nice to tell the current lady how I hurled myself into the war for a free world in an airplane "named for you!" And a new paint job wasn't required if I switched ladies, or got the boot, which was usually the case!

Prominently displayed around the ETO were pictures of lovely Marge, the movie doll I had met earlier, exhorting the troops to write home. Fin-

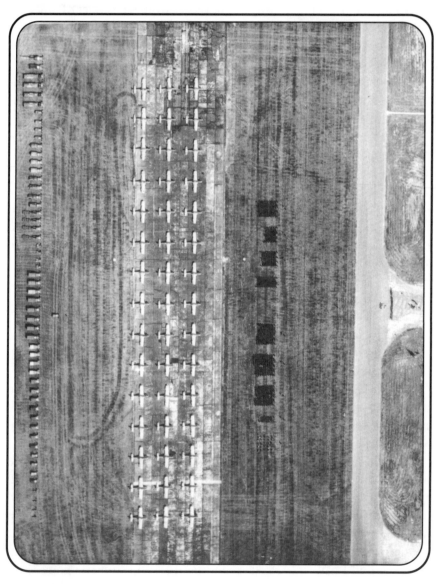

The final impressive line-up revue of the 55th Fighter Group before assignment to the Army of Occupation, Germany.

Marge Stewart, of the movie *Bombardier*, with Jack Hayes in *Love of Mine*, at Wormingford Army Air Base, England, April 1945.

ally having some clout, I got the PR Joe to locate her and arrange for a visit to the 55th. I have a picture of her sitting in my lap in *Love of Mine*, which Doak had shined up so much that reflections made picture-taking difficult.

Always unselfish, I let Marge spend the day, lunch and dinner, with the working men, and thence to my quarters for a friendly visit. Things began to come unglued when my service group CO, Joe Huddleston, an All-American football star and one of my greatest friends (even after this!), found that he and Marge had mutual friends in Indiana. They tripped down memory lane until the late hour reminded her of the busy day coming up and she had to go "beddy-by." The cologne and special plans were wasted. At breakfast, I was a little grumpy with her and wanted to kill Joe! Back in the States a year or so later, I called her in Hollywood and laid on the charm. She was as sweet as ever, but by then was married and seven months pregnant.

But she'll always be the Number Two Marge/Margee. If only she and Joe hadn't both been from Indiana!

The "big bomb" helped to end things, with the formal surrender in the Pacific on September 2, 1945, and our orders were changed to Army of Occupation, Kaufbueren Army Air Base, southwest of Munich. Joe Huddleston ran the moving of all kinds of available aircraft — DC-3s, DC-4s, B-17s with bomb-bay platforms, plus ships and trucks.

I was leading 60-some P-51 Mustangs to the new home on a beautiful day, with an awesome look at the massive destruction. So fascinating was the view that I wandered about 60° off course, for which I bought the pilots a beer, and their first meal at the new base.

We beat up the field real good on arrival with low-level passes, not aware that there were more than 5,000 SS prisoners of war in a stockade on base, and there was mass hysteria. There were no injuries and the Army guards maintained control.

We were uniquely fortunate in that the POW camp had some senior German officers and civil officials and our officers and non-coms had the opportunity to meet them and ask questions. I was especially privileged in meeting German General Adolf Galland, one of the greatest fighter pilots of all time, and with a career unmatched by any. He had commanded Luftwaffe fighter forces under Hitler, and later the West German Air Forces in NATO.

Kaufbueren, an officers pilot training base, had only slight damage from

August 1945, just after landing the 60 Mustangs at Kaufbueren, southwest of Munich.

Jack Hayes and *Love of Mine* at Kaufbueren, September 1945.

earlier "just passing by" strafes. The sod field had been improved with pierced steel runway and hardstands, laid by Allied engineers. And the quarters were unbelievable. Enlisted men lived in what we would call non-com billets, non-coms were housed in former junior officers quarters, and officers were in "senior" officers quarters. Joe and I lived in a two-story house behind the O Club.

When we smoked into Kaufbueren, I noticed a brewery just off one end of the runway — not operating, for obvious reasons. I mentioned to Major Paul Akst, my legal/military government guy, that I felt this was a shame and was pleased that he shared my distress. Three days later, the suds dispenser was at full blast, for U.S. troops only, and GIs were having free beer with dinner. To satisfy the temperance "hatcheteers," troops had to prove that they were: 1. 18 years old; 2. American citizens; and 3. members of the U.S. Armed Forces. Only one beer per customer; non-coms were not limited.

These laws were inviolate, but we did close our eyes for other Allied troops, none of whom qualified under rules 2 or 3, and some were ineligible under rule 1. Some philosophers, including me, have vehemently said, "If a man's old enough to fight, he's old enough to drink!" (Other words are sometimes substituted for "drink"; the only clean one that comes to mind is "vote!")

The idyllic life lost something with the realities of demobilization and the influx of inexperienced people. Some of the Old-Timers, God bless 'em, stayed beyond their departure dates to help train replacements: not many — some had served over four years — but those who stayed were appreciated.

The Army of Occupation was faced with many questions: Would there be a second front, guerilla warfare, sabotage? I was directed to maintain maximum-strength guard and security patrols, particularly at night.

Because Military Police were as under-manned as the rest, guard-duty requirements were levied on all group and squadron units. This critically lessened the availability of mechanics and aircraft, and caused a reduction of flying time and flight safety problems.

In one of my more Solomon-like decisions, I directed that all personnel, excluding maintenance, would be detailed for guard duty. Joe and I were on the first shift, with corporal partners. My tour was energized when we heard noises in a warehouse. Through a democratic process, we determined that the corporal would investigate while I maintained vigilance

Jack Hayes addressing a joint German/American meeting at Kaufbueren in the fall of 1945.

outside. The cause of our alarm proved to be a very protective mother dog. We left her with her newly delivered children to the cares of the day shift when she chased us out of there!

Replacements soon arrived, enabling us to retain combat posture without further use of the officer corps as guards.

There has to be mention of those stalwarts who contributed so much to the postwar records of the 55th Fighter Group and 442nd Air Service Group: Joe Huddleston, of course; Major Paul Akst, about whom not enough could be said; and another "mover" named Dick Smith. An international-level diving performer and coach, Dick had the title of "Special Services," and was responsible for troop morale and welfare.

Between Paul and Dick, I was the "Emperor of Bavaria!" I owned two lavish ski chalets in the Bavarian Alps, complete with staff, skis, instructors, *et al*. I did rescue Dick's military record when I cancelled his bid for a plush riding stable upon learning that he had beaten General Patton's bid!

I mentioned one day that it would be nice to have a base football team, and two weeks later, Dick produced equipment for a 30-man squad — A-1 stuff. It was a small team, but everyone went both ways, offense and defense.

Major Macauley Clark, one of the finest fighter pilots in the group in P-38s and P-51s, was head coach, and a great one. I played halfback, and assured Mac that I was just one of the players, except when the starting line-up was named! Joe Huddleston was line coach.

With demobilization came problems finding enough players, so even Joe and Mac had to suit up for the last three games — real pros. In Joe's first game, the officials laid on him a 15-yard penalty for "unnecessary roughness." Then came the protests: "Four years high school and four years University of Kentucky football, and I get a penalty for roughness in this rinky-dink league!" But the fact that the roughed-up one was leaving the scene in an ambulance did weaken Joe's argument.

On the subject of roughness, there was eye-gouging, fists to the face, and knees to other places. A considerable amount was inflicted on yours truly, the lieutenant colonel group commander — even in our team scrimmages! These were the days of demobilization and revolt against military rank and discipline. There were not many penalties called, probably because the officials were of the same cloth, and sympathies, as the rest of the team.

We played a memorable game in Linz, Austria, against a P-47 fighter group commanded by a good friend of mine. He played on his team and mouse-trapped the hell out of me — in pre-game maneuvers, not on the gridiron. He insisted that I stay at his villa and partake of sumptuous food, drink, and the charms of a voluptuous lady of nobility — a duchess or something.

I'm not sure whether the lady was suffering from years of imposed celibacy, playing Delilah to my Sampson, or responding to my "friend's" bribes, but I played hell with the training rules that night!

At pregame suit-up time, I found the pads much heavier than I remembered, and tied my shoelaces with head erect so I wouldn't faint. As I expected, the opening kickoff came to me, accompanied by many large football players.

Despite me, we managed a tie, and I gave myself a two-day sick leave. When I was best man at his wedding several months later, my friend was still chuckling!

Love of Mine, with only 25 hours of flying time!

I applied for Regular Army commission and was ordered to Munich for a Board Interview. I thought I had done pretty well, until just as I was dismissed, an Infantry lieutenant colonel who was probably in his forties asked, "Son, how old were you when you made lieutenant colonel?"

Being well aware that promotions in the ground forces were slow, especially prewar, I was pretty sure that the Old-Timer wouldn't enjoy the answer, and I said, "Twenty-four, Sir." Boy was I right!

He launched forth an awesome explosion of curses, and I figured I'd had the kiss of death, even when the brigadier general board president said, "Now, John, we should congratulate this young officer." The majority must have prevailed, because I made it.

One fall day, the major general commanding tactical air forces in Germany dropped in, and I met him with split lips and a beautiful shiner. After I convinced him that they were caused by football, he announced that he had good news and bad news.

"Here are orders promoting you to temporary colonel." Not at all bad for 26 years old!

But then came the bad news: "Here's a copy of a wire from Washing-

P-80 First to land in Germany 1946

Jack Hayes climbing out of the first Lockheed P-80 Shooting Star to fly overseas and land in Germany, the new *Love of Mine*, March 1946.

The new P-80 Shooting Star *Love of Mine* at Giebelstadt, Germany, June 1946.

ton, same date, suspending temporary promotions, and, of course, orders cancelling your promotion, also same date."

There was more: "The 55th Fighter Group has been selected as the first United States Air Corps Unit overseas to convert to the Lockheed P-80 jet fighter."

I have to add this modest note. Another group in Germany had been selected previously, but the outstanding record of the 55th in occupation duty dictated the change.

"You will move your group from Kaufbueren to Geibelstadt Army Air Base in central Germany. There is a 10,000-foot cement runway, taxiways, and revetments. The rest of the base is badly damaged."

That was a fair description, except the "damaged" really meant "destroyed!" So, early 1946 came and Joe was tackling another move, while I prepared to turn Kaufbueren over to Army ground forces, nearly ruining my career in the process. It seems the "grunt" two-star couldn't understand missing things like a dry cleaning plant, stoves, and kitchen equipment, and "the goddamned tiger that was on the front wall of the Officers Club!"

I pleaded ignorance to all of the above thefts — falsely, but got by with help from above (*military* help, not divine). I never did find out what happened to the tiger. Knowing fighter pilots, it probably found its way to the States and adorned/adorns some jock's home.

The Shooting Stars were unloaded at the Allied port of Bremen, Germany, and assembled at the patched-up field, using German mechanics. I flew up, met the Lockheed test pilot, and had *Love of Mine* and my name on my first P-80. And there were good christening parties!

I had two check-out flights and flew my first P-80 to Giebelstadt, with loops and rolls off the deck.

Only a month later, I was going home after three and a half years. We had *the* farewell party, and the 55th Fighter Group was deactivated a month later.

Chapter 8

Training Command to Command and Staff School

AND SO I WAS TO return to the Zone of the Interior — and the U.S. of A! I had a captain and warrant officer from the 55th with me and we sat around Le Havre Redistribution Center in France for a week before sea transportation was available, a tired and rusty tub.

We did wangle three days on the Riviera — nothing like the movies — with lovely rooms, but lousy weather, food, and service. This was somewhat compensated by beaucoup wine, but even that gets old after so much!

We finally boarded our "scow," which had a civilian captain and crew with a Transportation Corps looie as liaison with us Army types. I was immediately informed of my designation as commander of a thousand or so troops, and ordered to ensure that there was no drinking, smoking

It was obvious that there would be no trouble in devoting my career to flying, . . .

only in designated areas, and a daily headcount! I questioned the last —
how in the hell could we misplace anyone? I was tartly informed that some
did disappear — falling, jumping, or being thrown overboard!

This responsibility I handled rather well by locating the senior non-
commissioned officer and laying the job on him — with guidance, of
course: "Don't be obvious with the booze and explain any drunks as 'combat fatigue.' Smoke if there aren't open fuel tanks around and pick up the
butts. The only gambling will be Old Maid, Go Fish, Bridge, and dice.
Post look-outs to warn of unfriendlies so players could hide the cash."

As for the headcount, I suggested that they investigate bunks unoccu-
pied for 24 hours, bodies unmoved for the same period, and for any other
reasons that might come to mind.

It all worked beautifully because the Merchant Marine guys couldn't
have cared less and the Transportation John said, "To hell with it" after
being locked in closets, finding hand grenades in his bunk, and many near
misses from heavy falling objects!

We came to New York in the early a.m., and some of us exulted in the
sight of Miss Liberty. Our tub docked in Brooklyn, and we were touched
by people trying to maintain the "Welcome Home, Hero," atmosphere
with a few nice ladies handing out coffee and doughnuts and a scratchy
record playing "It's Been a Long, Long, Time."

Then I reported to Fort Eustis for processing, assignment orders, back
and advance pay, and leave orders of 45 days, if desired — and I desired!

I soon realized the extent of the hostilities felt by many GIs toward officers. The uniform was still mandatory, on and off duty, so we were denied
the disguise of civilian garb. We were warned that some discharged GIs
hung around the gate hoping to encounter one of the detested officer corps
and wreak vengeance on his person. MPs even escorted us to the train, saw
us to our seats, and gave a "yer on yer own" farewell!

I used my leave — and most of the money accrued overseas — visiting
friends in Texas, Montana, and California, ending up in San Diego with
the folks.

For some reason, my being single was a challenge to married friends,
especially the wives, and they felt that I was the answer to the problem of
their unmarried friends or relatives. Any socials included girls, "*the* one"
who would lead this boy to the blessings of matrimony. They were all
dolls, with one exception, and were much better than I deserved, but I
managed to retain bachelorhood, if not my innocence!

A rare picture of a P-47 Thunderbolt (bottom), P-51 Mustang (left), and P-80 Shooting Star — the P-47 and P-51 "prop" fighters, the P-80 jet fighter. Jack Hayes is flying the lead in the P-47, July 1946.

The "exception" was a Physical Ed major at the University of California — bigger, tougher, and meaner than me. She insisted on driving her car, which should have been a warning, but all went well until she was taking me home. She stopped at one of the local "petting spots" and wanted to know my intentions regarding matrimony. I felt my answer was appropriate — smoothly evasive — until she hung a wicked embrace on me to show me what I would be missing, threw me out of the car, and told me to hit the road!

I reported to Headquarters, Air Training Command, back at Randolph Field outside of San Antonio, Texas. In my flying cadet days, the command consisted of six civilian Primary Flying Schools, then to Randolph for Basic Flight Training and Brooks or Kelly for Advanced. After the war, the Command was extended from coast to coast.

It was obvious that there would be no trouble in devoting my career to flying, with the personnel gent's opening pitch being, "Now, I know that you probably want staff experience, but we have to fill duties primarily involving flying."

There was great relief when I said that I wanted cockpit duties — fighters only! My orders were cut to the fighter training base, and I was on my way the next day to Williams Field in Chandler, Arizona, near Phoenix. My mission was training in T-6s, P-47s, P-51s, and P-80 jets, and a fighter gunnery research squadron, flying all the fighters.

I received my commission in the Regular Army while home on leave. Great news, but it delayed my resumption of flying. Awaiting me at Williams were orders placing me on a Regular Army selection board, interviewing applicants for commissions. With only two months of Regular Army duty, I felt unqualified, but was informed that request for relief would not be accepted.

For two and a half months, eight hours a day on a five-day week, I helped decide who would be granted Regular Army commissions. Each interview lasted 20 to 30 minutes, and by afternoon, individuals became fuzzy. This was not fair to the applicants, but the new Regular officer posture had to be established, for budget proposals.

We only had access to application forms and service records, and we were to evaluate appearance, bearing, and initial impressions from the interviews. Undoubtedly, some slick Johns were over-rated, and the solid, quiet types suffered, since we were not privy to efficiency reports.

But the Central Area Board did find it necessary to advise us of some glaring inequities. One smooth, natty, All-American boy, rated by us in the top five percent of all candidates, was found to be awaiting general court-martial on most of the offenses in the book. But he was *smooth!*

I was assigned command of a P-47 Thunderbolt "Jug" training squadron, flying the "N" version with clipped, square wingtips. This Jug served in the last days of the Pacific War, long-range ground attack missions, led by B-29s doing the navigating, ticking off the fighter jocks to no end! But they had to admit that it was a hell of a bunch of water and a real scarcity of checkpoints.

Like all Jugs, it was a beaut of an airplane, once you accepted the lack-luster takeoff and climb performance, especially in the Arizona heat. As altitude increased, so did performance, and the prop jock who tried to out-dive you above 20,000 feet had a real shock coming. Our ground crews wore heavy gloves to avoid blisters, and so did we, or you couldn't touch anything in the cockpit.

We were training navigators and bombardiers of two categories: wash-outs from pilot training, and those assigned directly to non-pilot training upon entering the service. The former were cocky "hot rocks," I suppose because most had some combat experience. I never understood why, after the war, we discharged qualified fighter pilots who made it the first time, only to give wash-outs a second chance! Most made the grade, mainly because the Jug was so forgiving.

Prior to one of the class graduations, I was cleared to fly a 16-ship squadron formation, four flights with instructors at flight and element leads. A fly-by, strafing passes by each flight, another fly-by, and separation for flight peel-offs and landings. At which point, things got dark brown!

As my flight turned away from the field, I signaled for right echelon. The stud wingman on my left, instead of waiting for element to make room, crossed under and pulled up into element lead, whose prop cut the student's airplane in half, just behind the cockpit. The stud leaped out and his Jug crashed in the desert.

Element lead punched his canopy off and was about to make a "nylon letdown," when I pulled up on his wing and talked him back to the field and a landing — my safety record couldn't take another one!

Jack Hayes standing on the wing of a P-47 Thunderbolt at Williams Field, Chandler, Arizona, just before leading the last squadron to the "Boneyard."   U.S. Army Air Forces

All this with the students' wives looking on — many with child, in imminent "salvo status!" I understand that things got to a high degree of hysteria, but there were no "early releases," or whatever you call them!

Next came the smallest class in Army Air Corps, or Air Force, history ("small" referring to class numbers, not individual heights!). *Three* newly qualified P-47 jocks were the total input to the fighter pilot fraternity! It was called "Demobilization," but there was a deep concern about the reduction in the size of the armed forces, and the fighter numbers in particular.

Training with "the littlest class" were Brazilian and Bolivian cadets, whose countries were still receiving P-47s. They were fine Joes, even if their activities outside of training seemed to be dedicated to getting all the single female employees at Williams in a family way. It was rumored that the Latin Lovers had about a 75 percent success — or kill — rate, depending on your outlook!

There were language difficulties in flight training, and we relied lots on liaison officers. On one night cross-country, I assigned one of the Latin cadets to work with me as an airborne monitor at two checkpoints in the navigation triangle. Our mission was to provide early warning of a lost or downed stud, by missing check-in call, or receiving emergency transmission. The liaison officer was to act as a relay interpreter, if needed.

I was not aware that the liaison officer had aborted with radio glitches and, being half asleep and flying in shallow circles, I hoped that my charge was sticking to assigned altitudes and not infringing on my airspace. Then came a call, "Coronel Hayes, no oil pressure, *bailing out!*"

No aircraft identification, pilot name, or location was given. It's always nice to have really important information in an emergency!

I responded, "Hold on. Who are you, where are you, and what are oil and cylinder head temperatures?"

The temperature readings would indicate whether it was oil system or instrument failure. If those were normal, it was instrument; if on the high, red line, oil was gone and the alligators were back!

The reply came, "No oil pressure, bailing out. Goobye Coronel Hayes!"

Our Latin friend lit in a soft field close to a farmhouse and called in. The Jug flew around for almost three hours before making a pretty fair wheels-up landing, 150 miles from being left to its own devices. What an airplane! We even salvaged some parts from it!

It was pleasing to find that there were still carryovers of the relaxed wartime attitudes as late as 1946-1947. We finished one P-47 training program with over two weeks to spare and, as a reward for "hard work," I proposed to the Director of Operations an eight-ship Jug cross-country with — get this — a DC-4 (C-54 transport) to accompany and carry maintenance folk who would be on orders and drawing *per diem*, as would the flight crew!

I figured, rightly, that the fighter jocks would go for the hell of it — for the great flying and other "fringe benefits" — without reimbursement. Most were married and I understand that there were harsh words exchanged, marital rifts, and the Hayes name blasphemed by the officers' ladies!

Suitable coverage of our odyssey would fill a separate book, so I will merely touch on some of the printable highlights, like the Brazilian liaison standing his Jug on the nose at Memphis and completing the tour as a rider with the mechanics. And yours truly, the fearless leader, delayed takeoff from Houston one morning because of difficulty breaking away from some of the baser elements of Houston society!

It would require several chapters to recount the experiences in New York City, but suffice it to say that there were MPs on hand to assure that all of our noble party were accounted for on departure time from Mitchell Field. Talk about poor sports!

There were some hairy penetrations of weather in the Northeast, all done at low level, on different headings, and without coordination, and, somehow, we rejoined! The formation, minus one, landed at Willy Field as the two-week authorized time expired. I was *so* glad that I didn't have to present a smiling face and healthy body to a loving spouse. I needed all of the two days available to me in the BOQ to recover.

Back to my real duties, I led a 12-ship Jug formation at a graduation fly-by. We were followed by Mustangs and P-80s, since we were the slowest. Then, a sad day came — flying the Thunderbolts to the graveyard. It was the close of a wonderful era, but one with an outstanding place in fighter history.

My next command, beginning in February 1947, was of a P-51 Mustang squadron training Chinese pilots, who were the good guys then. But I'm sure we saw many of them in the MiG-15s and later editions as the enemy! The Chinese pilots had a low wash-out rate and high motivation — due, I was told, to the importance of "saving face." They flew with four to six cushions, and with the parachute burden, they barely made it to the airplane. But they were damn good pilots!

As a wartime measure, some West Point cadets received flight training as part of the Academy program and graduated with pilot rating. We were to train them in the P-51 and grant the rating of "Fighter Pilot, Single-Engine" to those qualified. Therein lies a tale of a very unpleasant experience for me.

I was forced to eliminate a son of one of the greatest Army Air Corps generals, and I had served under his command in Europe! The general's son had had six accidents in pilot training and had obviously made the grade because of the high respect and regard for his father. I fell into the same pattern and kept him in the program, even when he scraped a wingtip early on, after receiving extra dual instruction in the AT-6.

But with P-51 night flying qualification came the end of the road. On his first landing, he ground-looped, buckling one landing gear and damaging the prop, and he damn near ended up on his back, which could have been fatal. I went to the hospital where he was getting the routine check after an accident and told him that he was disqualified as a fighter pilot. I recommended that he apply for multi-engine training, or maybe even consider an Army career in something besides flying.

I honestly think that he was relieved; he had had more accidents in training than on a normal combat tour, and he didn't know how much longer he could luck out! But, God, how he hated facing his old man. He told me that the general was in Phoenix to see him join the ranks of the fighter pilot fraternity and he didn't know how he could tell him. So, I called him and asked for an appointment. He probably suspected the reason, but just said that he would come to the base the next night.

I met him in the visitor's lounge at base Ops, laid out the history of his son's flying, and his disqualification from a Fighter Pilot's Rating.

His only question was, "Is this your decision?"

I answered, "Sir, if you're asking if I had permission from my superiors, the answer is no. But you know that no one could afford to reverse the decision."

He replied, "I asked the question to confirm what I suspect — that you're the only one with the brains and the guts to do what should have been done a long time ago."

Before I could reply, he followed up with, "But you weren't so damned smart when you didn't wash him out earlier! Good luck in your career." What a man!

I met a challenge and got lots of thrills "instructing" (read "giving check rides") in the Mustang modified to the two-place configuration. We had had "piggy-backs" overseas by removing the fuselage tank and armor plate, rearranging other things, and installing a seat, but the function was passenger carrying — giving deserving ground troops rides and transporting couriers.

The trainer P-51 came about when some yard bird was shocked to discover that military pilots, starting with World War I, had been checked out in fighters without dual instruction! Incidentally, this practice continued through the first jets: P-80 Shooting Star, F-84 Thunderjet, F-86 Sabre, and F-100 Super Sabre, the latter being the first supersonic aircraft.

The fact that no problems were encountered was due, obviously, to the fact that only the finest pilots were selected for fighter assignment! But it was still deemed necessary to correct this deficiency in training, and the two-place Mustang was born by "field modification." The rear instructor's seat ("cell") had a stick that was restricted in movement, a throttle but no prop control, rudders (also with limited movement), and no brakes! This abomination was met by scorn and laughter from P-51 instructors, and they made it clear that they would never, ever, comply with assignment to the "idiot seat!" In the face of pointed remarks from my seniors regarding lack of leadership, discipline, and command example, I announced that I would use "The Thing" — as it was fondly referred to — for elimination check rides.

I thought that my example would shame instructors into some utilization, but it only evoked questions about their leader's judgment in using an airplane that was unsafe even for an average stud, to allow the inept a chance to affirm disqualification with an "auger job!" There were some thrills, until potential eliminatees chose to resign rather than face the challenge of "The Thing!" It was used for morale flights until the demise of the Mustang.

Some of us at this time thought it would be keen to have an aerobatic team, but neglected to request official sanction for many reasons, the paramount one being that approval would certainly be denied. And, the Army rule was "If it's not prohibited, it's permissible."

And so, our aerobatic team departed Friday afternoons and returned Sunday evenings, sometimes home on Saturday long enough to change team members and give the wedded members a chance to lower the home heat.

I flew right wing and made all the trips, as did the leader, who was married to an understanding lady (or maybe she didn't like him!). We stopped at military and civilian bases, sometimes with shows at two or three places

Margee Lou Roby Hayes.

in a day. Aircraft control regulations were loose in those days. Local traffic was notified of our antics by a tower operator's transmission, "We got some fighter pilots playin' around in the area. Ya'all be careful!"

We did our best to minimize publicity, for reasons of "military security," and it worked, except for one time — and that's all it took. It seems that the chief of staff called the commander of Training Command, who called the commander of Air Training Command, etc., until a message was received by the commander of Williams Field: "When the chief of staff decides to have a goddamned aerobatic team, you will be so advised!"

I understand that the prospect of general court-martial had lots of appeal to those in authority, but the question soon arose, "How did an aerobatic team exist without the knowledge of senior officers?" In other words, "Who the hell's running the store?"

Being that I was the senior, I would have had my head on the block, but miraculously the incident was not even mentioned in my efficiency report. Must have been that lots of senior gents were still reflecting Army Air Corps and World War II spirit!

The high point of this duty, and my life, was meeting the second and final Marge. She spelled it "Margee" — Margee Lou — and I found her at a nightclub in Phoenix, the "Gilded Cage," in February 1947. One look and I knew, "That's for me!"

It took a while before I got the first date, but I really impressed her — so much that we were finally married on February 4th, 1950, three years later!

In June 1947, I reported to Air Command and Staff school in Montgomery, Alabama, where I gained less than a distinguished scholastic record — pretty well fitting the norm for me. Life in the bachelor officers quarters did detract from academic endeavors, as I was trying to determine my readiness for matrimony.

Nothing in Alabama approached Margee, my "Arizona Doll," but I seemed to attract ladies already committed to officers senior to me, who generally desired action on the field of honor! I avoided final confrontations, at loss of pride and requirement for treatment of ulcers!

The flying was less than thrilling — the T-6 Texan trainer, the C-45 cargo transport, and the B-25 Mitchell bomber — though I had some good times with Joe Huddleston and a solo to New Orleans.

In the meantime, the U.S. Army Air Forces officially became the U.S. Air Force in September 1947, of which I was now a member.

I graduated — barely — from Air Command and Staff School and received orders to March Field in Riverside, California.

Chapter 9

March and George AFBs

I arrived at March Air Force Base in June 1948 and was assigned to the 67th Tactical Reconnaissance Wing as deputy wing commander — a totally superfluous position, and another example of over-manning/over-ranking of Air Force units.

We were a tenant on a base under the command of the 1st Fighter Wing and had two squadrons, RB-26 Invaders and RF-80 Recon Fighters, equipped for the photo mission. I never could get excited with picture-taking, but hasten to acknowledge the invaluable contributions of aerial reconnaissance in all the wars. Just not my cup of tea.

I did some research and

> . . . *I would soon be joining the ranks of unemployed fighter pilots, so I talked the First Fighter Group commander into a squadron command.*

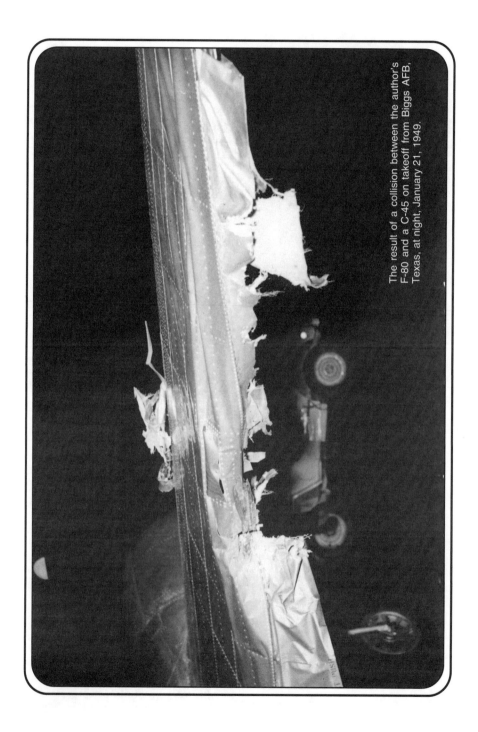

The result of a collision between the author's F-80 and a C-45 on takeoff from Biggs AFB, Texas, at night, January 21, 1949.

found that the 1st Fighter Wing CO was a "jock-strapper" (athlete), and made an appointment with him without permission of my CO, but I figured that he wouldn't miss me (I was right). My offer to coach a postwar March AFB football team was received enthusiastically, and it was agreed that I would also play. He submitted a request to my wing CO for this additional duty. The commander was probably influenced by memories of wartime days, for all services fielded teams of college players and there were games with several All-Americans on the field. Those days were over, but we put out a great team!

With command backing, I had no trouble getting time off for the candidates, but I got the cold shoulder from various commanders. We played Air Force, Navy, and Marine teams, and I might as well have been wearing rank insignia, the way I was worked over! I barely managed to be present for duty on Monday mornings after a Saturday game, until later in the season.

During one of the last games, I broke my ankle. Wet field, mud cleats, and one of my warriors let the runner go by, then showed "hot pursuit" in hitting me and the ball carrier, after my tackle and before we had gone down. All of our weight was on my right ankle, that foot being implanted in the mud. I heard the snap, and felt considerable pain, which increased rapidly when the tacklee was slow in unpiling. I started to peel skin from his sensitive parts and managed to convince him of my severe injury, just before he leaned on my face with a couple of fists. And there were no face guards then!

The team finished up with the title of "Western Air Force Champions!" I was coaching from a wheelchair, and at the big game was asked to serve as official time-keeper. I have absolutely no idea why there was a variance between the stadium clock, which I also controlled, and my official clock. Nor could I explain why this error resulted in three extra plays for March Field before the end of the first half!

It is true that March Field did score the winning margin as a result of the extra time, and the losers protested that the second half was "The shortest goddamned half ever played!" Suffice it to say that the other team was from Eighth Air Force, Strategic Air Command, and was made up of the best from several bases. Whereas we were the few gathered from only one base, but a *fighter* base — OK, reconnaissance, too.

With pending deactivation of the Reconnaissance Wing, I would soon be joining the ranks of unemployed fighter pilots, so I talked the 1st Fighter Group commander into a squadron command.

In this squadron, we flew the F-80 Shooting Star, the first U.S. jet, but transitioned into the F-86 Sabre — the first swept-wing fighter, also with the first aileron boost and high-pressure hydraulic systems, *plus*, the first ejection seat for emergency bail-out.

There were some problems with the seat; a couple went off on the ground with severe damage to a mechanic and one pilot. The high-pressure hydraulics also had growing pains, costing us several airplanes and pilots in the first year. But what a sweet flying bird, and it looked better on the ground than most do in full flight!

We lost one outstanding flight commander when he went in on takeoff from the factory on a ferry flight. He was single and recognized as a Don Juan, but not to the extent demonstrated at his funeral! The pall bearers formed two lines outside the chapel, through which mourners passed for the ceremony. Somehow, the somber mood and sense of loss were lessened when three lovely ladies, all clad in mourning blacks complete with veils, passed through our ranks. We didn't even exchange glances for fear of the chuckles, and I've always wondered about the feelings of the dolls when they spotted each other.

North American Aviation made the F-86 Sabre, the F-100 Super Sabre, the P-51 Mustang, and many others, all good. The greatest people to deal with, they threw a party for flight and squadron commanders in the first "swept-wing" group — 1st Fighter — at a Los Angeles bistro, the name of which I have forgotten. I do recall that the flight commander mentioned above and I were at the famous corner of Hollywood and Vine watching the sun rise and debating the name and location of our hotel. I've forgotten who was right, but we finally found it.

I was later ordered to the command of another fighter squadron when the CO there was relieved, and I should have recognized another omen! But I was involved in *the* high point of my life — I married Margee Lou on February 4, 1950, at the March AFB Chapel. A fraternity brother, Harry Hodgetts, was an usher, as was Joe Huddleston from the 55th Fighter days, troops from Williams Field and 1st Fighter guys and dolls attended.

The wedding was a real blast, though we almost had a bad ending. As we drove out the main gate, honeymoon bound, we were followed by cars

Margee Lou and Jack Hayes cutting the wedding cake, February 4, 1950. Note the F-86 on top of the cake!

containing soused fighter Joes, and all of us were stopped by the Highway Patrol for speeding. A patrolman was sympathetic to our honeymoon status, until confronted by our inebriated followers voicing things like, "Sum bitch, thas are boss an' you better bug-out, er we'll have yer ass!" I reached my height of diplomacy by getting them headed back to March, and the cop let us all go. But the headaches were only starting; when we returned from a fabulous honeymoon, I was informed by the group commander that my fighter pilots "damn near wrecked the Officers Club!" I managed to smooth it over, but that was another omen!

It became my squadron's time for a maneuver. I was ordered to Moses Lake, Washington (fondly named "Moses Hole" by fighter jocks before us), for Air Defense Command maneuvers testing effectiveness of radar and controllers against B-29 bombers. We had a great time, and set records for time between takeoff — scramble — orders and takeoff.

Strategic Air Command weenies put so many restrictions in the rules of engagement that it was ridiculous: no head-on passes, and all attacks would be broken off at our maximum gun range, not minimum range. You could hardly see them at that distance, so the rules were often violated, if not ignored completely, and the bomber pilots' wails and moans were sources of merriment at bar sessions!

There was an unusual amount of gun-camera failure, precluding action against rules violators. Back at March Field, some of "gun-camera malfunction" footage was uncovered and displayed at private showings. These scenes were gratifying to the fighter types, but would have caused massive cases of fear of flying for the Big Friends!

We were usually released from Alert in mid-afternoon, and to keep busy, I led an unofficial aerobatic team putting on impromptu shows at fields and towns around Moses Lake. There was no fuel, nor starting units, in the area, so we had to stay close to "The Hole." Even at that, we sometimes landed at Moses Lake after dark. I was waiting for questions about the extra activities, but there wasn't a word until when we went back to March, I was informed that aerobatic teams would be approved at group level, and squadron commanders would not be considered as leaders. My rule that "if it ain't forbidden, you can do it" worked again, and gave me some fun flying!

We returned after our maneuver to March in elements of two, and it was caustically pointed out to me by the group CO, and his adenoidal deputy, that it would have been peachy if we had arrived in squadron formation, with a fly-by before landing. But there were some problems that made it impossible: limited range without external tanks, bad weather, refusal of air traffic control to allow any formations over element (two-ship) size, and coordinating the support transport aircraft with fighter movements. But I recognized the futility of argument and made with the salutes and "Yes, Sirs."

The 71st Fighter Squadron received glowing commendations from Air Defense Command for outstanding performance, and North American Aviation featured the squadron in the company magazine. The Strategic Air Command Wing, which owned the base, forwarded the communications with the following (paraphrased) message: "Not our mission, but

A 71st Fighter Squadron party. From left to right: Jack Hayes, Chief Master Sergeant Joe Gilligan, and Margee Lou.

that's nice." The group commander's "enthusiastic" endorsement also came: "Noted." *Sheesh*!

The group commander and I never seemed to find the same frequencies — probably my fault, but the relationship was aggravated by his suspicions of my activities when I was still a bachelor. I must admit that social activities were much livelier at the BOQ than among the family types, and my leader was always in my squadron area the morning after a fine *soiree*.

He was obviously conducting a breath-a-lizer test of his own, and it continued after Margee Lou and I joined the married community. When I saw him coming, I made a ramp intercept, hoping fresh air would dispel any alcoholic fumes. I was backing around the ramp with him in close pursuit trying to catch a whiff, and the jocks at Operations enjoyed the show.

And then came the day of reckoning. The squadron was throwing a farewell blast at a local bistro for a flight commander who was transferring out. All was well until our several-car convoy headed back to March Field, in close formation. Soon came the gendarmes — one car, initially. I was doing fine with the smooth talk, and convinced the top cop that all cars would be driven by the sober, or most so, at the most reasonable speeds, directly to the home base.

We didn't realize that the other officer was an unhappy former GI who detested rank, and had placed the highest order "Help!" call. There followed lots of flashing red lights, the police cars descended from all quarters, and we were off to the local jailhouse.

The "squealer" hastened to vent his spleen to me on a nose-to-nose basis, resulting in an outbreak of hostilities, instantly subdued by local authorities. We were released to the base legal officer in the early morning, and I exposed my bride of four months to the first of many travails — responding to her anxious queries with, "I been in jail." But she hung in there after that one, and more!

I waited a couple of days for the ax to fall. Finally I was summoned to the group commander's office and a sepulchral atmosphere. The outer offices were empty — I'm not sure if that was to save the culprit embarrassment or to protect the innocent from contact with the "unclean."

I was given "At ease," and the commander read from a lengthy police blotter. After a couple of sentences, I interrupted with, "Sir, I know what it says, I was there."

After I left, I went back to the office to clean out and wait with the new wing commander for news of the future. A dismal outlook, but a pleasant surprise!

The new wing CO, a football player, boxer, and frustrated fighter pilot, was a kindred soul. Most important, he was a former policeman and member of the Police Officers' Guild. He had been called by the good cop, who had initially been in charge of the fracas, and informed, off the record, of extenuating circumstances.

I was told that I would assume duty as wing Operations officer, had better stay on the "by-God" straight and narrow, and that he had refused to allow the group commander's submittal of a Special Officer's Effectiveness Report — the kiss of death! After thanking him deeply, I saluted, and as I reached the door, he added, "Wait a minute, Hayes. Did you really swing at the cop with the billy club?"

"Yes, Sir, and I was saved when the good guy grabbed my arm and deflected the billy, or I would probably be in intensive care."

He chuckled, and then said, "Get the hell out of here and remember, if you pull something like that again, I'll personally kick the crap outta you!"

And he would have, but I felt such loyalty to him that it *was* the straight and narrow! We checked him out in the T-33, a two-place version of the P-80, and he was killed taking off in bad weather a few months later.

The Air Defense Command decided that it would be keen to operate under the separate squadron concept — not an original idea. The Royal Air Force had developed the arrangement prior to World War II.

Two squadrons of the 4th Fighter Wing were transferred to Eastern Air Command, Wing Headquarters and the remaining squadron moved to Victorville, California, which later became George Air Force Base. Quarters were not available for us at Victorville, so I had to leave Margee Lou in the off-base hovel we were luxuriating in at March, while I flew T-6s, C-47s, T-33s, and F-86s, just to fly. I drove a T-6 to March on weekends to see her.

Finally, we were assigned quarters at Victorville — a redone contractor's shack! It was the home of our first-born adopted son, Timothy Michael, born nine months and four days after our marriage.

After losing my friendly wing CO, I was trying to keep busy as the wing Ops officer, with only one squadron and base Operations to "test my mettle." One of the best things to cross my desk was a slot for the Fighter Gunnery Instructor's course, which was ten weeks at Nellis AFB, Las Vegas. It was fighter pilot's heaven, and flying the F-86! I talked the new wing CO into assigning me, and "Off we go!"

The course was one of my greatest experiences. And it was even a ball when things got a little dicey! On one occasion, the quiet of the deserts and mountains northeast of Las Vegas was broken by the roar of a twin-engine World War II light bomber, followed by screams from a flight of four F-86 Sabre jets, on our air-to-air practice gunnery mission. The sounds rising and falling in crescendo, as fighters made individual attacks on the aerial target, were punctuated by staccato bursts of the six .50-caliber guns on each fighter. The native animals, long accustomed to this cacophony, proceeded with their daily routines, only briefly disturbed by the explosive and grinding sounds of a mid-air collision!

Now in those days, *circa* 1951, air-to-air gunnery practice was accomplished by firing at a nylon banner, 20 feet long by 6 feet wide, towed by a B-26 whose pilot was spring-loaded to dump "the rag" in the face of any attacker if the angle off the tow ship's flight path approached anything less than 15°.

The geometry — or is it algebra? — involved in fighter gunnery is complex, especially to one who failed those courses, after initial difficulties with multiplication and long division! So briefly (and probably imprecisely), the air-to-air attack problem requires maneuvering your aircraft to a position 45° off the flight path, behind the target, tracking and firing until reaching the direct astern position, or zero degrees angle off.

In combat, the dead astern position is the maxima for the attacker, but is unhealthy for the tow pilot in training, which is why he does not hesitate to dump "the rag," even in the face of his best friend.

The attack should be terminated at between 10° to 15° off, when the attacker reverses his turn to cross over the target, calls his number and "Off," reverses his turn, and climbs back to the key position (the "perch") to initiate his next attack, in sequence.

So, I was Red Two and heard lead call "In," and saw him enter a left diving turn to the initial attack point. With his next transmission, "Red One Off," I observed him crossing over the target and reversing to a steep, right-climbing turn back to the perch, clearing me for a diving left turn, calling, "Red Two In." This being a four-ship flight, Red Three and Four *should* have been outside of me, at the same altitude, and slightly behind. What happens when someone is not where they should be will become clear shortly.

As I approached a position 2,000 to 3,000 feet above target altitude and 45° angle off, the turn was reversed and the gun sight positioned at the top, leading edge of the target. It's essential to track smoothly, no slip or skid, pulling a smooth 3 to 4 Gs. I'm sure that an explanation of "G forces" is superfluous these days, so I won't.

As I squeezed the trigger, I entered a series of violent snap rolls, with no feeling of a collision, leading to the conclusion that I had either been pulling excessive Gs or was totally uncoordinated on the rudders. The error of my analyses became evident with a high-pitched voice in the headset, *"Numbers Two and Three collided!"*

I realized that I was "Numero Dos," and looking to the right, I could see that less that four feet of wing remained, well under the design specs of the Sabre.

I then experienced a series of outside inverted snap rolls, interrupted by an inverted flat spin and back to the snaps. Both maneuvers threw me against the straps, with my feet off the rudders and hands against the canopy.

This position prevented me from starting the ejection procedure, known as the "Jesus Christ" or "Oh Shit" maneuver, depending on your philosophical bent! It was a simple maneuver — all that was required to "give the ship back to the manufacturer" was to pull out a red handle on the right armrest 90°, ejecting the canopy and exposing a two-pronged handle, the squeezing of which ejected the seat, pilot, and any loose paraphernalia in the cockpit.

My motivation for personal survival has always been high, but was increased by two transmissions, both at high decibel levels: *"Pull the red handle, pull the red handle!"* Advice as necessary as telling Custer to watch out for Indians!

The other attention-getter was "My God, he's going in!" The latter could have been directed to the jock who had occupied the same airspace as me, but I couldn't believe he could be in worse shape, so, ignoring prescribed ejection procedures, I grabbed the red handle with both hands, pulled up, and squeezed. Things worked perfectly, except the fact that the airplane was inverted meant that I was being shot toward the ground!

The surviving flight members stated that the collision was at 12,000 feet, my seat came out at 4,000, and the chute opened at 800 feet. But the altitude of the valley was 1,000 feet, and altitudes given were above sea level, making my actual height above ground lower.

I contributed to the problems of ejection when I had loosened the seat belt to allow the twisting and turning required to keep the target and rest of the flight in view. So, I was hanging on the belt and, rather than receiving a shove from the seat, got a real "boot in the rear," snapping my head forward and temporarily disengaging some teeth, as well as inducing a short nap.

Rejoining the living, I unsnapped the seat belt, shoved the seat away, and pulled the rip cord. An old tradition, probably started by someone who had never bailed out, held that bringing the rip cord handle back was the mark of personal coolness in an emergency. Mine probably ended up in California!

The chute opening was quite a shock, but it felt good! I heard the airplane explode on the ground as the chute opened, looked down, and I was directly over the burning wreck.

But the ordeal by fire turned out to be the least of my worries, with a

35-knot wind blowing on the surface. I had attended required lectures on parachute landing techniques, with minimal attention, since, like all fighter types, I assumed "It'll never happen to me."

While exulting at being among the living, I sensed that there was a problem, moving rapidly over the ground and swinging violently from side to side.

Due to the oscillations, my feet missed the ground; the chute landed first, followed by my ground impact in the horizontal position! The sensation can only be compared with the imaginable shock of a pro linebacker hitting you after a 20-yard start! I fondled and tasted the dirt and made all kinds of grateful, but ridiculous, promises to the good Lord.

With the diminishing of terror came the nicotine cravings, in bunches. By combining a slight bend from the waist with gentle and gradual knee-bending, I managed to reach my flight suit leg pocket and found the faithful Zippo lighter, but no smokes! The doctors told me later that this might have eased the injury shock symptoms, since my body was having enough trouble handling the nicotine withdrawals!

The only position I could tolerate was standing erect, hands on hips, which I was doing when I spotted the tow ship coming toward me on a low pass, bomb doors open. To my horror, a large object was dropped and came hurtling toward me. After all this, I was being bombed!

I was a ludicrous sight, shuffling from side to side, peering up from my hunched over position and trying to estimate the trajectory of the oncoming object. I should have known that Snapper Knapp — the tow pilot and one of the best fighter types to come down the pike — had planned it so that the bundle stopped about three feet from me!

It was the extreme hurts getting by hands and knees to the winter flying coat they had dropped, with its arms tied together. I finally managed to open it and there was a note from Snapper: "Hope this will keep you warm, but ef yer still cold, ya started a good fire 'bout half-mile down the hill. By the way, if you need medical attention, lie down on your chute."

He didn't realize what a problem was involved, but I did shuffle over to the chute. The tow ship circled to verify my response, then notified Nellis that a Sawbones would probably be nice for my morale, physical condition, and general well-being.

From all this came the realization that a chopper had not been dispatched, or was being recalled to pick up a doctor, and there I was in January, snow patches on the ground and I was wearing a light, summer flying

A helicopter at the F-86 crash site north of Nellis Air Force Base, Las Vegas, Nevada.

suit (not having anticipated this demise), at the farthest northern point from home base, with no idea how long it would take for the Cavalry to arrive! It was an hour or more; the cold was bearable, either from shock or the lack of nicotine.

I found life fairly tolerable if I adopted a posture similar to that of Quasimodo, so I figured I might as well check out the scenery. The first attention-getter was the biggest damn barrel cactus I had ever seen, about six feet from my ground impact point. It was five to six feet in diameter, needles four to six inches long, like a porcupine. If I had hit that hummer, besides the hurts, I would have lost so much blood that by the time the chopper arrived, their transportation problem would have been simplified — I read somewhere that empty blood vessels are very pliant, so it would have been no problem folding me into the body bag.

Finally, the sounds of a T-6 came, along with the "whump-whump" of a chopper. (There are some who think that "fluckata-fluckata" is a more accurate description. Whatever.) The T-6 led the Roto-Rooter pilot to me and he landed a ways down the hill — I suppose to survey a closer landing area. The doctor climbed out, ran up the hill and asked, "How are you?"

I figured he made the trip to find that out, but just said, "It's my back, Doc. How about a cigarette?"

With an All-American boy manner, like he was touting celibacy or other virtues, he announced, "I don't smoke."

There was a temptation for violent action, but I realized that he could ease the pain, so I laid on the agony. He shot me up with morphine, helping the wait for the chopper driver while he brought the whirly-bird up closer — with, I hoped, cigarette packs in every pocket!

After the young pilot turned off whatever you turn off in a chopper, he ran up to our position and was greeted by my querulous request for a cigarette. In those days, there was little possibility of two Air Force types in the same airplane being non-smokers. But I had had lots of bad luck that day.

In my desperation, I was convinced that there *had* to be a smoker at Nellis, and headed for the rescue craft. But with the first step came the massive hurts, and I couldn't move. The doctor pumped some more of the good stuff in me, and then life was beautiful! I floated to the chopper, was helped into the litter, strapped in on top of my chute, and we took off.

At that point, I felt that all this adventure had justified flying pay for a few months, but it wasn't over! We were flying at about 8,000 feet to get over the mountains, it was January, and I was still in a summer flying suit. I have no idea what happened to the heavy coat the Snapper dropped on me — the Doc was probably wearing it! I should have been miserable with the cold, but I was still on cloud nine with the morphine giggles. That is, until I sensed the parachute starting to be pulled from under me in the wind blast.

With my limited aerodynamic knowledge, I deduced that the chute would not hamper the main rotor blades above us, but was sure as hell going to screw up the tail rotor — with bad, probably fatal, results.

I started pounding on the doctor's door; he couldn't hear me and was giving me the "V" for victory sign, for Christ's sake! He did notice that I was frantically grabbing and stuffing under me errant parachute bits, and advised the pilot that there was a problem. We landed on a mountain side and they did much better securing the chute.

We started over and took off, sliding down the mountain! I found out later about the diminishing performance of choppers with increasing altitude, and was informed that we would never have become airborne without the downward slope available! I am unable to address that grim picture.

When I was unloaded onto a litter at Nellis, I refused any further movement until "I get a damn cigarette!" All kinds of packs were offered and I took five, just in case!

I was then transported to the "quack shack" (hospital), and the commander was an orthopedic type who was intensely interested as long as it looked like my back was broken, or badly bent. He did ask if I had any desires, and I jokingly mentioned a martini — at 10:30 a.m.! Shortly, an ambulance driver came with a large dixie cup filled with the devil's brew, and many olives. I had a sip or two, out of courtesy. They didn't help the pain, but I no longer gave a damn!

The x-rays showed that my back was not broken, but major muscles had been ripped loose and were "slithering around like a bunch of snakes," as one of the doctors (probably a muscle man) put it. They gave me shots in the back muscles, and put me to bed. I was given a top bunk — while lowers were available — I suspect by the ward nurse, who had the hates for officers.

She came to clean my "owees," or contusions, on my face, by direct order, I'm sure. By the time she finished with me, I was bleeding more than I had on the desert, so I laid back with a towel on my face, and asked my fellow patients to call someone (not her) if my breathing became shallow or the bleeding seemed excessive! In my multiple exposures to the profession of nursing, she was the only blot on the world's greatest.

One of my first concerns was getting the word to Margee, in the least traumatic manner possible. While unloading from chopper to the meat wagon at Nellis, I recognized a guy from the Jug days at Willy, asked him to call my assistant wing Ops officer at George to request that he and his wife see Margee and let her know that I was bent-up and bruised, but OK. The Nellis troops would have done the same thing, but his was the first familiar face I saw.

Margee called me a few nights later to say that I had been promoted to colonel. I made her spell the name and read out the serial number, and sure enough! This was one of those situations that make or break a career; if the now-deceased wing CO had allowed the Special Officer Evaluation Report (OER) to be submitted over that police incident, the "Hayes" would have been redlined and another name typed in. I'm humbly grateful, but have been informed by those who know me that any humility was well disguised.

After three days in the hospital and four at home, convalescing, I was back to Nellis. The maximum rank for course attendance was lieutenant colonel, so this was my last shot. I really laid the sweet talk on the flight surgeon, who begrudgingly okayed flying status after applying yards of tape, from navel to armpit, and this guidance: "If I get the slightest indication that you're having any trouble, yer ass is on the ground!"

He must have been aware of the devious acts that enabled me to finish the course, and I'm forever grateful for his understanding!

I was back to the training squadron and strapped an F-86 on to see if I could handle the bodily movements and the G forces. I could twist and turn by maintaining rigidity from hips to head, but found G forces a problem: at three Gs the smarts started, and four was the maximum G force I could handle. My report to the Training Wing CO was "No sweat!"

The question may arise as to my endangering other pilots in formation, but we were in close formation only to and from the gunnery ranges. My low G tolerance made my gunnery patterns looser than desired, but not a hazard. When we engaged in rat races, I dropped back to the last position, which gave me room to maneuver without getting in the way.

The critical problem of getting in and out of the Sabre was solved by the non-coms and airmen — another reason for my high regard and affection for the enlisted ranks! The Sabre was mounted from the left (as were most fighters, observing the Cavalry!), using two hand holds and three long steps up — no challenge unless you've got a sore back. On the first flight after being clobbered, I hadn't gotten up the first step or hand hold when the miseries took over. I let out a gasp, moan, or scream, depending on who's telling the story, and resumed a crouched position on the ramp.

So I was about to shuffle back to Ops and turn in the suit, when I realized that I had underestimated the "can do" of the Air Force maintenance man. Along came a crew chief stand, wheeled and with six-inch steps, ending just below the cockpit. They figured I could hack it with a man supporting me on each side, since my attempts to raise my arms to the side-rail level brought forth whimpers and obscene language!

So up the stand we went, but I was unable to go beyond the standing position in the cockpit — looking like Ben-Hur in his chariot! They solved this by having a man straddle the cockpit canopy and lower me into the seat, while I eased my legs into the rudder channels and dismounted with a reverse process. I stressed that a sharp eye had to be out for suspicious observers — colonels, and especially doctor colonels.

They set up the damnedest flight-line spotting and reporting system.

The second day of our operation the call went out, "Brass on the flight line." Me and my helpers were halfway up the stand when I was whisked off and away, to behind a maintenance supervisor's truck. From the troops swarming over that F-86, it looked like it was being rebuilt!

But finally came the moment of truth — "start engine time" — and they handled that. I was well screened until being strapped in and the engine started. We probably didn't fool anyone, but what friends! I paid for a keg to be delivered to the maintenance squadron at a time and place they chose. Hope they had a great one!

These procedures got me through the rest of the course, but I dropped from Top Gun competition slot to also ran. Just as a clarification, the "Top Gun" rating originated at Nellis AFB, years before the Navy movie with that title. But the Air Force held the fighter community as unimportant in the "Wild Blue Yonder" concept and subservient to bombers, missiles, and space command!

I had flown missions, and qualified, in all categories of fighter employment, but had less than the minimum sorties required for course completion. The informal word was that I could not be graduated with "Fighter Gunnery Instructor" rating, and that an unofficial rating of "Top Guts" had been turned down.

Margee drove up to Nellis a few days before the graduation ceremony with our four-month-old Timothy. It would be unbelievable, if you didn't know Margee Lou, that she had planned and set up a cocktail party, with snacks, for students, instructors, and staff, while taking care of the baby and me! (I only saved her from the French and Belgian students because they were fighting among themselves!) This *soiree* was a couple of days before graduation, and it was there that I learned of a solution to my lack of qualifications.

At the party, the commander of the fighter gunnery instructor's course announced, "You are free to depart the next day and, by the way, the signed Graduation Certificates, minus names, will be in the office of the school secretary and his office will be unlocked and unmanned, tomorrow from two to three p.m." And that's how I graduated from the Fighter Gunnery Instructor's Course.

And so I was off to the next assignment . . . onward and upward!

Chapter 10

Hamilton Field and Korea

*J*N 1951, it was time for another of the reorganizations that came about with every change in Air Force hierarchy. The most prolific of reorganizers were the disciples of the Strategic Air Command, known as SAC — and by other descriptions of varying obscenity.

This particular scramble, an obvious ploy to increase the number of generals in Air Force blue, created a Wing Headquarters over fighter and combat support groups, staffed with people trying to keep busy. The 78th Fighter Group CO became wing commander, and I was ordered to Hamilton Field to command the fighter group. We were flying the F-84D/E Thunderjet, but were scheduled to convert to the F-86 Sabre and the Northrop F-89 Scorpion; we had some of the greatest fighter squadron commanders ever.

. . . it was time for another of the reorganizations that came about with every change in Air Force hierarchy.

Hamilton was one of the first Army Air Corps fields built, pre-World War II, across the Golden Gate Bridge from San Francisco and near San Rafael. It had beautiful and spacious quarters, and ours was one of the best, across the street from the Officers Club, which I thought was nice.

An important chapter in our life took place at Hamilton. In May 1952, Margee, Timothy Michael, and I took off for San Diego to await the arrival of our adopted twin boys, Patrick and Stephen. They had some digestive troubles, so it was nine days before Tim and I put Margee and the new ones on an airliner at Lindbergh Field.

I was in uniform and carried the two-place basket to seats across from Margee. A couple of nice little old ladies across the aisle asked Margee the twins' age, and when the reply was "nine days," they looked startled — Margee looked so good for supposedly having just delivered twins! But then the explanation came when one stated, "They're service people, you know!" Apparently we had more *endurance* than civilians!

I worked in two more years of service football while commanding the 78th Fighter Group, abetted by the Western Air Defense commander, Headquarters at Hamilton, and an avid football fan. I signed lots of papers, made command decisions in dirty practice togs, and worked many an evening keeping up. This was only possible because of a strong staff, the squadron COs, and, of course, the head man's attitude!

The first year was the best of my four years of service football. The head coach was a former pro, Captain Glenn Johnson, who suited up for practice and played in most games. We had several high-caliber college and high school players and found a former high school coach to coach the backs and scout opponents. I couldn't devote time to coaching, and was grateful for the chance to play some more. We were the Air Force Pacific Conference Champs, and one of the finest post-World War II teams.

But the second, and last, year was grim. We had some new college experience and a generally new squad, with a West Pointer as coach — from whom came the "Grimsville!" He pictured himself as Vince Lombardi, or a coach equally famous, and screwed up what could have been an outstanding season. He didn't play and I was told that it rankled the hell out of him to see me down in the mud, blood, and cleats!

Just before the next to the last game, he came by my quarters and asked if I would stop playing, and simply coach. Since my "coaching" contribution consisted of listening, taking notes, and nodding agreement to his words of wisdom, I notified him that I was hanging up the pads and made definite and succinct suggestions as to where he could put his football team!

I don't imply that my departure caused that dismal record of Hamilton Field — there were only two games left and he had already screwed things up beyond salvage. My sympathy was for the squad, and what could have been. I have no bad memories, just real gratitude for four years of service football.

Air Defense Command established the Western Air Defense and Air Division Headquarters at Hamilton Field, with 78th Fighter Group the subordinate command. Now that's close supervision that wasn't needed, nor deserved.

We continually had flights on Air Defense Alert, numbers dependent on readiness status, which rose and fell with world tensions. The squadrons rotated the Alert mission, maintaining fighters and pilots on varying response requirements. The other squadrons were training in gunnery, formation, tactics, and new pilot upgrading.

For some reason, probably a carryover from World War II, it was necessary to provide dusk and dawn patrols over the San Francisco area. Since zero-zero klag — zero visibility, zero ceiling — was predominant at Hamilton during those hours from 75 to 90 percent of the time, there was a problem, which was solved by the following plan: Travis AFB, which was well inland, and was owned by Military Airlift Command with SAC and had tenant units, was tasked — or rather asked — to furnish facilities for two F-84s and pilots, who would fly the dusk patrol and land at Travis an hour or more after dark.

The same aircraft would launch at least one hour pre-dawn, patrol, and land back at Hamilton. The 78th Fighter would furnish ground personnel and equipment. Hard to believe, but the negotiations for that piddly job were more complicated than the Yalta Agreement!

Not long after we started the mission, there were unofficial rumblings from the Travis brass that fighter pilots were making passes at unaccompanied ladies in the Officers Club. With some of their transport and bomber men always away on TDY (temporary duty), there was concern —

not regarding the virtues of the ladies, but that they were exposed to ungentlemanly conduct.

Naturally, I was shocked, so I put myself on the next Travis roster, and found no evidence of any misconduct. I was a bit concerned, however, when my young wingman asked to be excused before dinner, but he assured me that he intended to use the library and study for some off-duty courses he was taking. Being greatly impressed by this dedication to self-improvement, I only reminded him of our early takeoff time.

I heard him come in shortly after I retired, and the next morning I expressed concern at seeing lipstick stains on his shirt and handkerchief. The situation didn't improve when he corrected me: "Those are blood stains." That ended *that* interrogation! After much deliberation, I concluded that pilots landing an hour after dusk, having dinner, and rising two hours before dawn, certainly wouldn't be interested in sexual pursuits — even fighter pilots!

It wasn't until much later, when we were safely home, that I realized I had never seen any textbooks or writing material!

But further to my dismay, as we taxied out the next pre-dawn, I noticed two F-84s in Transient Aircraft Parking, and I had a revelation! The Don Juan fighter pilots who were on authorized cross-country obviously were planning to spend the last overnight at Travis. And thus, a brief directive was published: "No F-84s at Travis unless on official duty, or some careers will be redirected to the transport/bomber vocations!" There was some suggestion that automobiles replaced the F-84s, as "vehicle of choice," but surely not!

When I flew Air Defense Scrambles, I scheduled myself in the number two, wing position, ostensibly to maintain formation flying proficiency, but really because I had a helluva time describing civilian transports — airliners. The controllers expected definitive description of the "unknown," like, "DC-4, DC-6, DC-3," etc., rather than my descriptions: "Uh, it's got four engines, kinda long and slinky, twenty or more passenger windows, and the damnedest tail you ever seen! Oh, yeah, a sign on the side says TWA/PAN AM" — or whatever.

Intelligence was always scheduling me for aircraft recognition sessions, but I could never get enthused over airline pictures, after the wartime photos. I didn't fly many interceptor missions, anyway, and I wondered why we played air defense when the Big War was so long past, with no bad guys on the horizon.

I eventually realized that the Air Force was trying to maintain a semblance of the mighty force of old and the various arms, *i.e.*, Training, Air Defense, Tactical, and Strategic, with their support, supply, and maintenance branches. This was aided by the Korean conflict, but the military was still trying to reverse the disarmament trend and out-shout the "peace at any price" do-gooders. And too many still haven't learned.

We Old-Timers — World War II vets — had difficulties with a scientific/technical approach to the Jet Age. We automatically assumed that when you got an airplane, it would be within the performance parameters, like weight, takeoff and land distances, obstacle clearances, and stuff like that, no matter where you were sent to fly. Suddenly, we were burdened with the responsibility of determining if we could take off and land under varying weights and atmospheric conditions.

An example follows of this virginal approach to the mysteries of jet flight occurred when I was leading a flight of four — me and my squadron commanders — returning from a commander's conference in Colorado. We had a fuel stop at Albuquerque, New Mexico, a very high place. This high altitude would probably cause lots of problems in our getting airborne — or so we thought! (I later learned that there were charts available to precisely determine takeoff distance required at our elevation and pressure altitude, whatever that is.)

Our solution was to flip a coin to determine the unlucky soul who would resolve the question, "Go or no-go?" Phil Joyal was selected by this scientific manner, and after he pointed out things like, "I have the most kids, one on the way, and a wife who needs me," he recognized the futility and strapped the F-84 on.

The guidelines were simple: if he became airborne before he ran out of runway, we would follow. If he aborted the takeoff by ground looping, or pulling the gear up, we would wait for better conditions and take up a collection for his bus fare home.

Finally, if above scenarios did not transpire, and his takeoff attempt resulted in a fatal crash, we would arrange for the proper services, have his aircraft number deleted from the inventory, and have our three F-84s placed in temporary storage until winter, when three low-ranking lieutenants would ferry them home!

Ole' Phil vanished in a cloud of dust at runway end. We were preparing condolence speeches, when there came a calm voice: "Wait 'till the very end, don't try to pull off the ground, pull the gear up and nose down. There's a real good downslope and a valley to fly down."

It worked! It took a while to climb over the next hills, but we were soon home and ready for the next challenge in the Jet Age!

There was not a gunnery range available for air-to-air gunnery practice, so Western Air Defense HQ reopened the former Yuma Army Base, with its miles of ranges. Squadrons were rotated through and we reached a high combat readiness rating, in what could be charitably called "field conditions!"

I could never approach my former proficiency, which wouldn't have won many competitions, but was respectable. I finally figured out that high scores are tough to get when you're looking over your shoulder for potential mid-air collisions! The Air Force let the base go, figuring "Who needs gunnery?" The Marines do, and it's now their base!

It eventually became boneyard time for the F-84 Thunderjets. We were re-equipped with F-86 Sabres, which were no problem, and the Northrop F-89 Scorpion, which was a different story. The F-89 was an ideal air defense weapon, with pilot and radar operator, good instrument platform, and a revolutionary control, the decelleron. This was a split aileron dive brake with instant response from pilot inputs, allowing the pilot to fly formation or change airspeeds without changing power.

But there were problems caused by the proximity to the ground of the engine air intakes, which earned the Scorpion the designation, "The Vacuum Cleaner!" Despite constant ramp and runway sweeping and death penalty threats for littering, there were continuing engine failures, usually in flight! For that, and other reasons, the F-89 had a short Air Force life. But before its demise, there was a tale that became part of the F-89 saga, featuring a radar operator of the 78th Fighter Group.

With the unexpected requirement for a non-pilot rated radar operator, the Air Force laid on an intense recruiting program for backseaters — with glamour, white scarves, and "Wild Blue Yonder!"

From this recruiting there came to the 78th a captain, a former supply officer, exemplifying the fighter pilot image. He passed the qualification tests, and was assigned to a pilot (hate to use "crew" in the fighter business!), and was put on the Alert roster. During his first scramble, at 500

In late 1951, Jack Hayes led Republic F-84 Thunderjets, with the newly assigned F-89 Northrop Scorpion following.

Jack Hayes shows the Commander of Western Air Defense Forces the first Northrop F-89 Scorpion Interceptor assigned to 78th Fighter Group, Hamilton Field, California, 1952. Hayes was the Group Commander.

U.S. Air Force

feet, the gear and flaps were coming up, and the right engine exploded! Both ejected, with minor injuries. The captain underwent a short hospital time, then performed local flights, and was put back on Alert.

On the second scramble, there was an engine check on the runway, and the right engine blew before they even started rolling. Our hero fired the canopy, climbed out on the left wing with parachute (his "Mae West" life jacket, dinghy, and survival gear still attached), ran to the wingtip and jumped. Because the wing of the F-89 was ten feet from the ground, his landing caused damage to his knees and hands, but didn't slow him down in getting as far as possible from what he described as "that *@#X%§+¢?* piece of *&¢#@!*"

I visited him in the hospital the next morning and made a jovial comment about how his tour of duty was bound to improve. His response was, "Colonel, you're talkin' to the best damned supply officer in the United States Air Force!"

And that was that!

By fall 1951, the average fighter jock was getting the unhappies if he hadn't had his tour in Korea. But we were all well aware of the dangers in volunteering, which plunged you into the personnel hopper, the "round peg in the square hole chaps." An abundance of bad stories were being circulated: fighter pilots assigned to administrative duties, as supply officers, mess kit repair squadrons, even *bombers!*

By-name requests from fighter units were discouraged, and not honored anyway, because "You go where you're told to in this man's Air Force and commanders take the replacements assigned, not just those personally requested!" Now there's a typically profound personnel dictate.

I was anxious to take a look at this new war, but didn't feel that Margee Lou needed any more trauma, for a while at least. It had been a rough enough year and a half. So I was resigned to however the ball might bounce for future assignments, when along came Bud Mahurin, who had been assigned someplace in wing or air division. Bud was one of the greatest fighter pilots of any country, or any war! We met when I was flying missions in P-47s during World War II with the 56th Fighter Group.

Recognizing a kindred spirit, Bud suggested that we request TDY to Korea, for "combat experience," and then wangle permanent assignment.

The commander Western Air Defense Forces thought the TDY was a good idea, but for no more than 90 days, and "no fast ones over there" — meaning don't do what he expected, *i.e.*, request permanent reassignment.

This was a golden opportunity for me — a chance to get experience in a different war, while Margee could stay in base quarters. But Bud allowed that he had fingers crossed when we said farewell to the two-star boss. He was assigned to an F-86 wing and was lighting up the skies until the Sabre was given the ground-attack mission. But ground fire did what no fighter pilot could, and Bud spent some tough times in North Korean prisoner of war camps.

I was assigned to the 4th Fighter Wing at Kimpo, Seoul, another F-86 wing, and mine and Bud's two wings went neck-and-neck on MiG kills to the end of the war. There were great aces in both wings and it was sad that some were killed in non-combat accidents, back in the States. But saddest of all was the death of George Davis in his first combat tour in Korea.

Early in his tour, he was breaking every record in any war, and was still the same unassuming gentleman. He could have been assigned the most experienced wingmen, but George insisted on taking the rookies, to contribute to their indoctrination in aerial combat.

Later in the war, when I was flying P-51s, I found out that George had been shot down and was carried as missing in action, but that he was hit in the cockpit with 20- or 37-millimeter shells and was followed to ground impact with no chute. His wingman had lagged in the battle, through no fault except inexperience, and a MiG had fired from close range. The MiG attacker was well known to F-86 drivers — bright red, known as "Casey Jones," and the pilot was probably Russian or Chinese.

What a way George went out! He had shot down two more MiGs before being clobbered! I flew back to Kimpo to talk and commiserate with his mates and to write his lovely wife.

But during my stint with the 4th Fighter Wing early in the war, I attended tactics and procedures lectures and flew missions — usually numbers two and four slots, to element and flight lead, and finally section lead, two flights and the largest formation flown at that time. There could be several sections up, separated by 5 to 30 minutes, but they were integral fighting units.

I was in some hassles while flying wing positions and saw some kills by leaders, but I was too busy covering their rears to get a shot. While flight lead, I had a head-on encounter with a MiG. I didn't get any hits, but

An F-84
formation
from
Hamilton Air
Force Base
in 1952.

had a couple of impressions: the cannon round from a MiG is as big as a bowling ball, and you can get completely behind the F-86 stick and still use the gunsight, and squeeze the trigger!

My first encounter with artificial restraints placed on combat forces came as we were sweeping north to the Yalu River at 35,000 to 40,000 feet. We saw miles of supplies with no covering, camouflage, or gun protection. Then we watched the MiGs take off, climb above us, cross the river, and attack. So combat engagement, for us, was always entered on the defensive!

Most critical was the fact that the MiG was fighting close to the home base, while we had to conserve fuel for our long haul back. They could sit above us and make passes until we were forced to turn into the attack, and continue this until flameout or bail-out time!

One of our flights was a late afternoon F-84 cover. We started home after the Thunderjets had withdrawn, and were bounced by one wildly painted MiG, rapidly deduced to be a "Sierra Hotel" (a term we used often, the initials of which stood for "*shit hot!*") Russian instructor! He would smoke down into the attack until our -86s had to turn into him, stay until being out-turned, and return to altitude. He repeated this until he had to go home, and the -86s were running on fumes. They had to shut down engines and glide until restart became necessary. The lead flamed out turning in to the hardstand, Number Three flamed out on the taxiway, Number Two entered the "quiet period" on the runway, and Number Four punched out safely, three miles north!

During all flights, we were not allowed to cross north of the Yalu River, which we called the "Goddamn River," or "GDR," for short. The Yalu "no-no" line was hard to take, but was reluctantly accepted, with some transgressions. We had a young, red-hot captain who never seemed to be on the schedule when there was a fight, and he tried everything. He scheduled himself on every mission, if there was enough time between the morning and evening sorties, but no joy! He tried flying missions when the aces were flying, but it would be a quiet day! He tried astrology, numerology, even made all kinds of commitments to Satan, since the Good Guy hadn't come through!

On his last mission, he was leading a section on withdrawal support for P-51s, who had beaten up communication and radar sites south of the GDR. MiGs were climbing out to the GDR after being dispersed by the target-support Sabres. Along came "Lieutenant Dumbjohn," or whatever the North Koreans called them, and all he could see was Antung Main Airport, and home.

Our hero, heading south over the Mustangs, spotted the MiG heading the other way, smartly executed a split-S, and ended up directly behind and closing rapidly. There was only time for a short burst.

Back at Kimpo, we were celebrating for the Tiger when he identified himself as the guy doing the victory roll, and he got a combined "end of tour" and "I got me one" party — that is until a snoopy intelligence type got the boss' ear and said we had better see the combat film. It was wisely proclaimed that there would be no combat reports, or film, forwarded to Headquarters for the time being!

A few of us gathered for a private showing of the killer's combat film. The first frames showed a MiG rapidly filling the screen, a fast overtake, and some hits. Then came beautiful shots: the MiG-15 on final approach for landing, gear and flaps down, taking hits all over. But in the background was Antung Main, with parked MiGs, red flags, and everything but a follow-me jeep with a sign saying, "Welcome to Antung!" The MiG went inverted and splashed, and our boy broke off to the south. No flak — not even small arms — in this secure area! Obviously the killer had violated the "no-no" and had crossed the GDR!

The pictures were unbelievable in clarity and detail, which is why they were burned and the mission report labeled "camera malfunction!" Since he was not supposed to be on that side of the GDR, he would likely have been court-martialed if the film had not been destroyed. And so he would have to go home without a kill to his credit.

The next morning, we poured a hung-over, thoroughly ticked-off captain into the transport for the "Land of the Big BX," the Zone of the Interior. He said that if he had been smart, he would have "gone back in and strafed the whole damned Antung Main!" That would really have been hard to hide!

After my F-86 missions, the Fifth Air Force attached me to the 49th Fighter Wing, flying F-84s farther south. I knew lots of troops there in the fighter game, and we had a ball! The most important was Bud Andres, a top fighter pilot and friend, who played football for "Alabam'," and was a squadron commander. I stayed in his quarters and flew most of my sorties with his outfit.

After a couple of orientation flights, we were off. The Thunderjets flew railroad cuts, with two 500-pound bombs. We occasionally hit truck parks and troop concentrations — hard to see, but you knew you were in the right place when the 20-, 40-, and 87-millimeter (mm, or "Mike-Mike") boiled up.

The North Koreans and their Chinese friends moved almost entirely at night and planned train movements to be in tunnels or steep valleys at first light. Truck convoys were the same: spending daylight hours in valleys, wooded areas, or with no attempt at concealment, in villages, since attacks on them would be on "helpless civilians" (a well-exploited procedure later, in Vietnam). Before hitting these areas, we circled and made dry runs to enable civilians to disperse, and, incidentally, alert all anti-aircraft units!

The dilemma was that if the enemy makes maximum use of civilian areas for concealment, and these civilian areas are declared sacrosanct, it's fold tents and surrender time! The Korean and Vietnam wars raised problems and moral decisions unheard of in the World War II European Theater.

The North Koreans used another means of keeping supplies moving in daylight, which really unnerved me, as a Cavalryman in the first place, and an animal lover in the second. Horses and oxen were loaded with ammo and supplies, covered with foliage, and casually moved along the roads. After cutting rails close to the Yalu (GDR), we would reconnoiter to the south looking for targets and always finding these beasts of burden.

I would have nothing to do with attacking these targets, until I was forcibly reminded that the United States Air Force, in general, and the Fifth Air Force, specifically, had been assigned the mission of interdicting North Korean supply lines, and if I had some goddamned problem with shooting at animals, it would be simple to relieve me of my commission and pilot's rating and reassign me as a veterinary assistant!

So it was back to work, and damned if the first animal target didn't blow so high that my bird had dents all over and it spent the long trip home trying to ingest or upchuck various pieces of metal! Thus ended the Hayes Korean Chapter of the SPCA!

Most F-84 targets were close to the GDR and we had F-86s for MiG cover, high and in position prior to our target time, and protecting the withdrawal. It grew considerably dicey if the MiGs came across just as we reached the target, since this called for the drop fuel tanks command from the F-86 lead, (in order to lighten the load and increase the speed!) and we had to try to evade the barrage of tanks.

There was one wing, to remain unnumbered, and the wing commander, nameless, who always made things interesting with a shower of tanks, but reassured us with, "Don't worry -84s, we're up here."

A squadron lead finally acknowledged with, "We know it ya sonofabitch, you're dropping tanks all over us!"

There followed comments referencing radio discipline, but because *none of us* heard the transmission, much less admitted sending it, it was obviously a case of enemy use of our frequencies.

There was no doubt that we were on enemy radar on climb-out and over North Korea, plus visual tracking in the target areas, so it was decided to use darkness and low-altitude penetration to attain surprise. Without aircraft external lights we couldn't fly formations, and attacks had to be made on penetration headings, without circling and alerting ground defenses. Most fighter jocks evidenced total disinterest in the new tactic, and, when volunteers were requested, were totally preoccupied with other matters, *any* other matters.

I found two sorties a day tiring, and figured that I could fly a morning and another that night. The next day, I'd fly an evening, then repeat the first day without dragging too noticeably.

The night flights were spooky and lonely. We were allowed cockpit lights only, flying in and out of clouds, radar vectors to letdown, in the clear, and you were on your own. It was so dark outside the cockpit that bombs were dropped on elapsed time. The villains responded violently. As soon as your stuff went off, they threw everything they had, from light to heavy, all over the sky, and you had to duck down in the cockpit to keep some night vision. And it helped not watching!

The North Koreans had a trick that showed they knew something about perspective. They would string lights up a vertical cliff, narrowing the distance between lights until the illusion was of an approaching line of vehicles on a flat surface. We suspected that a couple of our guys may have bitten and did not return (DNR); when night reconnaissance reported the scene, they were pinpointed by radar in *mountainous* terrain.

I only flew one night frolic. The next afternoon, I led a flight on rail cuts and armed reconnaissance back. I climbed to 25,000 feet for home, started letdown, and up jumped the devil! I had no inkling of a cold until my eardrums and sinuses started raising all kinds of hell. I told element lead to take the flight in, climbed back to altitude, and tried to clear things up.

I blew so hard, holding my nostrils closed, that I felt I was going to induce a hernia, diarrhea, or both. Nothing worked, and fuel was scarce, so it was bite the bullet time. I had awful pains from ears and sinus, and tears blocking my vision. It was so bad I asked for a flight surgeon to meet me. Turning initial for landing, I felt an eardrum blow and an explosion — honest — over my eyes, and goop gushed into my throat. So here was the Doc expecting a combat casualty and all he got was high-ranking ear and headaches!

Then it was back to Kimpo by train. I imposed on Ben Preston's hospitality (who was wing CO of the 4th Fighter Wing) for ten more days, got TDY extended by that much, and returned to finish the F-84 missions.

After completing my 20 F-84 missions, I flew a T-6 to the P-51 Mustang wing, at K-46. I've forgotten the base location, but remember that this was the last place where they still coded friendly bases. I didn't expect an honor guard and brass band to meet me, but was surprised when a first lieutenant — first "John" — identified himself as greeter, assigner to quarters, issuer of flight equipment, airplane checker-outer, and overall major domo!

After being taken to my quarters in the wing CO domicile, I had to ask where in hell the brass were. I was informed, with a straight face, that this was, after all, a weekend, and senior officers used those days, at a plush resort to the south, to restore over-worked minds and bodies from the ravages of war.

An obvious question, "You shut down on weekends?"

"No, Sir. Captains and lieutenants run the show." And with much greater efficiency, I soon found. (Incidentally, the first John retired from the Air Force as a general, a rank never more deserved!)

Once my new friend had satisfied himself in my proficiency in formation, weapons delivery, and aerial combat, he assigned me as his wingman, and off we went. Not much had changed, except in the airplane — we flew road and rail cuts, followed by armed reconnaissance and attacks on transportation, supplies, and troops — and this young Tiger rung me out! The lowest altitude and highest Gs I had seen in a long time.

The terrain surrounding K-46 was so mountainous that radar-directed letdowns and approaches were impossible, and the base facilities, and Mustang equipment, were no help. So flight lead put the wingmen into close trail, found a valley fairly certain to point toward home, and whistled on through. If ground and clouds merge, then maximum climb and hope you break out before you spin out!

I had flown some two-a-day missions when back to the fray came the "command" echelons, after a long weekend! The wing CO expressed his regrets at not meeting me on arrival, but it was essential that he get the staff and commanders away from the pressures of combat, to really solve their myriad problems.

To ensure that I was getting an accurate combat picture, the wing CO directed that I fly his wing on the morning mission — not the early one, but a "tennish" takeoff. Like he was laying on a frapping tea party! Our targets were suspected command and control centers in the Pyongyang outskirts, and we were carrying 250-pound high-explosive bombs — with following flights dropping incendiary bombs, setting on fire the ruins left by our precise bombing!

We crossed the 38th Parallel at 25,000 feet, slid into trail formation, as briefed, and then came the familiar heavy flak, barrage type. Lead pulled up into a wing-over and shallow dive angle, maybe 35°, *and dropped his bombs!* We were supposed to drop when he did, like the bombers in World War II, but my altimeter was only going through 20,000 feet, and seasonal field burning put out a smog so bad you couldn't even see the city!

Being certain that the bomb release was accidental, I throttled way back and steepened the dive, hoping for a visual. I didn't know where Three and Four were, until "Red Lead, this is Three. Red Two is still diving."

This brought chastisement: "Number Two, drop immediately and rejoin south of target."

Even going through 14,000, I wasn't seeing anything but flak, but ever the disciplined Air Force officer, I pulled into a climb and salvoed when I was certain that the bombs would land in fields, not the city.

I rejoined the flight to carry out the remainder of the field order, "Conduct armed reconnaissance south of Pyongyang, attacking military targets to the limit of fuel and ammunition. . . ." We did, but at 15,000, not at 2,000 or 3,000 feet! This charade was carried out until our leader decided that, because of poor visibility, the mission should be terminated and so informed the Tactical Air Control Center.

It was a real kick when the controller, obviously a frustrated fighter pilot who was familiar with our leader's voice, said, "OK, Tiger, cleared to home plate. Ya'all be careful now, ya hear?"

After landing, we wingmen were picked up by jeep to go to Intelligence debriefing, while the wing CO climbed into his air-conditioned staff car. I stared at the captain and looie, element lead and wing, without a word. Then one said, "Geezuz, Colonel, we gotta live with this or face grounding, maybe disciplinary action. The bastard only flies once a week; we share that shit detail and fight the war the rest of the time."

I made no contribution at the interrogation until our "Scourge of the Skies" marked the target map with direct hits. That did it! After politely asking that the wing CO and I be excused for a moment, I led him to a corner of the Nissen hut, and, to paraphrase, said that if he kept up the crap he was handing out, not only would I drop by his quarters and inflict bodily harm on his person, but I would make personal reports of his dereliction of duty to every command echelon, including the Pentagon!

Back he went to the debriefing table and stated that I had reminded him that the "setting sun" (at noon) caused reflections that looked like bomb bursts, and he really didn't know where the bombs had hit!

As we left, I mentioned that I would like to fly the rest of my missions with junior officers, "to feel the pulse." No sweat. A couple of days later, he was back on R&R and I never saw the weenie again.

There was one most memorable and satisfying mission in the Mustang. We were on a sweep, with rockets and guns, in the Sinanju area, south of the Yalu, when we were directed north and west for air rescue support. An F-84 had been hit close to the Yalu, and the pilot had reached the coast before punching out. The rest of his flight was low on fuel, but they would stay over him until we could get there. More -84s were being scrambled, as were MiGCAP F-86s — our combat air patrol against the Russian planes — but we were essential since we could stay in place longer.

When we were in the area, an F-84 lead pinpointed the lad for us by radio. The shore was strewn with rocks, ranging from head-size to house-size boulders. The most immediate and critical problem was that a North Korean division was in the area and was closing in. We strafed around him, as close as possible, and put rockets on the Bad Guys farther out.

The "object of our attentions" had a "grease gun" — a shortened machine-gun that broke down to fit into the pilot's survival kit. It was like watching cowboys and Indians, or, Lord forbid, Custer's last stand! We could see the Tiger raise up over a boulder, fire a burst, and get out of there as the North Koreans lobbed grenades where he had been.

The rescue choppers came on the scene with lots of goodies — F-84s, F-86s, and P-51s. We were getting a little short on fuel, but had ammo and wanted to see the end. The F-84 lead took over traffic control, just as it was getting congested. There had been no strafing closer than 50 yards; we were not that sure of our accuracy and had to figure on ricochets in all the rocks.

The Sabres held at medium altitudes, close to the GDR, to intercept MiGs coming across high or on the deck. We expected them, with all the activity, but they probably figured it was too big a collision risk. And it was!

The primary chopper was held out until ground fire diminished and troop movements into the area had stopped. It was still too hot at the pick-up point for the chopper to land, so an extraction seat, on a long cable, was dropped, and they got the hell out when the pilot was in the harness. A fresh flight of P-51s took up rescue escort, and everyone else plastered the pick-up point, which had been a sanctuary. Total North Korean losses were estimated to be in the thousands.

After landing, we got the story. As the jock reached the chopper, still on the cable, he took a .30-caliber in the face, and held on! The bullet entered the left lower jaw and exited the right cheekbone, taking bunches of teeth with it.

The nearest general hospital being in Seoul, near Kimpo, the chopper landed there, and he drove the doctors wild. On the second day, he was nowhere to be located, and was finally found in the Kimpo Officers Club, drinking Scotch from a straw, through a missing tooth hole. It hit the fan, in all directions. The head Doc said, "You crazy fool, with your jaws wired together, you could drown on your vomit if you got sick!"

The patient wrote "Naw" on a piece of paper and held up wire clippers, pointing out the guys to work them! That hero spent his remaining hospital time under guard.

There was only the F-80 Shooting Star left, for me to have flown all the combat fighters in Korea, so I asked the Fifth Air Force to put me on TDY with them. Luckily, the chief of staff called me in and mentioned that I obviously hadn't noticed the name of the current wing commander, and might want to reconsider. He called that one right! We had only met a couple of times and had to be separated both, once when we were sober!

Acknowledging the superior wisdom of the chief of staff, I was granted permission to visit ground forces, observing close air support and the problems of ground warfare. It was an interesting experience, visiting troops of several nations, and I found opinions of air support fairly uniform, expressed most graphically by U.S. grunts: "You sum bitches hit three miles ahead, or right on our asses! Ain't there some way you can bracket? How come yer all over the sky when things are quiet and stay in the O Club when yer needed?"

There was more, which can't be quoted due to obscenity levels. It was obvious that drastic action was required to boost the Air Force image, so I volunteered for a ground patrol.

It was surprising how fast approval came from Army Headquarters, but I suspected later that nothing went above company level, knowing that the request would be turned down. Night patrol was decided as the lesser hazard, so I was off in a weapons carrier with a squad, blackout condition, and a rough ride.

Our location was a total mystery to me when we stopped and unloaded, and silence was strictly emphasized. It is unbelievable what soldiers carry: flak jacket, .45-caliber gun and belt, webbed jacket with supplies, first-aid kit, grenades, ammo belts, canned rations, and canteen! (That was what *I* carried; later developments led me to believe that the rest of the squad was considerably less equipped!) Oh, and a rifle, or whatever they called it, and a helmet — which were the proverbial straws to buckle my knees! And someone, for Christ's sake, whispered, "Move out!"

As instructed, I was holding the belt of the trooper ahead (us old Cavalry men still call soldiers "troopers"), down the roughest ground imaginable. With the load, I could barely stay upright with legs spread, and a slow shuffle. This was up and down, and over rocks. Finally, we stopped, which I recognized by walking up the back of the gent ahead, and did *he* break the silence! This got him a belt from the sarge in charge!

We clustered around our leader — actually they all clustered around me, since I could hardly move, much less "cluster!" We were given whispered orders: "Within hearing of the enemy for the rest of the patrol. Strict silence or we will receive fire! Arm weapons, round in the chamber, safety off."

Thence came the blackest moment of a military career stuffed with gray to black moments. I had been shown how to slide the thingamajig on the .45-caliber automatic back, slowly and quietly, letting it ease back the same way, so that a bullet was in the chamber, I believe it's called. I was doing good, until the whatchamacallit slipped and pinched the skin on my thumb.

Without thinking, I blurted out "Ouch!" Then came panic, and the order, *"Hit the ground!"*

Some time elapsed, then came the whispered word, "Withdraw." It's amazing how fast, and far, you can go backwards. Finally we were allowed to turn and crawl forward, then walk, or shuffle to the weapons carrier, unload gear, and climb on.

I was amazed at the hilarity among my fellow soldiers and felt that I should express my apologies for screwing up the patrol. When this produced mass hysteria, I discovered that I had been set up! No confessions were forthcoming, but I must have a big part in some GI diaries, maybe even a company history!

There was another, stronger, impression from my time with the ground forces. In visiting troops from four nations, I always asked who they would most want next to them on the battle line. Without exception, it was "Turks." "The Turkish Brigade!" I found their combat record unexcelled, and verified their place in history as the fiercest of warriors. I was privileged to serve a tour of duty in Turkey later, which strengthened these impressions.

When my TDY was up, I went back to Hamilton. The commander of the Western Air Defense was shocked by my accounts of a few incidents of poor leadership. He ordered me to direct my words of wisdom to the three-star director of Ops, Air Force. I did, and got a record ass-chewing: "I didn't assign them there! Who the hell asked for your opinion?"

Chapter 11

Turkey and the Pentagon

AFTER MY STINT IN Korea came lots of uncertainties at Hamilton — another Air Defense Command reorganization in 1952, with people and units splintering in all directions. I served as base commander for a few weeks and didn't set many records for that command echelon; it was well known that it was temporary duty, and I couldn't wax enthusiastic over housekeeping and other functions of support.

I then became Director of Operations for the 28th Air Division, which was responsible for Northwest Radar Identification and Control Stations, operation of Central Control Agency, plotting and identifying traffic, and scrambling fighters against unknown targets. My office over-

> *I figured that the Russians would be quite comfortable watching us deplete our forces, . . . they had no requirement to hurl bodies and bombs at us!*

looked the Combat Control room and its large area map, with traffic, unknowns, and fighter intercepts plotted by enlisted airmen and WAFS, using shuffleboards to push identification discs around, like in the Battle of Britain. Only this was 1952!

I found it difficult to imagine any threats to the Free World in general, and the Northwest U.S., specifically, even with the threat in Korea. I figured that the Russians would be quite comfortable watching us deplete our forces, and those of our allies, and that they had no requirement to hurl bodies and bombs at us!

Still, I worked hard at the job and was fairly successful, except once when there was egg all over my face. We held an exercise with B-29 Superfortresses to penetrate our area — Hamilton, Paine, and McChord. We had been beefed up with extra fighters, and I was running the scramble/intercept show. Briefly, the fighters were assigned base identifier names, followed by colors, *i.e.,* "Tiger Red, Tiger White, Blue, and Green." I didn't assign identification to more than four flights per base, because I just figured, "No sweat" — a term that has preceded many total screw-ups!

I knew I'd had it when the bombers poured into the area, rather than dribbling in, as usual. I was scrambling everything, and was through the four colors fast. Not being of an artistic bent, I was groping for more colors and had fighters and controllers in hysterics, and lost complete control with, "Tiger Aquamarine" and "Eagle Chartreuse!" Worse, the bombers kicked the bejeezus out of me, and I *hate* to lose to the heavy metal guys!

Not long after came consolidation of Air Defense areas, deactivation of the Hamilton Division, and I was back to the Colonels Assignment Group at the Pentagon, where I seemed to spend lots of time. Lieutenant colonels and majors ran things, and they knew they had you where it hurts and you had to be nice. And so, in 1953, I grabbed at the first suggestion — duty with the United States Air Force Group, Joint American Military Mission to Turkey — to assist the Turkish Air Force in converting to their first jets.

Margee Lou had only been in Texas, Arizona, and California in her life, and off she went to Turkey with seven-month-old twins, two-year-old Timothy, and me. We drove to New York, visited friends and relatives, and spent a short time in dumpy quarters at the port. We boarded the *Private*

Eldon B. Johnson, a World War II troop ship. He may have been a great soldier, but that was one lousy scow! The first night, before Margee took to her bed with the "queasies," she was putting clothes in lower drawers, when a metal folding desk dropped about three feet onto her head, knocking her out cold! Our first of a few trips to the dispensary for stitches, and my girl was back to the rack for the rest of the trip; she arose only to take some nourishment, or to help me with diapers when she heard me crying.

We docked in Istanbul, but weren't able to see much of the beautiful city until later. We rode the Orient Express overnight to Ankara, and were met there by the chief of staff and lady. It was a warm welcome until one of the twins threw up on him, but he was great and they were two of our best friends in the tour.

We were given all the time needed to settle in. We stayed in the guest house, Margee looked for places to live, and I went through orientation — most of which was history of Turkey, with no description of how we would be helping their armed forces, or the problems awaiting solution.

We found a new apartment building with State Department families, a missionary, and other foreign types. I discovered early that the Turks love kids, especially boys, so we had it made. We hired a live-in sitter, beautiful as only Turkish ladies can be beautiful. We became great friends, even after it was pointed out that she was a renowned high-level paramour. She only worked for us while we were in the apartment, but she called on us often and we and the lads visited her until we left Turkey. These visits always ended with her in tears and showering the boys with kisses, but only a handshake for me! She epitomized the theme of what the Turkish people displayed to us throughout the tour — friendship, always friendship!

I was to lead a field training team of four officers, eight non-coms, two civilian technical representatives (Tech Reps), and two interpreters — Turkish nationals. We usually left on Monday, and were back to Ankara Friday. This depended on the C-47 Goonie Bird, and the sporting blood of the Headquarters types who were flying them, but I only spent a few weekends away from hearth and home.

Our Turkish base was Diyarbakir in eastern Turkey, 125 miles from the Russian border. Fabulous! It was the only walled city in known history that had never been taken by siege. There were underground aqueducts built by the Romans, which enabled the city to withstand a three-year blockade and assault by the Numero Uno Hun, Attila. Roman walls, bridges, and aqueducts are still in use and functional. (Historians compelled to challenge facts, names, and circumstances above may expect my total surrender!) What a contrast — jets operating over this antiquity!

The base had been modernized under the Assistance Program with longer runways, cement hardstands, and some additional buildings — the second wing to convert to the F-84 Thunderjet. It was a kick to see examples of their World War II fighters, remembering that they were neutral: an American P-47, a German ME-109, and an English Spitfire. Only the Spit was flyable, and I got some flights — and thrills — in the beauty!

The Turkish Air Force had kindly allowed the construction of separated living quarters, messing, and recreation. We furnished the food and the mess was operated by the Turkish cooks and soldiers. We had our own bar, and we brought five days' worth of movies. I felt guilty about not opening the movies to everyone, but solved this by loaning out the films, and all were happy. Just after reporting in, I talked the U.S. Army HQ into "extra rations," got additional cooks and help, and threw a "blast" for all the officers; everyone had a great time. I made friends there and throughout Turkey who will always be among my fondest memories.

The Turkish pilots were outstanding; some had gone through the U.S. of A. pilot training as well as the Fighter Gunnery Instructor's Course at Nellis Air Patch. The Diyarbakir Wing had one squadron starting weapons delivery, bombing, air and ground gunnery, and rocket delivery. Other squadrons were being outfitted and in transition phase. I was delighted to find something at Diyarbakir not to be found, as far as I know, at any other fighter base in the world — a ground gunnery range located *on the field*, on the opposite side of the runway from work and living areas. Imagine sitting in the arbors outside most buildings and watching all kinds of ground gunnery, one mile away!

I usually had an English-speaking pilot in my flights, or in the tower. The first few months, I was betting on who would buy the tea (*Chi*), or coffee (*Cafe*), according to scores in strafing, medium- and high-angle dive-bombing, skip-bombing, and rockets. I showed off for a few months, but finally decided I had to either stop flying the missions or stop betting. Because my job called for flying, I stopped betting before I went broke!

A couple of their pilots came to me and said that they wanted to form

The aerobatic team at Diyarbakir, Turkey, 1953, left to right: Lead, Jack Hayes, and Slots 3 and 2.

an aerobatic team, but that our Air Force advisors had opposed the one formed at the first jet wing (which showed what kind of fighter pilots we had over there), and would probably fight this one all the way to TAF HQ. I responded that I would not go to my boss for approval if they could ensure "under the table" consent from their Headquarters. I got the "no sweat" ("*Telas Yok*" in Turkish), but I was told an American on the team would connote American group approval. I flew the slot and helped develop the sequences, even though they needed no help. They were magnificent!

The wing commander, Colonel (later Brigadier General) Suat Eraybar, became the best of the many friends I made. I flew his wing on gunnery missions and in night formation. We were having difficulty including night flying in their training ("We aren't night fighter pilots, for Allah's sake!"), and I was sympathetic, but directed to fill those squares in the training program. And all it took was one night formation flight!

There was only one unnerving thing about flying on Suat's wing. On every flight, we headed for the Russian border at 25,000 to 30,000 feet,

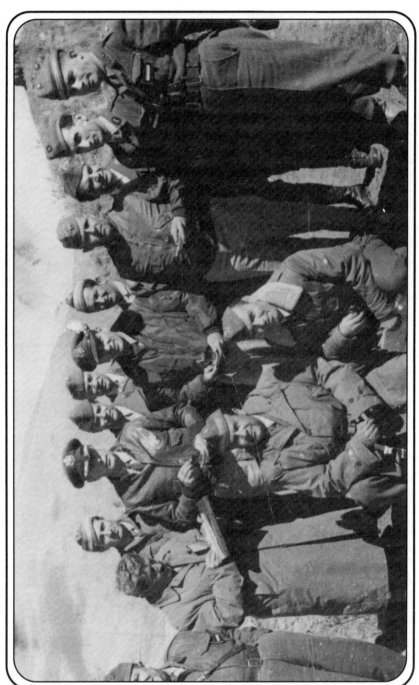

The Russian Front, 1954, with two other USAF officers and Turkish Army and Air Force personnel. Jack Hayes is standing in the middle row, third from left.

Jack Hayes at Diyarbakir, Turkey, 1954, demonstrating maneuvers to the Wing Commander, General Suat Eraybar, with the number three man on the team translating, at the Turkish Air Force Officers Club.

and flew up and down the border, paralleled by Russian MiGs. Suat insulted them in Turkish, English, and German, and dared them to come over and fight — we were armed with two .50-caliber guns loaded with 100 rounds, and maybe a couple of practice bombs! Thank God for Russian discipline!

During a joint Turkish Air Force/Army maneuver close to the border, I was directed to observe and assist in TAF forward air control and response to army requests for close support. This would have been performed, as always, in an outstanding manner, but riding a jeep from the forward air strip where I had parked our Goonie to the Tactical Air Control Center, our driver skidded and rolled to the left. I was thrown from the jeep and landed on my head, and was out cold!

With me was one of my pilots and our interpreter, who, with the driver, delivered me to the army hospital. When I awoke, my head had been put back together with stitches and a neat bandage. The Air Force brigadier general, chief of our advisory group, was there with the chief Turkish Army surgeon, which meant I had been out for one hell of a long time. I mention that only because this was the record length of all my many temporary comas!

I had learned of the deep pride that Turks have in all things Turkish, and I hadn't been in their country long before I shared the feeling. So I was concerned at what their reaction might be to my being taken to an American hospital. I asked my interpreter to explain that I would be proud to recuperate under their care, but I had to think of my wife and three boys in Ankara. Being great family people, I think they accepted that, but when back on duty I flew up and presented a plaque of gratitude and some goodies, which were scarce on the "frontier."

I was so intrigued with the beauty and history of the area that I asked for permission to fly our wives out to see the base and Diyarbakir. They were taken to the ground gunnery range and watched all kinds of weapons delivery, closer than the average Air Force type will ever be. We had lunch in our area, which dispelled the illusions of our "tough life" in the field! Turkish Air Force buses took them, with interpreters, into the city for shopping and sightseeing, and the natives did some sightseeing of their own. The only requirement was that the visitors be off the base before sunset, for religious reasons.

As new bases were being converted to jet fighters — with more F-84s plus Canadian F-86s for the air defense mission — I found the requirement for large advisory teams at each location had lessened. To be honest, the only reason there was an Air Force Advisory Group at all was to convert their supply and maintenance systems to compatibility with the USAF, for re-supply and logistics purposes. Otherwise, they could have done it on their own.

I reduced the teams at the bases to a field grade fighter pilot as commander, and non-coms in armament, supply, and maintenance, and Tech Reps, as required. I was assigned a C-47 and visited two bases a week with a larger group of technicians and Tech Reps. Also, I had to drop off and pick up the permanent folks so that they had some time at home. I experienced the usual great cooperation from the Turks, and developed more friendships.

During the last year of duty in Turkey came an announcement from NATO South Headquarters of the first ever NATO Gunnery Meet. The contestants were Italy, Greece, and Turkey, with Italy to be the host. Some of us had concerns about how to keep the Turks and Greeks firing on the targets, rather than each other, but all went surprisingly well. I was desig-

nated as chief umpire, with staff from the other advisory groups and
NATO South Headquarters.

We went to southern Italy for air-to-air gunnery competition. I had
anticipated control and security problems in recovering and scoring the
nylon targets, but not to the extent encountered. The tow-target pilots had
trouble releasing in designated areas for pick-up and return to the scoring
area. Oddly, the nationality of the pilot dictated the release point, which
would happen to be in an area surrounded by his countrymen! Competi-
tors fired bullets with designated colors painted on the nose. It was amazing how many additional holes could be marked from the drop to the time
we received the target in the scoring area! After two missions, I halted
activities and asked the senior officers — all general officers — from each
country to meet with me.

I handed them copies of new rules in procedures for scoring of air-to-
air targets: Target release and recovery points were off limits, except for
umpires and assigned personnel. Targets dropped outside designated
recovery points would be invalidated, and the mission would be resched-
uled. The scoring area was off limits, before and after scoring, and this
included general officers! Did *that* hit the fan! But the situation was solved
when I announced: "Sirs, I shall have to report to commander, NATO
South, that I am unable to function as chief umpire and recommend cancellation of the meet." Amazingly, most of the brass grinned as if to say,
"Ya got us!" and off we went.

After air-to-air gunnery, we went to Brindisi for air-to-ground competition. Umpires were in place with a couple of us in the central control
tower, and others in the towers that report violations — *i.e.,* below safe
altitude, firing before/after designated fire lines, and other things. Everything was in place before dawn! One of my sore points about wars was the
ungodly hours at which they're fought, and there we went, in peacetime.
To atone for the hour, the Italian general had delivered trays of rolls, pret-
zels, beer, cognac, and wine. I could picture a protest if booze was obvious on an official's breath!

On the second day, an Italian Air Force bus was taking officials to the
gunnery range, and at about 45 mph the driver reached to his right to close
the door, bringing the steering wheel with him. This caused a sharp right
turn, skid, and two rolls to the left, ending right-side-up in a churchyard. I
saw what was coming, and dove for the floor, wrapping myself around a
leg brace, while my compatriots rattled around the interior amidst moans,

groans, shrieks, and wails. One of the more "worldly" of the involved said later that the sounds reminded him of an orgy he went to, once. But I wouldn't know about that!

Those of us with some mobility were assisting the walking wounded out of the bus and making those with the immobiles as comfortable as possible on the bus. A young priest was doing what priests do, when he came to a jock I'd known for years who had a broken shoulder. This pilot had, in his words, "ejected myself!" from the Catholic Church! When he saw the priest, he panicked: "Don't let him give me the Last Rites, Jack! I can't confess in Italian. As soon as I'm home I'll be back to the Sacraments." Sure! I explained to the young man of the cloth that he was working on a *real* lost cause and, with hands clasped in prayer, this descendant of St. Peter left my friend, stepping on his face, shoulder, and crotch en route.

We replaced the wounded with staff from NATO Headquarters and finished the meet. Before the awards presentation, the Turkish Air Force major, gunnery team leader, and leader of their aerobatic team came to me and said that they would like to leave an impression on all those NATO members present and could they put on an aerobatic demo. I could imagine the "impression" they'd leave, and chuckled at the prospect! They got the OK from the two-star commander of NATO South, and then came the kicker!

I passed on the concurrence to the team leader and he said, "Oh, by the way. . . as you know, the number four slot man is not on the gunnery team, and we would appreciate your flying that position."

I pointed out that I hadn't flown with them for several months, that it should be an all-Turkish team, and that there was nothing wrong with a three-man team. All this evoked grins, and the response, "Well, guess we'll have to cancel."

So I gave in. Another of my more brilliant decisions! On our second loop, parallel to crowd line, it was obvious that if I stayed in the slot, I'd be wiped out by severe ground impact! So, I had to pull up, through lead's jet wash, to a slightly high position. I survived that, but damned if the lead didn't start a roll as I was pushing back through his wash to the slot!

On the last maneuver before break-up for landing, we came out of a cloverleaf, heading directly toward the reviewing stand on the deck, and I prayed for everyone in the stands, and me — not necessarily in that order. We passed over the stands and the hangar behind so low that I took off the windsock!

I was told that the two-star general asked, after our low pass, "How do you turn this goddamned show off?" I can imagine the reaction when he was informed that we were on a discrete frequency — we couldn't be reached by radio! After our demo, I hid, in my sopping-wet flight suit, in the Turkish C-47 until we were airborne and had no repercussions, but got a "good show" from my Turkish friends. The flight lead did say, in great humor, "Albay, we almost bust yer ass!"

A final note of Turkish fighter pilots' sense of humor. Usually, when I returned from field trips — which was practically every weekend — Margee would open my bag and arrange for washing or cleaning. Someone Up There liked me, because Margee was late getting home! I opened the bag to find two pieces of black lingerie, with my briefs neatly folded on top of everything, and reeking with cheap perfume! I got them washed in time to save Margee Lou from another crisis in our short, not idyllic, married life. She had been informed about the jeep accident on Army maneuvers and the bus accident in Italy, but this would have been the "straw!"

Before leaving Turkey, I visited their Air Force Headquarters and presented trophies for the fighter wings, to be presented to the outstanding fighter squadrons, under whatever rules and time periods they desired. We left Ankara with me wearing Turkish Air Force pilot wings, Margee with a beautiful arrangement of flowers, and some of the greatest memories of our lives!

I didn't spend much discussion on the problems encountered by those of us in the field trying to get support from Air Force Advisory Group Headquarters staff. Briefly, those people were interested in the good life — golf, sightseeing tours (outside Turkey), and selling household goods to Turkish civilians. One of my Turkish friends asked, "Why do they come over here to have a good life?" I had no answer, but I know now, these were the "Ugly Americans!"

After the umpire bus accident, I had sent a "personal" message to the brigadier general commander of the Air Force group, advising him and assuring him that the gunnery meet would go on. I wondered why he had no comments when I returned, until he was discussing my last efficiency report before I departed Turkey (not very shiny, by the way), and mentioned that he was stunned that I would be driving a car full of drunk umpires, and rolled it over! He had left me in the job all these months, when I should have been relieved, if the allegations had been true. I explained the personal message and got as a reply, "I'll be durned!" That's leadership!

I left his office, and command, and met one of the real contributors to the mission — the head of maintenance and supply, an arrogant "slick-chest" (a term used to describe someone with no combat medals) golfing buddy of our leader. When confronted, he flashed his buck teeth, acknowledged intercepting the personal message, and ducked into the Command office. My two regrets from the Turkish tour were not kicking the crap out of him and the sergeant who got my orders changed from the First Fighter Wing to the Pentagon!

Pentagon

In June 1955, I reported to my first assignment where flying wasn't my primary duty — or at least not on or near an airfield. In 15 years of service, I had never felt so incapable and out of place than in the "Puzzle Palace," or "Concrete Complex," among other more obscene titles. But I can report that I left the joint with one of my highest efficiency reports, after many ups and downs. I was somewhat humbled, though, when one of the professional staff types explained that the endorsement to the "Outstanding" category was from a two-star of another service (Army) and was therefore downgraded one block by promotion boards. The reason was that everybody knows that reports on other services are *always* inflated!

I don't know the general reaction to the first encounter with "The Big Picture," but mine was severe shock! The less important the matter, the more lenient the due dates and time allowed for staff work and coordination. But barn-burning, world-shaking subjects requiring extensive research and staff action demanded immediate completion. Not because the requesting agency of government — executive, legislative, cabinet, *et al.* — established a short suspense, but because each subordinate level imposed minimal preparation times and tightened the screws to impress his seniors.

Other impressions included professional staff officers who were on second and third tours, and loving it. When not in Washington, they had staff duty in major commands, and most got stars — a much higher percentage than those in field and command duty. At times there have been Joint Chiefs of Staff made up of members with no combat experience!

I soon learned not to coordinate subjects with State Department action officers when invited to "lunch at Fort McNair." Great roast beef, but the main attraction was the martini before lunch: triple the normal martini size, and so dry you could blow dust off of them! They insisted on at least two, and preferred three, which leads me to believe that the State Department had an automatic "afternoon off" policy after lunch at McNair.

The problem became obvious at my first such lunch, when I was sticking the roast beef up my nose when not spilling it down my shirt. By the way, the dining room is populated by senior officers attending the National War College, and I recognized trouble when I saw it! I forced down the beef, mashed potatoes, and coffee, coffee, coffee, until I was asked to leave at closing time. I went back to work and got through the afternoon, although I was later asked why I giggled so much and if I had any idea how many fannies I had attempted to pat. I wasn't going to explain why I giggled and I had no idea of the fanny count, until I started getting sexy notes and phone calls! I don't know how I got through the latter, but I did. And I *did not* respond!

It's amazing what careers some folks developed and enlarged in the "Palace." I was working in the "Base Rights" area for the Air Force, involving negotiations with other nations for use of their land area in deploying U.S. forces. I dealt with a civil servant who was adored by members of that service, but abhorred by U.S. Army staff personnel. Seems he had "left" the Army, was accepted by the civil service, and initially occupied a closet-sized office. On my first visit, I passed through *two* receptionists' offices before entering his office. Now *that's* career progression!

I reported to the International Branch, War Plans Division. This name raised some questions in the neophyte brain: I thought *all* war plans were "International." Who are we fighting in the USA? With my tour in Turkey, I became the Middle East expert, and I was amazed at all the countries in that area!

I sensed that my performance of duty was something less than exemplary — maybe lousy? I never had the right words, or always took the wrong position; I even had a secretary with the "moodies" (whatever the hell that is) who managed to type an important paper front and back, duplicated pages several times, and assembled the finished product, for my presentation to one of great authority, with great confidence. I shall not dwell on the subsequent bloodletting (mine), but it was shortly thereafter that I was reassigned to the staff of the Joint Chiefs of Staff — deep, deeper, into the recesses.

I had a hunch and asked the brigadier general in charge if I had been found wanting. He didn't reply directly, but read what he told me was guidance in assigning officers to the Joint Chiefs of Staff: "Only the most qualified and capable officers of the military departments will be assigned to duty with the Joint Chiefs of Staff. . . ." Maybe, but I noticed that when I cleaned out my desk in War Plans, I was the Invisible Man to the professional staff of weenies!

You had to be a dedicated "fly-boy" to maintain proficiency in aviating. Fighter pilots flew T-33 T-Birds out of Andrews AFB, a 45-minute drive if traffic was light, which was never! I had to schedule weeks ahead of time, and then rescheduling was usually necessary because of Pentagon "short fuse" projects. I soon learned that flights were always available nights and weekends (great for family life), but flying during duty hours was unheard of on the Joint Staff.

High priority was given for flights on "official business," but required a certified and notarized statement that commercial transportation arrangements were inadequate. The last statement above your signature read, "I realize that inaccuracies herein constitute a false official statement and will result in disciplinary action." All that just for saying that utilizing commercial transportation might keep you away from your desk a couple of days, with detrimental effects on the operation of Department of Defense, and upsetting your boss to no end! This, at a time when low-ranking military and civilian officials were signing multi-million dollar contracts, and we're signing our lives away to get a damned T-Bird to fly!

During my three years in the Inferno, I averaged 100 flight hours *per year* on the books, the maximum allowed. But I still managed to keep up with new developments; I checked out in the North American F-100 Super Sabre, the first pure supersonic fighter, and the F-84F, a swept-wing version of the Thunderjet. It was a little complicated: I flew the T-Bird to the fighter base, went on leave status during the check-out, meaning time did not count for pay or proficiency, then flew back on duty status. I would explain this, except that I don't understand it.

The staff types found a solution to the problem of some pilots insisting on maintaining proficiency, at personal sacrifice, by "excusing from flying" — like flying was onerous, not a privilege. I was, and am, amazed at how many of my vintage retired with the minimum flying time required, and *no* combat flying. And they wore the "I was there" badges, with "Battle Stars!" Before I left the "Wild Blue," I counted 23 ribbons that could be accumulated without danger to life or limb. Ribbons for years of service, marksman status, *ad nauseam.*

The Joint Staff was a pleasant change. I was treated like a gentleman, although many of my associates might question my qualifications for such treatment. I was assigned to the Gold Team, Joint Strategic Plans Group, Joint Strategic Plans Committee of the Joint Chiefs of Staff. Our team was responsible for Joint plans and base rights! I made great friends on the Joint Staff and from the other services. I saw some great minds, but "free thinkers" were eased out.

Our "action papers" required coordination with comparable staffs in the services, which was not always easy. Sometimes you couldn't get your own service to agree, or thought you were nuts, so you had to write a unilateral position. The services submitted individual views, or "purples," which were hashed over, and final positions, or "splits," were given to the action team to finalize. We were taking notes furiously for changes, "splits," conclusions, and recommendations. I was lucky to have my two teammates taking notes so that we were able to publish a coherent paper for the Pentagon.

I feel that I didn't give a blazing performance on the Joint Staff, which showed consistency in my Pentagon tour. For each "paper" our team handled, one of us was the "action." We sat next to the director, Joint Staff, with reams of background files, and fed him documents quoted by the service representatives. I could never find the proper reference and got an, "Oh well, forget it" from the director. I suppose I became known as a "patsy" and could see expressions of sympathy, or scorn, on the faces of the working-level guys.

But I redeemed myself on a particularly complicated paper, and I treasure the memory. The three services were throwing out, amending, omitting, deleting, and canceling various parts of the paper before them. I was writing furiously when the director said "Next item," and the action officers started to leave. I could see that the "approved" product was gibberish, and barked out, "Hold it!" Then came the well-known "deathly silence," and the director said, "Yes?" (I swear he almost said "Sir").

I said, "If this paper comes out as approved, it will make no sense. I recommend that this wording be approved." Which was quickly done, but most satisfying was the respect I felt and retained for the rest of my tour on the Joint Staff. The "dumb fighter pilot" wasn't so bad after all!

I enjoyed two rather crude descriptions of the Pentagon, in general, and certain residents, in particular: "The Pentagon is like a log floating down a river, swarming with piss-ants, and every piss-ant thinks he's the one steering." And, with reference to an individual, usually senior in rank: "He runs around stomping on piss-ants while elephants are stampeding the camp!"

As my sentence approached its end, I called on the colonel's group yet again and got a major shock: "Fighter commands contacted expressed 'No interest' or 'Too senior!'"

Just before slitting my throat and wrists, my bomber commander in World War II called and said that Strategic Air Command was recruiting senior fighter pilots to assist in training B-47 Stratojet bomber pilots in nuclear weapon delivery methods, which involved such maneuvers as the Immelmann turn and one-half Cuban Eight. In an Immelmann, the aircraft completes the first half of a loop and then rolls over to an upright position, thus changing direction 180° with a simultaneous gain in altitude (a half-loop). A Cuban Eight is a figure "8" maneuver, but one in which the aircraft dives down and pulls up, so that when you look at the figure, it is sideways from the ground rather than flat/parallel. Needless to say, problems were anticipated indoctrinating pilots who had never encountered more than a 45° turn!

Rather than drop into the personnel hopper, I accepted the offer, and was assigned in June 1958 to the 341st Bomb Wing as vice commander, at Dyess Air Force Base in Abilene, Texas.

When I reported, I found out that the aerobatic program had been discontinued long before. It seems that a wing commander decided to play fighter pilot in a B-47 without the expertise, tried a roll off the deck, and busted his rear — with the crew and an RAF air commodore observing. You know what? They named an Air Force Base after him. *Sheesh*!

Onward and upward!

Chapter 12

Strategic Air Command

I FIND THAT WRITING ABOUT SAC to the uniniti-
ated, or unbelievers, is tantamount to describing the
agonies of childbirth to the male, the "stonies" to the
ladies, or any travail unique to one group to "outsid-
ers." You have to see it to believe it!

The bomber boys were so completely supreme that Tactical Air Command (support of ground forces) and Air Defense Command were fighting for their survival and had few
bases in their control. Being tenants on SAC bases, they were
treated as second-class citizens.

We new guys had to go
through the "SACumcision," as
we called the orientation, and
were introduced to the "jutting
jaw and steely gray eyes" expected of SAC folks, especially
senior ones! I had six weeks
temporary duty to the Air Force

*The bomber boys were so
completely supreme that
Tactical Air Command
. . . and Air Defense
Command were fighting
for their survival. . . .*

Maintenance School to learn an idiotic maintenance system, about which more will be described later, then went to SAC Headquarters for the brain-washing and B-47 school, six weeks and 30 hours of flying time. Then an exhaustive ground school and a pre-flight inspection which took three hours.

Halfway through B-47 school, I was summoned by the brigadier general in charge with this: "Understand that you *were* a fighter pilot. I want you to know that last night, fighter pilots in B-47 training here wrecked the Officers Club, tore down all SAC insignias and burned them in the middle of the dance floor, and locked the school secretary and some instructors in the ladies' powder room!"

So I called a mandatory meeting of the brethren, and explained that "These bomber weenies allow only one chance, and yours has been used up. So go along with the system, always keeping in mind that 'This, too, shall pass!'" I think it was fighter pilot pride rather than my golden words, but what gratification to see most become "select" and "lead" crews, the highest rating bestowed in the multi-motored command. And lots finished their careers as fighter pilots, bless 'em!

Realizing that I may cause ennui and lose some readers, while also subjecting to boredom those who hang with me, there must be some explanation of the organizational concepts developed by SAC and forced on other USAF units as "The Believers" came into power and authority.

Units of Tactical Air had operated in World War II and Korea, and very nicely, with a two-group concept per base: the flying group commander was assigned flight crews, aircraft, and basic maintenance personnel; the service group CO was responsible for housekeeping, support activities, major aircraft maintenance, and was *subordinate* to the flying group commander.

The "new look" was as follows: the wing commander (the guy with the airplanes) was responsible for primary functioning of the base and commanded a higher echelon, but worked with the combat support group commander, who was given the title of base commander, because "He was given authority for administrative functions to relieve the wing CO and enable him to concentrate on flying matters." SAC really went to all the trouble in order to circumvent Air Force policy with the directive that "Flying units will be commanded by pilots only." This opened up homes and rank for over-aged navigators/bombardiers, slick-chests, and pilots found wanting in Wild Blue activities!

This was not a problem on single-wing bases; there was no doubt who was in the saddle. Somewhere in the reams of directives, guidance, and policy were these golden words: "Base commander can appeal to next higher authority." This may have happened, but only once per base! Wing CO couldn't fire his ass right away, but the "appealer" had trouble sleeping, ate and drank in the club alone, and continually looked behind him to determine who was following! So he requested reassignment, which had been expected, and he went into limbo.

The two-wing base would usually have a division Headquarters present, but the support group CO still had the accolade, "base commander," which ticked off the wing and division commanders and confused the local civilian gentry as to whom should be granted obeisance. In its infinite wisdom, SAC granted an "entertainment fund" to this lowest ranking commander on base so that he could carry out his responsibilities to the civilian community. The division commander scooped up most, and the two wing COs persuaded him to divide the whole fund three ways, leaving the "base commander" with just enough for coffee and a few doughnuts!

Obviously, the senior elements of the SAC organization were screwed up, but you can't imagine how they screwed up the working level! Bomb squadrons lost all mechanics, including crew chiefs, most Operations types, and became glorified Operations officers! They were assigned aircraft to fly daily, and told missions to fly, the next day justifying any lack of accomplishment. No matter their effort, operator error was the norm for failures, maintenance error the exception.

Besides stripping the flying squadrons of their mission and people, all maintenance functions were placed under a deputy commander for maintenance — organizational maintenance squadron (formerly Tactical squadron maintenance), a field maintenance squadron for specialists and major maintenance, electronics squadron for all radar and communications. Director of supply replaced squadron and wing supply officers.

The deputy commander for Operations was not only assigned all Operations and plans staff, but the squadron commanders reported to him!

The connotation of "deputy commander" is of primary responsibility for that area, maintenance or Operations. These responsibilities rest solely on the *commander*, and cannot be delegated, nor assigned to subordinates. A *deputy* position, by military definition, exists to "carry out the policies of the commander in his absence" — not to assume his responsibility and authority, on a day-to-day basis.

SAC wings were often found "wanting" in many areas, and wing commanders' heads rolled, while the deputies clucked in dismay and displayed a "who me?" attitude. The only deputy commanders fired for poor performance were those canned by the wing CO and, for some reason, this action was bitterly contested by staff at numbered Air Forces and SAC Headquarters. The rejectee was never reinstated, but, by subtle discrediting of the rejector by senior staff types, some good wing commanders "bought the farm!"

Finally, it was comical to note the treatment given wing/division commanders by senior staff in the higher echelons of SAC. They had an uncanny recognition of the "Goers," "Teacher's Pets," and kept their paws off and had only good things to say. But just let the wind shift, find a weakness in the MCS (Management Control System), maybe a marginal staff visit report, or, horror of horrors, a low score in an operational readiness inspection (ORI), and out came the jackals for the kill! But I seem to remember that jackals come in *after* the kill, and that's apropos for the herd I'm describing!

I completed the bunches of training/orientation, which barely qualified me for duty with the "elite forces" (I got tired of that phrase!), and it was continually voiced that I was only starting my SAC education. This boiled down to "beating the system" — a veritable art, bringing success to those capable of its mastery, and dismissal for those naive enough to go "by the book!"

When, finally, I was stationed at Dyess AFB in 1958 permanently as vice commander of the 341st Bomb Wing — a position as necessary and useful as the well-known appendages on a boar — my main function was to stay inconspicuous, do as I was told, and never, *never* say anything except what identically reflected the positions and attitudes of the commander! A problem of all vice commanders, not unique to the 341st.

Besides coordinating efforts for charities and bond drives, etc., I was to keep an eye on the venereal disease and re-enlistment rates, keeping the former low and the latter high. My success would have been laudatory had not the rates been reversed! Anyway, that's how they came out.

My primary responsibility was ensuring smooth transition to the new maintenance organization, and I was smart enough to keep my feelings to myself, or my career in SAC would have been shorter than it was. That wouldn't have been so bad, except we wouldn't have had the opportunity to meet the many wonderful people we did, who greatly overshadowed the other kind — and there were bunches of them, too!

One of the most flagrant examples of misusing personnel and equipment lay in the requirement for flight crews to report to the aircraft *three hours* before takeoff time. Recognizing that the fliers had to eat and draw flight equipment before pre-flight, fly a minimum of six hours, attend maintenance de-brief, and turn in equipment, it was a hell of a long day!

But it didn't seem so bad when you compared that to the maintenance, services, and supply men. They were at work two or three hours before crew time, then had to scramble to fix things that broke or wouldn't work during pre-flight or taxi out, sit through post-flight debriefings, and help prepare work orders for the next shift. And no rest after takeoff; they worked where required or spent hours on the goddamned unending SAC paperwork!

As the first to have jets, it was plain to fighter people that these things were going to be easier to maintain and operate because there were less moving parts to rub against each other (or whatever parts do), but not in SAC! Ground crews operated everything they could before flight crew arrival, whence they combined to turn on/off everything and actuate whatever they could without the airplane collapsing or becoming airborne!

SAC Headquarters maintenance weenies were baffled by the low in-commission (availability) rates and short parts life. If they had just had the humility and common sense to solicit comments from the field, we could have said, "Quit testing and operating all the systems." Or, more cogently, "If it ain't broke, don't fix it, test it, or touch it!"

I understand that some of the working level, knowing that there was no staff access, wrote anonymous letters to the commander of SAC (CinC-SAC — pronounced "sink-sack"). Without reference to SAC, it was mentioned that commercial airlines had been in the jet business for a while and that all you had to do was watch activity in any civilian airport to learn that jets could be serviced and re-launched after an aircrew walk-around and if there were no major "gigs" from the previous flight.

I have difficulty with the fact that a four-star will take action on an anonymous letter while his be-starred staff refuse recognition of comments and suggestions through military channels! Anyway, teams were dispatched to study methods of the major airlines. Shortly thereafter, at a SAC commanders conference, a "new" maintenance system was unveiled, highlighted with a theme written in fire on the walls: "If it ain't broke, don't fix it!"

At the 341st Bomb Wing, I went through more B-47 training — what an airplane! There was nobody around who had been in the Immelmann/Cuban Eight weapons delivery methods, but I found another misplaced fighter pilot who led an instructor crew, and we had the same thoughts — aerobatics.

The -47 did a beautiful barrel roll, from small, to medium, to a heavenly cloud-burner covering 180° and thousands of feet. Once you got through the super-slow vertical movement, pulling 1.25 to 1.75 Gs, the plane did a nice Immelmann and Cuban Eight. But the loop almost wiped us out, and had us pulling a "brown contrail" on the first few! The airplane was so sleek and high-powered that acceleration was unbelievable as your nose dropped from the inverted to the vertical and back to level — hopefully!

We had, to some degree, anticipated airspeed problems during the loop, and I was throttling back as soon as airspeed increased, going through 45° above the horizon, inverted, and I really had to pull back as we approached the vertical. Even all throttles at idle position was not enough to keep the airspeed from heading for the red line. My friend in back was calling our airspeeds in increasingly high pitches, so I extended all landing gear! This was an emergency procedure performed only as a last resort, which this was.

To explain the missing landing gear doors, which blew off at that speed just like they're supposed to, I concocted a tale about us in high-speed descent with fighters on collision course, forcing me to make a hard break left and down, exceeding airspeed, etc. The USAF tried to locate any fighters who might have been in the area, but couldn't. In the process, my name leaked out as the bomber jock and we had many late night calls from the brotherhood of fighter pilots — many drunken, and most obscene!

I didn't do many loops after that, but it was possible by dropping the landing gear earlier and throttling back faster. I didn't mention that some engines "flamed out" in that first loop, but we got most started again. We explained the engine failures by blaming "compressor stalls" from the high speeds. The new procedures worked, and we hardly lost any engines after that. But we had to curtail the fun things when an airline pilot incoherently reported seeing a "Goddamned jet bomber doing by-Gawd aerobatics!" I was sorry to hear that he had a tough time getting back on flying status!

Besides the aerobatics, I completed B-47 qualification training, including air-to-air refueling on the KC-97 Stratofreighter and KC-135 Stratotanker. Like anywhere in the Air Force, the bomb people and families were tremendous — the usual oddballs seemed concentrated in the higher ranks, for reasons I cannot explain. Aircrews and ground types put in long hours, but most devastating were the days per year on temporary duty overseas, or being restricted to the Alert area on base.

I also have to recognize a unique breed, the KC-97 air refueling squadrons. Boeing Company took the C-97 Stratocruiser and made it the KC-97 Stratofreighter, a flying gas tank, the first air refueling aircraft in the inventory. I'm sure that the KC-135 tanker outfits were great, but my only "connection" with them was on the receiving end.

The techniques of air refueling aren't complicated, depending on whether you're doing "probe and drogue," on most fighters, or "boom," on bombers and the F-4 fighter. In the boom technique, you ease the B-47, in this case, into a steady position directly under the tanker, formatting on him. Out comes this long round tube from the tanker heading for a hole in the upper fuselage. When asked my impression of my first refueling, I said, "I felt like a bride on her wedding night!"

I meant to devote this to lauding the KC-97 tanker squadrons, especially the 11th Air Refueling, which was assigned to 341st Bomb at Dyess. They walked off with a majority of performance awards from SAC and the Fifteenth Air Force, but most impressive was their spirit and "can do" attitude. As I told Dave Gray, who was commander for most of the glory days, the 11th Air Refueling Squadron was "the closest thing to fighter Operations I have seen!" He knew that I could say nothing better than that.

After 11 months as vice commander, I had my annual physical exam and I finally found out why the doctor carried you around the room on two fingers, saying "cough." After my second cough, he grinned like he had found gold, which was impossible where he had his fingers! "Yes, Sir. You *really* got one," he said, as he let my feet touch the floor again.

"One what?"

"A HERNIA!" he shouted, as if he had made the medical discovery of the century. He proceeded to tell me that this was a "grounding" condition (which meant I would be off flying status), but that he would give me a few days to get my affairs in order.

I stalled for a while until the quack asked if I enjoyed flight pay, because I was gonna lose it if I didn't "go under the knife" in a couple of days. I won't describe the rigors of the operation, since even the strong of heart would quail. I was starting the second week of a 30-day convalescent leave, and loving it, when the stuff hit the fan!

The SAC inspector general sprung a no-notice inspection on the 341st, to check all the workings — with emphasis on combat crew performance, aircraft maintenance, and security. To put it briefly (and kindly), we failed! This I learned from a brief phone conversation with the commander of the Fifteenth Air Force, Lieutenant General Old.

"Are you gonna lay around on your ass the rest of your life? The leave is over, you command the wing, and I'll give you ninety days to get things unscrewed or I'll fire your ass, too!" Now *that's* miracle healing!

My first actions were to gain instructor pilot rating in the B-47 (the crews would know I spoke the language), attend crew proficiency inspection briefings, and gain certification of crew Emergency War Order responsibilities. I visited the overseas Alert stations where our crews pulled temporary duty. Most essential was riding the ramp and visiting work areas in late night and early mornings. I dropped the word that I wanted to see one helluva bunch more officer's insignia and non-com stripes in those work areas of our group. Whatever, we maxed the follow-up inspection!

We had a great competition with the other B-47 wing, the 96th ("great" because we always won), and you may recall that this was the group number that General Old had formed and took to England during World War II. For those interested, I will furnish statistics on the competition, but will only mention the highlight!

The 96th had somehow found a B-17 to be presented to Abilene, Texas, as a monument. While it was in place and awaiting dedication, I suggested to a few maintenance commanders and non-coms, in the strictest secrecy, that it would be a shame for the great Flying Fortress to be enshrined without the insignia of the greatest bomb wing ever!

A couple of days later, I thought it was going to be me and the other wing CO in a good old butt-kicking contest. The city fathers had called him and informed him that the 341st Bomb Wing insignia were all over the B-17, and they thought it was hilarious! The template of our insignia was two and a half feet long and two feet wide — hard to miss seeing, since they covered every blank space!

All that stopped blood from flowing were the reactions of the division and Fifteenth Air Force (General Old) commanders when the highly agitated 96th CO called. They thought it was the funniest thing yet, and it was all over SAC that day. And by the way, the paint is weather resistant and non-fading. I'll have to stop by Abilene and see the great folks, and check that B-17!

We received word that the 341st was to be deactivated, but even before the first transfer orders came, I was reassigned. Another SAC wing CO had been fired, and I was ordered to assume command. It was just like the First Fighter Group days at March Field in California, with the same results, except these were wings, not squadrons.

I was to report immediately, so Margee and the boys remained at Dyess until I could come and get them. A C-47 Goonie Bird (which I seemed to be either flying or riding until retirement) flew me to Schilling AFB — named after one of the greatest fighter leaders of World War II — at Salina, Kansas, a city I would rank in a tie with Abilene, Texas, for military-civilian relations!

I could see the vice commander and staff waiting for me as we taxied in, but I don't think they were awfully impressed with my entry! I had everything buttoned up, hat squared, and a properly severe expression on my face; it was all spoiled, however, when I caught my heel on a step and sprawled on my face in front of the greeters! One of the greeters, though, treated my entry as business as usual — hospital head nurse Bernie Armstrong, from the First Fighter Group days, nursed me through the broken ankle, and said, "You ain't seen nothing yet!"

This was the base that had been our jumping-off point for England in B-17s during World War II. And the same stairs in the Officers Club down which I had tumbled with another captain, engaged in fisticuffs over a local damsel, who left with someone else!

The wing CO had been canned because of hanky-panky in the Management Control System. The MCS functioned as follows: every wing activity was assigned a point scale and graded accordingly. This may help to explain SAC, but probably not; there is no way that SAC can be understood. To illustrate SAC logic, rating periods were divided into "quartiles" — first, middle, and last. And, you know, *three* quartiles make sense when you're in SAC!

Schilling AFB had been on top in SAC for years and wing commanders had gone on to greater things. This was very suspect to the rest of the command, but questioning the "fair hairs" was suicide. At the first staff meeting, when I delved into the inspection, purity and innocence abounded. I found it inconceivable that the wing CO was the bad guy all by himself. I did fire one colonel when he blamed everyone else; if his boss couldn't see what was going on, he should have clued him in.

I reorganized the wing into the consolidation of Operations, which I hated, but it was the only way to keep control. I emphasized that Emergency War Orders were top priority.

I had found a problem at Dyess which was even more critical here, and · was solved the same way. Touring the ramp late Friday nights, and early Saturday mornings, I found flight crews still debriefing or turning in personal equipment, and maintenance crews correcting "gigs" and putting the airplane to bed. Early morning Monday, around 0100, maintenance was readying aircraft for early takeoff, and flight crews were busy flight planning.

Genius was not required to figure out that a bunch of folks were getting a mighty short weekend. And you bet morale was at rock bottom! So I told the staff that aircraft were to land no later than noon on Friday, and take off no earlier than noon on Monday. Operations guys were in total shock and hyperventilating, but got the word.

My first commander's call put it on the line to airmen and air crews:

"This is the goal and it's for everyone's benefit. If we don't have the training and flying time by the last quartile, then we'll go to a seven-day week, and twenty-four hour day, if necessary!"

Only once did we go off the five-day week, and that was during an inspection. As one of the old-timers said, "Jeezus, Colonel, I have never seen so many maintenance elbows and assholes around so many airplanes and working so hard!"

The flight crews more than held up their end. They never received less than "outstanding" on Operational Readiness Inspections. And what morale, across the board!

The wing was assigned one of the first Atlas Strategic Missile

Squadrons and was the first to become combat ready. A superior squadron CO handled it all, thank God!

SAC decided reorganization was necessary in view of the B-47 fleet phase-out. Among other things, a division was formed, initially at Schilling, but it was to move to Walker AFB, New Mexico, in late summer 1963.

I was ordered to assume command — a two-star job, which was nice, but it was unbelievably over-ranked! Initially I was assigned to Schilling and a B-52 tenant wing at Amarillo, Texas, trying to keep busy without over-supervising the wing COs. I was assigned a T-33 T-Bird, which was nice for fun, and helped keep me from going out of my mind. My division Ops officer, a SAC super-fair-haired boy, had fighter pilot delusions and browbeat his way into instructor pilot status, so I wouldn't have to go through flight checks with base jocks. He wanted to learn aerobatics and I tried twice, but he either got airsick or I had to take over to avoid "crash and burn." He retired with three stars, which should tell you something!

I attended the "B-52 Senior Officer's Transition Course" with a brigadier general, a former SAC Command Post director who, as the saying goes, "couldn't fly a box kite in a strong gale!"

The B-52 wing busted an Operational Readiness Inspection, and bad — the first one in my SAC purgatory, even though I was one echelon above the bustees! I had some difficulty in convincing the wing CO that he was *not* the only one in step, after measured guidance, including words like, "I'll fire your ass, get off your ass, get your head out of your ass, etc.!" And he came around, sort of.

About this time, February 1963, the brigadier general promotion list came out *sans* Hayes!

I had always commanded on a very personal basis, so in my infinite wisdom I wrote an article for the base newspaper explaining that the disappointment when an airman misses a promotion is no less, or more, than that felt when the more senior feels "passed over."

No one had ever told me that CinCSAC felt that it was sinful, arrogant, and incomprehensible for an officer to harbor, or worse, *express* a desire to be a general officer! I wonder that he never entertained those desires, but just blushingly said, "Aw, shucks," and accepted the promotions thrust upon him!

He told General Old to inform me that I was "that far from being a general" and that he had called the Pentagon to have my name removed from the promotion list due out in July. And some "friend" sent me a copy of the general's list with my name red-lined.

The hatchet was out! Three Operational Readiness Inspections on two bases in five months, and all rated "outstanding!" This must have caused severe stomach acidity and heartburn for CinCSAC — it sure didn't help my digestion, or blood pressure! The Inspector General finally got me on some O Club activities at Schilling. And I was just a tenant!

After I went all the way to March Air Force Base to be officially "canned," I received permission to keep my T-Bird and drop in on the Pentagon and the colonel's group. I called ahead, and when I reached the Pentagon was told that I was acceptable to run the Tactical Air Command Post, and warned that TAC was now being run by SAC folks! Nothing else was open, except in pro-kit disposal, mess-kit repair, and aircraft salvage!

So, onward and upward!

Chapter 13

Tactical Air
Command Headquarters

W HEN THE COLONEL'S assignment guys told me that there was an opening for the director, TAC Command Post, I questioned the requirement for the same: "Hey, I just left SAC, remember?"

I was informed that SAC apostles, senior ones, had taken over TAC and it was a new ball game. Immediately, some appropriate adages came to mind: "Frying pan to the fire," "Up to my ass in alligators and someone is draining the pool," "When things can get worse, they will," etc.

TAC Headquarters allowed as how I could drop by and be interviewed by the vice commander for determination of my suitability for the position. So I T-33'd to Langley and got the vapors and palpitations when I arrived at the Command Section and saw the VC's name.

SAC maintained control of

I was . . . given a lecture on how the position could be a turning point in my career. . . .

their forces, worldwide, even when deployed. The gentleman, three-star, who would be deciding my fate, had commanded the Alert forces in England and when I visited my crews there, we had had differences about crew treatment and conduct. And yet, we won all the awards he bestowed on the temporary duty Alert forces!

I knew that he had checked with cronies at SAC and I was amazed at the mild interrogation. It was loaded with comments that I knew how SAC operated, we were going to do all we could to whip TAC into that likeness, and that I could make great contributions to that endeavor. It's called rubbing salt into open wounds!

I was informed that I had passed the rigid requirements and that transfer orders would be cut. And he almost smiled. As I was walking out of the "head shed," I passed the office marked "Chief of Staff" and a two-star name. I was startled to hear "Psst, psst" from that office. That was the first general officer I knew who ever whispered.

He beckoned me in, and wanted to know if I had been accepted. I wondered why he couldn't ask the VC himself, but I replied in the affirmative, which exposed me to a lecture on how he and the commander had reconstructed the Command Post "in the SAC image," and were proud of it!

I was thence given a lecture on how the position could be a turning point in my career, which led me to believe that he had talked to the wrong guy at SAC, or hadn't been listening. The gist was, "Remember, you have a direct line to the commander, office and quarters, so when you have any information of command interest, pass it on immediately."

This I tried for a while, but it was soon evident that staff members or commanders were also passing information on, usually more than I was privy to. So, I usually got "I know that!" followed by questions that I was unable to answer.

That took care of rapport with the commander, except that he never stopped believing that his director, not the Command Post, would always have the latest. He even called me in quarters, and expected a coherent discussion of events that had just transpired. I developed fast footwork and gab; I never answered his questions, but had him so confused that he forgot what he was asking!

I reported in and found the SAC image, just like the chief of staff had said — maximum security, guards wore berets and pearl-handled pistols, elaborate briefing/conference room with multiple-screen display presentations.

The main difference between SAC and TAC had escaped the new command: TAC did not have a general war responsibility, except in those forces deployed overseas, whose command/control was transferred to the theater commanders. But an around-the-clock control room was maintained, with ticked-off fighter pilots on duty who had no authority and only a monitoring function.

This Command Post, command/control organization and layout was directive to the numbered Air Forces Headquarters and tactical units. And all facilities adhered to exact standardization, down to and including squadron personal equipment rooms.

I found myself in the middle of another inter-command dispute: TAC had a converted KC-135 tanker, adding extensive communications, and labeled it, "TAC Command Post." The command concept was that the CP would fly on all tactical deployments/redeployments, with a senior officer on board, as "Tactical Forces Commander."

SAC thought this the funniest damned thing they had ever heard. Because air-to-air refueling had become a concept, it was natural that SAC would furnish the "Task Force Commander" — they owned the tankers! (Note: If there developed an emergency in the tactical forces that did not involve refueling, the task force commander displayed monumental indifference — "They weren't SAC forces!")

I flew a couple of missions in the TAC CP and published a Manual of Operations, including the "Tactical Forces Commander" concept, realizing it was only a paper exercise. I was pleased that my effort climbed, unscathed, through the staff echelons until it reached the Command Section.

I was directed to report to the vice commander, he who had approved my assignment, and was met with: "I don't see SAC coordination on this."

Since he was not a joking type, I replied, "No, Sir. I know you are aware of the command/control policy differences and agree that SAC will never approve this concept."

"Hayes, are you suggesting that Strategic Air Command is unreasonable?"

I wanted to say, "No, Sir, they're a bunch of shitheads!" Instead, I replied more diplomatically, "General, the TAC commander has directed immediate publication and use of this manual. Additional coordination will cause delay of months."

"Well, uh, yes." He was a man of quick decisions! "Publish it as 'temporary' until SAC coordination is received." So I did.

Months later, said coordination returned and all that was left was the cover page, a description of the Airborne Command Post (ACP), where it would be based, manning, and a statement that "The TAC Airborne Command Post *may* accompany movements of TAC forces and *observe* the operation. Communications with elements of the Task Force are *prohibited* unless requested by Task Force Commander [*meaning SAC!*]."

My exultation was short-lived. The TAC commander was first to see SAC's comments. He then called the deputy for Ops (my boss), the VC, and me in and started the meeting with, "What stupid bastard sent this to SAC?" Even though my name was on the transmittal letter, in my naiveté I waited for the vice to bare his chest or soul, or something, and admit that he had ordered the report to be published.

The silence had to be broken, so I bit the bullet: "I did, Sir." By the time the meeting was over, I was hoping that I would be able to retire as a lieutenant colonel, at least. The deputy for Ops hadn't been aware of the VC's directive, and the VC never blinked when I laid eye contact on him.

I must admit there were interesting and rewarding experiences, and the Command Post folks were fabulous! Two additions to the CP had been approved: a larger battle staff room with additional command/control communications and aircraft movement and status displays, and a computer building for storing contingency plans and deployment/redeployment flight plans.

I had a lieutenant colonel assistant who was a computer whiz, plus bunches of civilians from the industry with thick glasses, unkempt hair, and slept-in clothes. They made me very nervous, so I stayed out of it.

I laid out the plans for the battle staff conference room and surprised myself! It's amazing what you can do when someone else is paying the bills. I quailed when directed to justify requirements for such a facility with Department of Defense civilians, but the assistant director of Ops, a one-star, had spent more time in the Pentagon than the janitors. I was only too glad to be his "horse-holder," the minion who carries the charts, flips same, and never opens his mouth!

I flew with fighter squadrons on deployments and redeployments, which made life worthwhile. I headed a team to Europe to determine the status of standby bases marked for TAC forces when increased readiness directed, and I thought I might get shot before the visit was over. This was my first realization that there wasn't *one* Air Force; once a demarcation line was crossed, the theater commanders took over and you better keep your cotton-picking hands off! Conversely, specialist functions, *i.e.,* weather, communications, security — even the damned *postal service* with their separate organizations in D.C. — maintained authority over those units, wherever they were deployed!

It was glaringly clear that the Air Force Headquarters in Europe had barely given lip service to the mission of supporting TAC forces deployed in support of local hostilities. I actually had to sneak out and make clandestine inspections of two bases! My report was destroyed and I was told, "Forget it!"

Because one of TAC's missions was close support of ground forces, fighter pilot controllers, with enlisted radio operators, were dropped with the first airborne assault waves. This required that each fighter squadron maintain a minimum number of pilot graduates from the Army Airborne (read "paratrooper") school at Fort Benning, Georgia. Being fighter pilots, there were always more than the required number of volunteers.

It seems that the commander of TAC allowed that it would be dandy if senior officers, majors and above, in the Command pursued the Airborne rating. In fact, this would be an important factor in designating squadron and wing commanders. There were a bunch of bent and broken older types limping around, but an amazing percentage made it.

I saw this as an opportunity to gain more acceptance on the TAC team, and maybe lead to a wing command, so I was off on the daily 5:30 a.m. workout schedule: three-mile run, deep knee bends, chins, push-ups, and duck-waddle. I even quit smoking! I passed the fitness exam and was off.

But there was one hitch. My boss, the two-star deputy for Ops, gave the OK, but also some unintentional bad advice. He said to submit a written request to him because the VC would require lots of rewrites before approving, which he might not do anyway! With orders in hand, I was off to join the exclusive fraternity of the paratrooper.

I had just enough time to arrive at Benning, sign in, and get that godawful haircut, when the DO called. "He caught us, Jack, come on home."

It seems that the vice commander had called the Command Post for me — probably for some of his "wire brush" treatment — and my deputy told him where I was; there was no reason he shouldn't. Some secretaries in the Command Section told me what happened next: the VC walked into the commander's office and, in an outraged manner, asked, "Did you know that the director of *your* Command Post has gone TDY without permission of the Command Section?" He didn't mention Airborne school, but managed to make it sound immoral or unlawful, or both.

So I was recalled. I even got a speeding ticket in one of those little Southern towns that live on the income, to make it a perfect day. Two days later, I called the staff to attention, with my bald head on display, as the commander entered. I noticed he was startled at my appearance. I don't know what his reaction was, but two weeks later I resubmitted for Airborne school and the request sailed through. Hard to believe that it was so difficult getting permission to go someplace and hurt yourself!

There were six colonels in my Airborne class; we trained in a special section, and were assigned two top-notch instructors. There was no difference in treatment, just in language: rather than being given orders in loud and obscene wordage, it was, "Would the colonel be so kind as to give me twenty-five Airborne push-ups?" or "Could it be that the colonel(s) have difficulty with English words? We felt that the instructions were fairly clear." On critiquing a practice landing fall, I got "With the colonel's permission, rather than discussing each physical element, we would like to present the overall picture, which was that of a pregnant cow on ice!"

I was assigned to a training brigade made up of enlisted and junior officer candidates, which trained in the other half day as the "Clumsy Colonels." But needing all the practice I could get and wanting to dispel, in my mind, any trace of special treatment, I received permission to train with my brigade.

I only missed a couple of sessions, when my body refused more abuse. Not bad for a 45-year-old! They wouldn't let me take the graduation jump with the brigade, because I would have had six jumps, and the program only called for five.

I think there were two contributions I made to the training program. The first was that the young trainees, 18 to mid-20s, felt "If this old fart can do it, by Gawd, I can." The other was that I was permitted to counsel those wanting to withdraw, and managed to motivate enough that the brigade graduated a class well above the average number. Humility not being a virtue of mine, I have to say that I was awarded the distinction of being an outstanding graduate!

The first jump sticks in the memory. I was to be first one out, and after going through all the hook-ups, checking each other's equipment, then it was, "Stand in the door." I made the 90° turn in the "Airborne shuffle," and waited.

With your feet on the door edge and hands on the sides of the door, it's emphasized, "Don't look down," and so your eyes are on the horizon. For one whole minute? I don't think anyone can do it. Your neck gets a crick, and you can't overcome the fascination of looking straight down, which makes you wonder what the hell you're doing there! You land like they told you to, and you're pretty proud until you remember, "Oh my God! I gotta do this four more times!"

My next three jumps went fine. I did screw up one by getting my shroud lines ("shroud" — a hell of a name to use for people jumping out of airplanes!) wound up, but I had them untangled by ground impact time. I still had to do 50 push-ups for the faculty. Funny, it's not hard to do when you just had the bejeezus scared out of you!

On our fifth jump (I would say "last" jump, but that sounds terminal), we encountered a rare weather phenomenon, which resulted in the death of one of the colonels and put 15 jumpers in the hospital. It was a formation jump with three aircraft in formation, and we were to come out as fast as possible. When I opened my eyes — I always kept them closed until the chute opened — I saw that I was moving across the ground like nothing I had seen before. I pulled the shroud lines away from the direction of movement, like the nice men had told me, but still hit the ground so hard that I bounced back to my feet and collapsed the chute. Only a few contusions!

The jumpers were well scattered by the wind, and I was the only one to land directly in front of the bleachers, through no effort of mine, but no one believed that since the spectators were all coeds. I admit that I was late getting to the assembly area, but I had to acknowledge the applause, after all!

I knew that one of our colonels had been injured on the fourth jump, and dropped by his room that evening. He had a badly bruised hip, but insisted that he was going to graduate and was feeling no pain — undoubtedly due to the medicinal lotions he was consuming.

Landing in that wind, I figured that there would be casualties, which was verified by the heavy traffic in medevac choppers. Observers said that our friend landed from a backward drift, his head making hard contact with the ground, rendering him unconscious. Unable to collapse his chute, he was dragged into an embankment head first, and he never regained consciousness.

The Air Force control team, which furnished ground smoke for troop carrier pilots to fix jump point, and gave the go/no-go decision, found themselves in a real crack. The maximum wind velocity for a drop is 12 mph, and when the control officer gave the OK, their gauge was showing six, with gusts to nine mph. As the first jumpers exited, the wind velocity climbed to 20 mph, with gusts to 35!

There is no possibility of stopping a mass jump, since it's over in seconds, for that small of a formation. All they could do was watch the carnage and pray. These days we call it "wind shear," and that it was. The Air Force team was absolved of any responsibility, as they should have been.

The two non-coms assigned to instruct the Clumsy Colonels were crushed that they had lost one of their charges and felt personal responsibility. I submitted glowing letters of evaluation to their commanders, which I would have done without the accident.

There were a couple of more incidents before the Command Post tour was over. I saved a classmate's career twice, when he called TAC HQ late at night, let's say "tipsy," and demanded to speak to the commander and find out "why he wasn't on the by-Gawd brigadier general list whissh jest cum out, en if he wan't good nuff ta be a genrul...." Since Command calls came through the CP switchboard, those lovely ladies — and they were — rang my quarters. Incoherence was at a high level, so I hung up, and told the operators to give the "busy" signal until he passed out.

I gave him a day or so to rejoin the living, and then told him how his rear had been saved. As I said, this happened twice, and he never expressed any gratitude — which I didn't need or want — but it wouldn't have hurt to acknowledge the contribution of the CP operators! He was lucky that I was elsewhere when the next list came out, because he would not only have been put through to the commander, but I would have had the conversation recorded for posterity. He retired with two stars, so there must be a lesson there.

Finally, I wangled a slot in the Air Defense Orientation Course, and checked out in the F-101 Voodoo, F-102 Delta Dagger, and F-106 Delta Dart and qualified as a "Blip Chaser," shooting at drones. There was lots of misery from the oxygen systems in those planes. Rather than "demand" system, furnishing oxygen as required, these systems were "pressure," forcing the stuff into your nostrils until it felt like your eardrums were hanging out the lobes and sinus cavities permanently misshapen. Otherwise, it was lots of fun!

I had some great effectiveness reports, which I think unhappied the VC, so he had me assigned as chief of safety, figuring I might screw that job up — a fair assumption, since I had no experience there either, except for the wire-brush treatment applied to commanders!

Chief of Safety

I'm sure that the safety guys, who were all pros, were overjoyed that they had a virgin in charge. I stated that I would try not to screw things up too much, but wanted them to keep me posted, and to suggest and advise. My philosophy was that if I sink from sabotage or lack of support, I'll be the last one to sink because I'll be standing on shoulders until they run out. But if I screw up, I'll be first to admit it and will shield all from powder burns. And I got great response from great guys!

And I was introduced to the red telephone, a *direct* line to the commander, and vice versa, which was the bad part! Commanders were required to personally notify the TAC commander of a major accident, so I was usually called by our leader before I had the slightest hint something had happened. I tried bribery to the safety officers — booze, evaluation of local lady talent, use of my car when they were at HQ — but nothing could work. Since they were feeding the wing CO the information, he had to call the TAC commander.

I thought I had some pretty sound principles for evaluating safety programs, but I seemed to always be getting beat around the head and shoulders. Without going through the "head shed," I sent my teams on survey visits to the bases with the *best current* safety records, because that's where the next prang is going to happen! The best programs are where the latest accidents occurred.

The Command Section supported me (so surprising that I forgot the subject!), to include safety surveys in the no-notice inspections by the Inspector General. This would be an accurate evaluation, *versus* unrealism of scheduled surveys. So I was stunned when the Inspector General opposed the idea: "Commanders would feel that the IG is spying [*what the hell do you call it?*] instead of helping." This brought to mind the saying about the two biggest liars in the military — the IG who says, "We're just here to help," and the wing commander who says, "Glad to have you here."

I finally tried no-notice safety staff visits, but got bloodied up on that one, too. When some commanders protested, my question was, "If you have a good program, what's the worry?" The visits went down in flames. So, I published a schedule of visits and got the "eye wash" briefings. I hope I'm forgiven, but I exulted when, while getting the "sweetness and light" briefing by a wing commander, there were three interruptions: a mid-air collision with a safe bail-out and emergency landing; two aircraft locked wings while taxiing; and a DWI tried to park a staff car in the nuclear weapon storage area! With only a slight sneer, I said, "Let's cancel this briefing, Colonel. Looks like you have *lots* to do."

In spite of all this, TAC accident rates and safety records improved in all areas during my tenure as resident expert! The chief of staff wrote my effectiveness report and the commander signed — amazed, I'm sure, by my performance so glowingly described, but no more surprised than I!

I was then informed that there were greater things in store for me, which really bothered me — especially when the rumor was that my replacement, about my vintage, was said to have spent some "funny farm" time, showing how difficult it was to fill my shoes! Command Section directed that I brief the staff on safety status and problems.

My auspicious briefing had proceeded to the second chart when the commander spoke down to the "pit" — as we called the briefer's position — and said, "That's enough, Jack. After all, you're briefing as a lame duck!" He called me "Jack" so it wasn't all bad.

Working types in the pit expressed mute sympathy for another nose rubbed in it, which I acknowledged by quivering lips and misty eyes — yeah, right!

Director of Information

Never has a military man served in so many assignments — three, consecutively — for which he was completely unqualified! Amazingly, all effectiveness reports were in the highest categories, probably because the raters and endorsers knew that I had received the kiss of death and figured, "What the hell, let him dream."

Rumor had it that the vice commander was secretly advocating flagellation and fingernail extraction as acceptable military punishment, so I had a little concern when I was ordered to report to that worthy. I relaxed slightly when I was informed that the subject had to do with my reassignment, but I was stunned when told that I was to be Director of Information! It used to be called "public relations," but the primary function was representing the commander in dealing with the "media," — of which there were bunches — and, get this, *writing* articles for publication!

I then luxuriated in one of my few open guffaws while at TAC Headquarters, but seeing that I was laughing alone, I said, "Sir, I know you're aware of my demise in SAC brought about by alleged misuse of a pen. Surely you can't place the public image of the Command on one so lacking in literary talents."

The stern reply was, "The Commander desires that this position be occupied by a fighter pilot, well decorated, with Paratroop wings." The TAC image! (They were Airborne insignia, not Paratroop wings, but what the hell!)

So I was off to another "virginal" confrontation and inspirational talk: "Glad to be here, hope you'll accept me, I ask for your help," and other grovelings to no avail. That was the worst reception yet!

I found the journalism/media clique a closed society, and the bunch I inherited barely avoided open sneers and luxuriated in their language, placing me on the outside — but only for a very brief period!

With the outgoing chief scribe, I attended a convention of aviation writers and information officers from all services. What a reception! Never have I been so ignored, insulted, and scorned — and all those things have been laid on me by experts! Vengeance was mine in a well-oiled (me), pugnacious "up yours" address — which was unscheduled, but a great satisfaction.

I noted some resentment to my comments about slick-chests: "Noncombat experienced speaking as experts on aerial warfare," and "Many of the attendees are members of the limp-wristed society, making me gag!" I understand there was more, including invitations to fisticuffs, but I'm vague on lots of things!

Barely in time, the SAC element retired or was flushed by a change in command, and a TAC four-star was brought in with the right stuff. But I was almost in the dark brown stuff again; it seems I had incurred the wrath of a female scribe who had left high-heel marks on faces and personal parts of military information people.

The "charm" and jutting jaw (the only jutting part of her figure) were wasted on me. This led to my reassignment, thank the Lord! My newly assigned assistant, a colonel, a pro in the business and a top guy, took some of the flak from the female shark, and interceded for me when she went to the new commander. The commander called me in and said, "You are undoubtedly the most mal-assigned officer I have seen in thirty-five years of military service!"

So it was back to the joy part of the Air Force — being a FIGHTER PILOT!

Chapter 14

George AFB (Again!)

*M*Y REPRIEVE FROM THE misty world of journalism specifically, and the mysteries of higher Headquarters generally, became official with orders in May 1964 to George Air Force Base in Victorville, California. I was the division Director of Operations, another of the "try and keep busy" jobs. But the beauty of the assignment was that the 479th Tactical Fighter Wing flew the Lockheed F-104 Starfighter — the fighter pilot's dream, *The Missile with a Man in It!*

Margee and the boys stayed at Langley, in our home off-base, until the end of the school year. Shortly before I was to bring the family to California, I got a frantic call from the TAC personnel type: "Has yer family moved yet?" When I gave him the negative, I heard a sigh of relief, and "Don't move 'em, you're going to Vietnam."

This was another of Margee's

> *. . . I was the division Director of Operations, another of the "try and keep busy" jobs.*

The Lockheed F-104 Starfighter.

travails, handled with her usual class. Our furniture had been shipped to California and was in storage, awaiting the happy reunion, until Vietnam entered the picture. So it all went back across the continent, and you can't imagine the damage inflicted on furniture in "storage." Obviously, carpets had been spread around the warehouse with furniture tastefully arranged for the convenience of the warehouse men. Two sofas and a loveseat were broken and the carpets showed use by remnants of lunch and cigarette butts. They didn't even sweep before re-rolling the rugs for shipment! That should have been enough trauma, but the Air Force claims gent, a civil service grade whatever, was immensely bored by the process, and openly displayed his feelings that we were trying to rip off a hard-working civilian, eking out a living in the moving business.

The aforementioned "gent" experienced a total attitude reversal when he encountered Margee's reaction! Seeing it coming, I locked myself in a closet while the boys faded out. Before it was over, the president of the moving company personally visited to ensure that all was well, which it was. Amazing how a beautiful doll who is all class can transform a male into a milksop, with a slight display of temper. I know — I've spent considerable time in the "milksop" phase!

The F-104 wing was maintaining combat readiness and upgrading newly assigned pilots. The F-4 Phantom wing, acting as a replacement training unit (RTU), was training pilots for duty in Vietnam. After my Vietnam tour, I checked out in the Phantom and found its performance amazing, especially from such a big one! However, since the appearance of the Starfighter, I had a burning desire to don the spurs and join that exclusive fraternity.

It had been long recognized that there was a magical quality to the F-104, similar to that of the P-38 Lightning, the "Twin-Tailed Devil" of World War II. There was a most radical transformation in the personality, bearing, and attitude of any deemed fit to join the fraternity. Even the few of humble mien — although not many of them were interested — became swaggering, chip-on-the-shoulder, "up-yers" types, who were generally insufferable, especially to those not of the fighter pilot breed!

To explain the spurs: the Starfighter not only qualified as supersonic, times two, but was related to the Cavalry arm in a way not known to most. Part of the attire required to fly the Beautiful Bird was *spurs!* This was obviously not to induce more speed, but to hopefully provide for retention of ankles and lower legs in the event of ejection!

To accommodate the airspeeds, the horizontal stabilizer, normally positioned as an extension of the fuselage, was situated at the top of the vertical stabilizer and out of the vortices and shock waves of supersonic flight. Also, the artillery shell charge, which propelled the seat for ejection, could not ensure the jock clearing the tail — which had messy results.

The initial solution was to reconfigure the emergency exit/egress to the downward mode, which solved one problem but lost us some Tigers when there was engine failure just after takeoff. Unless the F-104 could be rolled well beyond 90°, approaching inverted, the seat and pilot were spiked into the ground. But it was still the best effort available at that state of the art.

It was also clear that, without restraint, downward ejection would bring the legs up around the head, divesting the pilot of ankles and bunches of lower leg, at least! Even when higher-powered propellants permitted upward ejection, leg retraction was still necessary, for the same reasons.

The solution, including introduction of spurs, called for a high-speed power winch located under and to the rear of the pilot's seat, with steel cables attached. At the end of each cable, running through the rudder channels, was a steel ball that fit into a ball and groove in the metal spur. In normal conditions, the winch operated under inertia and allowed free rudder movement. When the ejection process started with firing of the canopy, the winch retracted fully and at high speed, pulling legs under the seat. With seat separation, the winch disengaged, allowing free fall.

I love it! A Cavalry trooper and a fighter pilot, not only related in personality and attitudes, but both wearing *spurs!* The spurs, fitting under and around the heels and making a satisfying clink, or clank, depending on the surface material, were items of personal flying equipment, to be donned in flight operations or on the parking ramp prior to mounting — sorry, *boarding* — the aircraft.

Anyone of authority, even remotely aware of the individuality of the fighter pilot and his desire to stand out from the pack, should have recognized that the spurs would become a status symbol and be proudly exploited. In fact, they immediately became items of everyday wear and were seen and heard in offices, shops, and stores of the base. Ultimately, the crowning glory — wearing them in the Officers Club and mess, bringing on heartburn, even nausea, to support, administrative, and command officers. Some of the latter were of senior rank, most of the categories nonrated!

The initial complaints by the above were met, in aggrieved tones, with,

"You realize, of course, that we're on back-up Alert and have to be able to scramble with minimum notice." The more knowledgeable would have wondered why, if flight suits were to be donned before takeoff, couldn't that time be used to attach spurs? That logic escaped the complainers and upholders of military decorum and dress, but then came the dawning: "Scramble the whole frapping wing?"

As disciplined and dedicated Air Force officers, the F-104 drivers responded to the pressures by agreeing, as a token, that spurs would no longer be worn on basketball, handball, and tennis courts! But then came total surrender when the wing commander assembled the wearers of spurs and advised that he had been threatened with loss of command, commission, and career the next time a single spur was worn anyplace but the flight line. The commander stated further that his seniors had received complaints from other bases, "So, wipe the smirks off. This restriction applies at any base, of any service!"

Amazing results — there wasn't an incident for some time. Then, there were a couple of "clinks" somewhere off the flight line, and gradually, with the persistence of dripping water, the spurs were again a way of life.

Then came the commander's dawning, "Those SOBs are wearing those goddamned spurs all over the #*$%&@ place!" And so the cycles went; the conflict was probably a draw, unless a fighter jock was telling the story.

Along that same line, in the Army Air Corps/United States Air Force, and in the other armed forces, I suppose, there has always been a large and vocal element — usually non-combat, non-rated, and generally stodgy — whose main concerns dealt with uniforms, shoe shines, haircuts, proper storage and alignment of supplies, and other minutiae. And there were rebels with the temerity to suggest that the flight suit should be accepted as any other uniform, except for parade, formal assemblies, or after duty hours. When Strategic Air Command assumed a constant Alert posture, the Alert crews were distinguished, rightly, as "the Elite Force," but it took a four-star to begrudgingly allow these troops out of the Alert area in their *"work clothes!"*

But back to the F-104, "The Missile with a Man in It." Because only about 8,000 pilots became qualified during the airplane's life, every check-out called for a special party, including Lockheed brass, and enrollment in the select body. I had already been through Mach 1, the speed of sound, in several fighters, but the biggest thrill was the F-104! It was called "The

Missile," because without wing tanks, the wingtips were invisible and you were really in a missile!

On the first test flight, Tony Levier, chief test pilot, and one of the greatest, was reputed to have said, "If I was ten years older this would be a substitute for sex!" A little later the statement was revised: "Make that twenty years." No use hurrying things, but what praise could be greater?

These days, with the F-15 Eagle, F-16 Fighting Falcon, and F-18 Hornet, all Mach 3+, the Starfighter performance figures pale, until it is recognized that the F-104 entered the Air Force inventory as the Korean War was ending in the 1950s, and before the more exotic aircraft hit the skies in the '80s! The F-104 was that far ahead of the state of the art!

The beauty *really* couldn't qualify as a substitute for sex, but it came close: afterburner takeoff, maximum angle of attack and you swear you're vertical, level off at 40,000 feet in about three minutes, look down and the field's directly under you! To loop, 500 mph, 4 G pull up and afterburner "on." Over the top at 16,000 to 18,000 feet. Heaven!

There were symptoms of dry mouth and sweaty palms when introduced to the engine-out emergency landing procedure. Because the flame-out glide angle approximated that of a sledgehammer, practice was only conducted at Edwards AFB with miles of landing surface.

Speed brakes and engine rpm were set to simulate engine-out, landing gear and flaps "up," 18,000 feet, runway heading. The best glide speed allowed time and altitude for *one 360° near-vertical spiral, flare and drop gear and flaps!* It took only one of these gut-wrenchers for a unanimous decision — the emergency procedure for loss of power was punch-out, eject, and make a nylon letdown!

My departure date for the Far East was May 1966, leaving me with two problems: trying to keep busy as division Ops and working in as much time as possible with Margee and the boys.

The ennui I tried to handle in various ways; the first, setting up a realistic ground attack range simulating Vietnam, utilizing scrap trucks and tanks, building native villages, and simulating missile and gun emplacements. It had to be constantly rearranged to present a different attack problem for the pilots in training. To be honest, I had trouble with motivation for the project, and my assistant, Lieutenant Colonel Pete Popovich, one of the best, did most of the hard work.

I volunteered for duty on courts-martial and boards. I defended a "jock strapper" who requested duty at George AFB when I was assigned there, figuring that I would be coaching the football team. His commander had recommended separation from the service under "other than honorable conditions." Seems that he thought his magnificent body had been offered to the Air Force to carry the colors on the field of athletic endeavor.

He felt, therefore, that he was above the mundane activities of military life — like kitchen police, squadron activities, and anything not involving athletics. I beat the rap for him, because people had not done their homework. I left no doubt in his mind that he was on his own, but it didn't take. He was discharged a few months later by another board. Somewhere, he was given a false impression of Air Force life. Too bad.

Family relations were helped by my being authorized weekend flights to Langley for "navigation training," leaving Friday evening and returning Sunday — in the F-104, of course! I had to stop one or two times for gas each way, but improved on that, by chance.

On one of the trips, I stopped at a base that was home of the division from which I had been rudely separated and commanded by a brigadier general, a good friend of mine. We met at the O Club for some libations that evening, with my old staff. I solemnly advised that I was writing an article for the George Base paper and wanted their comments. Very cold reaction, but I don't know why. I was the one who got his ass burned!

I mentioned to the division CO that, in view of my blood contributions to SAC, I didn't see why they couldn't furnish just one damned KC-135 tanker on Friday afternoon to hasten the Old Warrior on his way to the connubial couch and his loved ones!

And from then on I tapped into a tanker every Friday evening, mid-USA, and made the trip non-stop! I had to use an F-104D, two-place, and my favorite instructor jock, Captain Delashaw, had to write me off as refueling qualified. I'm not asking, but I have wondered why there were no questions about a KC-135 configured for probe-and-drogue refueling, which was seldom used in those days, pumping up one Starfighter on Friday afternoons. And all those heads and eyeballs clustered at the boom operator's position — I assume for a look at the Beauty, but maybe to see if I could *really* still do it!

There was a little-known feature of the F-104, respected and avoided by those around her. The small wing had a leading edge of near razor sharpness, and at home base felt-lined wood pieces covered the area. On cross-countries, there was no protection, and, immediately after the engine was cut, the pilot waved ground crews away, not always successfully. The airplane sat so much lower than the average bird that the neophyte mis-judged, and in ducking under the wing, hit the leading edge, peeling back a good portion of the scalp!

Finally, because low airspeeds and the stall could be non-habit forming, warning systems were built into the Starfighter: a "Stick-Shaker," which did exactly that in the dangerously low speed realm, and a "Stick-Kicker," which knocked the stick forward just prior to full stall. These were fine when dog-fighting or in the landing pattern, but were disengaged in low-level attacks, strafing or bombing — you didn't want the stick vibrating while pressing in a low-level attack. On the other hand, without the warning, it was quite possible to high-speed stall and spread yourself all over the range. On one of those times, when the range control guy says, "Pull up, yer low," just you say "Oh, God," and you hope He doesn't answer! If you make it, on the way home, you offer the usual promises, which are mostly forgotten by the cocktail hour. The Man really has patience.

I made one last visit home, and had a great farewell blast by the Starfighter guys; then on to Travis AFB for the exotic East. Onward and upward!

Chapter 15

Vietnam and Thailand

Y NAME WAS circulated as available, and the commander of the Seventh Air Force, General Joe Moore, requested me as his chief of staff. He had been Director of Operations at Tactical Air Command, and I had worked for him running the Command Post. It was a short-lived pleasure working for him again; he soon departed for the U.S. of A.

The approach into Saigon was the first thrill in this combat zone. The commercial airline pilot, knowing that there would be ground fire, stayed high until it was time to dump flaps and gear, cut power, then a steep approach to landing. Not exactly according to the company book, but there were no complaints. Most of us knew the reason for the "kamikaze" approach, and we weren't paying customers anyway.

> . . . the commander of the Seventh Air Force, General Joe Moore, requested me as his chief of staff.

I had some doubts about how we were doing in this conflict when we couldn't protect airfields in "friendly" territory. The question was answered when the staff car driver handed me a .45-caliber automatic, placed a carbine next to himself, and locked all the doors. This was the capital of the country we were fighting with, the location of the American Embassy, and the Headquarters of the American forces, for Christ's sake!

It didn't take long to realize that there were no nice rules in this fight. Driving down a main street, I saw a young boy slap a satchel charge on a GI truck and run. The troops, both U.S. and Vietnamese, bailed out before the blast with no injuries, but it sure wiped out one truck and played hell with my complacency!

And it didn't help when an old lady tossed a grenade in the door of a GI club and disappeared down an alley, on a main drag! Lots of casualties resulted from that one, including confusion of the combatant and the civilian. The soldier who tried to recognize and protect that difference either died, or was found wanting by his superiors. The one who realized that there was no difference and fought accordingly was court-martialed and/or castigated by the media.

General Moore gave me whatever time I wanted to visit combat units in Vietnam and Thailand. I didn't ask if I could fly combat missions, but he didn't tell me not to.

At the U.S. and Vietnamese Army units, operations appeared standard, except that situation maps showed some areas controlled by the Viet Cong, others labeled as "unknown" or "questionable." And it was pointed out that there was considerable ebb and flow, meaning that the locations of bad guys varied daily, even hourly. This was worse than what the Germans faced from the resistance forces in occupied Europe. And they were the enemy while we were trying to help!

I met some fighter friends who were flying the A-1 Skyraider with South Vietnam units, so I got a checkout and flew a few with them. Our Air Force troops were carried as "advisors" to guys who had been flying combat longer than most of ours wore wings. We were sitting in a hooch after a mission and partaking of libations, for the nerves. One of our captains dropped the comment, with a sigh, "Another month and my tour's over."

Real class, passed over by a wry comment from a fighter jock from the Republic of Vietnam Air Force, "My tour will never be over until the war is, one way or the other!"

This brings up another point. The role of the armed forces of the Republic of Vietnam was hardly even acknowledged in descriptions of that conflict. Those brief passages that were devoted to the subject were extremely critical. I hope that sometime there will be recognition of the heroism, dedication, and sacrifice displayed by those noble forces.

I also flew some missions with the F-100 Super Sabres — "in-country," as the South Vietnam hassles were called. I flew the D model with two places, not having time, or permission, to go through combat training. I had been wearing glasses for a few years, but lost confidence in the "eye guys" when I heard the rest of the flight describe damage or destruction to all kinds of targets. I could only estimate damage to jungle because that's all I could see marked by the spotters. There were villages throwing up bunches of things that would hurt a fella, and we threw things right back, but it's hard to estimate damage to mud and thatch huts.

I observed on Vietnamese gunnery and medevac choppers, including relief of an outpost in the Delta. Scary! We were flying so low that all a chute would do was stream enough to point to your body, or if it didn't come out of the pack, it cushioned the ground impact — but not enough!

We picked up Vietnamese wounded, mostly leg damage from mines and some mortar. They were usually pretty well sedated, but obviously wondered what the Yankee fly-boy was doing so close to the ground. I lit smokes for all, and split a carton I happened to have with me. (I always smoked *real* hard when I was nervous!) There's no doubt about the damage done by the weed, but it does give a nice feeling when one is scared, tired, or hurting. It ranks along with medicinal, or "combat," whiskey. I didn't stop smoking until I had to give up flying airshows at the age of 63. I've never said I was smart!

I made a short visit to Thailand, long enough to recognize a beautiful country and people. This regard was enhanced when I was transferred from Vietnam and spent most of my Southeast Asia tour there.

I visited the A-1 and T-28 Air Commando Squadrons, not realizing that I would be flying combat with them soon. The F-4 Phantoms were flying MiGCAP (MiG combat air patrol) and suppression of SAM (surface-to-air missile) activity, with some ground attack missions when maximum saturation was deemed necessary.

The F-105 Thunderchief, a highly advanced and equipped fighter designed for long-range interdiction and ground attack, had the primary air mission in the theater. F-105s attacked targets in the Hanoi area, including north and east, and were suffering the highest losses, by far. Despite the odds, knowing that if they weren't killed they would face degradation and abuse from their captors, the "Thud jocks" fought on and left a magnificent chapter in the annals of fighter aviation — or any other combat arm, for that matter!

In every fighter wing I visited, my time was spent in combat Operations reviewing combat film, strike photos, mission summaries, and talking to pilots. It was evident that commanders and staff were flying missions on rotation, not selecting missions, which is the way it's supposed to be.

On my last Thud wing visit, I was met by the wing CO, who had served in a wing I commanded years before, and who hadn't impressed me then. He gave me a tour of the base, except for combat Ops, which culminated in his plush office getting a briefing on the Officers Club of the future!

I cut him short with a request to visit combat Ops, which was received with a hurt look and a call for someone to escort me. I don't think he even knew where it was — just that it wasn't at the Officers Club! I heard he flew 35 missions, when 100 was the tour, and all of them were "in-country" in South Vietnam!

Upon my return to the Seventh Air Force HQ in Saigon, I briefed the commander on my reactions, all good except dire comments about the wing commander in charge of O Clubs. But I gave some blood and portions of my rear when I was brusquely informed that "These things are important." To show how wrong I can be, that wing CO retired with two stars, as a major general!

After General Moore returned to the U.S., my duty as chief of staff was brief. The new commander of the Seventh Air Force wanted a general in my slot, so he had a one-star position in Thailand transferred to Seventh Air Force chief of staff position and requested a buck general to fill the Thailand slot, making me available for reassignment. See? General Moore, bless him, had insisted on approving my new duty station, which I shall try to describe.

The Seventh Air Force commander was responsible for USAF combat units in South Vietnam and Thailand, while the Thirteenth Air Force commander in the Philippines supervised housekeeping and supply of the Thailand units. This was a lot of spaghetti for the two commanders to eat with one fork, so an intermediate command was established in Udorn, Thailand — deputy commander of the Seventh /Thirteenth Air Forces — with a major general commanding. I was reassigned as the *assistant* deputy commander, Seventh/Thirteenth Air Forces, a colonel slot from which the brigadier general slot had been transferred to chief of staff, Seventh Air Force. Clear? There's more.

The ambassadors to Thailand and Laos had ultimate control and responsibility for combat Operations in those countries and had their own air forces, Air America and Continental Air. The military attachés, especially Air Force, answered only to the ambassador, and were resented by the commands in Vietnam. The Military Assistance Advisory Groups (MAAG) also had a tough job to do, under vague guidance.

I developed great respect for the attachés and MAAG Joes, and gained friendships that I would have liked to continue, but we just never seemed to cross paths again. Though I did have a run-in with one boy in blue, a colonel who was junior to me (but who wasn't by then?) in the Air Force Section of the MAAG — the kind of guy who would make you want to punch him in the mouth for just saying hello! I don't recall the subject, but if there hadn't been several Embassy types around, there would have been a fracas.

The next day, the Army general bossing the MAAG called me and said that he had been looking for a way to unload the dunce, had been informed of the incident, and assured me that the jerk would be on an airplane, soon! Wasn't that nice?

Our Headquarters had a Command Post and could monitor strike and search/rescue communications. We were "info" (informed) on frag (operational) orders laying out the next day's plans: strike forces, target assignments, air refueling, search and rescue, and specialized fighters for surface-to-air missile and radar suppression. The morning briefing covered the previous day's results and that day's efforts.

The U.S. Ambassador to Thailand was quite sensitive about the use of "his" forces and his relative rank with the military commanders in Saigon. There was a message from the top Headquarters in Saigon, convening a meeting at our Headquarters and inviting the ambassadors to Thailand and Laos. In a message to the world, our ambassador curtly stated that he "did not *attend* meetings in Thailand, he *convened* them!" Then he proceeded to invite the same people, at a slightly different date.

The Command Post had a rather unique feature, which caused embarrassment to any meeting attendees who were not forewarned. The chairs around the conference table had been ingeniously designed by one of the Thai contractors and had padded seats and arms, but also had an unbelievable center of gravity! The range of motion was such that when the seated one leaned back, there was the impression that he was going to end up on his backside, resulting in undignified scrambling and grabbing at the table sides.

I suggested to my two-star boss that we should get new chairs or warn meeting attendees of the thrill awaiting them. He didn't agree, and left for the Zone of Interior soon thereafter. The new commander wanted meetings held in a new Operations center, which solved the problem. I sure wanted a couple of those chairs to set up in my family room to deflate any of the pompous bent!

I had interesting dealings with the three-star general in charge of housekeeping and supplies, who had reached his rank in SAC. I sensed some inadequacies in the supply area when F-4 and F-105 commanders pointed out acres of tip tanks for the P-80, which was no longer operational, and the F-100, which was based in South Vietnam and was being phased out! I noted that he only visited Udorn every two or three months but never the fighter bases. Probably he had been so directed by the Seventh Air Force commander, the combat boss.

We had a photo reconnaissance wing, some A-1 Skyraiders, and a T-28 squadron, with a base commander reporting to our HQ. He was a colonel, a grounded navigator, who had the most abject fear of the general that I have ever seen. While he was sitting in my air-conditioned office, I would tell him that we would have a visit from *him*, and watch the perspiration saturate his uniform. And the general wasn't even there yet! I'm sure he went through several uniforms during his tour.

My commander seemed to be away during these tribulations, so I accompanied the base CO, mainly propping him up. The general would be happily ripping big hunks off someone for something minor (stacks of cans not precisely aligned, for example) then turn to me and say, "And what are you doing about these things, Hayes?"

My reply was, "Not a thing, General. I'm too concerned with how the war is being fought."

It then appeared that a stroke was imminent, but he managed to get out, "Where is your commander?"

"Off base, Sir, but I will be glad to put a call through to the commander, Seventh Air Force."

That made him blink, and he turned to the quivering base CO with, "Take me to my airplane." Which he did, and I saluted smartly. And you know, he never came back while I was there — for which the base CO thanked me effusively!

We had a fine troop and close friend, Mike Griffin, who acted as liaison officer in Bangkok. He probably had as many troubles as anyone in the theater; he had to babysit the civilian and military VIPs who found a trip to Bangkok essential to an understanding of the situation in Indochina. Most also found time for a token visit to Headquarters, then off to the night life, the beaches, Cheng Mai — Bangkok's famous market — for silk, and such. Mike handled it all, and we received nothing but outstanding reports on his performance.

I often imposed on his hospitality, on official occasions as well as a chance to break the routine. I don't think he knew that I used his name when I flew combat in the T-28s and A-1s — something about the Intelligence snoops thinking I knew too much to be exposed. The squadron COs were briefed to use my name if missing, or splattered, but I often wondered at Mike's reaction if he read that *he* was missing or bought the farm!

There has been lots written about Air America, the CIA's clandestine airline, so I won't discuss the pros and cons of the operation, just my personal contacts. The boss and deputy were tops, even if they were former Navy and Marine Corps! They told us what they were allowed to, and opened their club to us pending construction of our Officers Club. Lots of our pilots were saved in enemy territory when picked up by scruffy looking guys in dirty choppers and airplanes.

As part of the orientation, I flew to the U.S. Embassy in Vientiane, Laos, with Air America. Everyone wore civilian clothes and carried no identification on the person. Spooky. I visited some of the radio observation points, most surrounded by unhappies, and all lonely and isolated. An unofficial agreement, Air America moved their people in by air during the wet season, and got the hell out the same way when the dry season came.

I visited the HQ of the most outstanding guerrilla leader in Laos. Lunch was like nothing I had seen, with tepid native beer. The food was great, except that I mentioned that I hankered for hot food! The peppers are smaller than a pea and bring forth the tortures of the damned!

When I regained composure, and some relief, the general presented the *pièce de résistance*. We walked out to an enclosure of bamboo, about 20 square yards filled with prisoners. He handed me his .45, and said, "You shoot one?"

It was like a bad dream beyond comprehension. I tried to back out with, "No, Sir, I only shoot from airplanes."

He took the automatic back and shot the nearest prisoner in the head. It was the worst experience of my life, but most shocking was that there was no attempt by the other prisoners to get away. They were simply dumb beasts awaiting the inevitable.

I only wanted to leave, but the general had the body pulled from the cage, an elephant tail bracelet cut off and presented to me. I guess I hid my feelings, but on the way back to Vientiane and Udorn, no one tried to talk to me and I abandoned the "memento" to the slip stream as soon as we were airborne. This is an example of the inhumanity of that war, and for every case involving our troops and Allies, there were a myriad by the enemy, which were generally ignored by our "media."

I flew 49 combat missions in the A-1 Skyraider, most out of Thailand. The Skyraider was a fabulous airplane, hard to believe it was of World War II vintage. It carried every ordnance in the book, sometimes all at once. The squadron was at Udorn with advance facilities at Nakhon Phanom on the Northeast border of Thailand. The entire operation was later moved to Nakhon Phanom.

I flew as wingman on most missions since there was lots of territory to learn in Laos and North Vietnam. Weather seemed to always be bad and when night was added to the problem, the feeling became the "high pucker" and "Nearer my God to Thee!"

The Skyraider pilots were unsung and invisible heros of the war, flying the most demanding missions of any — except possibly the F-105 drivers, and even they had comparatively short target area times. The A-1s would spend one or two hours over the enemy, trying to locate targets, miss friendlies, and attack through clouds obscuring the mountains! Then rescue escort and cover required maximum time — all hazardous, since the enemy knew where the pilot was and surrounded the position with guns.

One of my last missions was in a flight assigned ResCAP — rescue combat air patrol — for an F-105 Thunderchief Tiger shot down 25 miles southwest of Hanoi. He had gone down in late afternoon the day before, and we were following a flight that had located him before dark set in.

All sorts of things happened, mostly bad, but this was a real effort: F-4 Phantoms on MiGCAP and SAM suppression, F-105s suppressing flak and SAMs, A-1s on close rescue chopper escort, others on area suppres-

sion, and eight for smokescreen cover of the pick-up. It was a good feeling to bring one Yankee home — we were, by God, doing something right!
Luckily, we didn't have to get White House or congressional permission,
or I would have probably retired in 1970 with an A-1 still strapped to my
rear awaiting the OK for pick-up!

One Sikorsky HH-3 Jolly Green Giant Rescue helicopter was shot
down, but we finally got the fighter jock out and to Nakhon Phanom. I met
him later in the O Club, and asked what his target was.

"Colonel, did you see a bamboo bridge about three miles northwest of
my position?" I had, because it was one of the hot flak points and we sent
a bunch to quiet them down.

"This is our fifth day against that sonofabitch and I'm the sixth Thud to
go down." Six Thuds for a bamboo bridge! It's called "interdiction" in Air
Force manuals.

It was never discovered that I was flying combat because of the cooperation and understanding of the combat folks, my explaining absences as
"field trips," and Mike Griffin's name on lots of combat reports!

During one of my combat flights, I lost a bunch of my right wing (about
four feet) from the big stuff attacking targets in Laos. I felt a pretty good
jolt and the A-1 tried to roll right — *real* hard!

The wing pulled up and said, "Boy, you really been hit!" I was tempted
to say "Naaah," or some other smart remark, but I bit my lip until he said,
"If you can just get back to Thailand, you can bail out."

Then I knew there was a problem! My name would have to be on the
mission summary as a combat casualty. We headed for Udorn, squadron
HQ, and I experimented with various configurations for landing. With
gear down, partial flaps, I could not overcome the rolling tendency at any
airspeed less than cruise. Udorn had a long runway, but *that* long?

I called for the arresting cables and lowered the tailhook, which didn't
come down! I touched down just beyond the approach cables — wheels
first, obviously — and went screaming down the runway. Even applying
maximum brakes, I still hit the barrier like a bat out of hell!

The squadron commander was waiting for me in his jeep and off we
went. I asked if there was an A-1 pilot about to end his tour and he said
there was, scheduled to fly the last one the next day. I met the pilot in Ops
and said, "Son, that was a great job of landing and what a way to end your
tour." We even drove him out to the shattered Skyraider, showered him
with fire hoses and champagne, and he and I celebrated in the Club. He

was a basket case the next morning when we poured him on the airplane for home. I've often wondered if he knew what the hell happened!

Combat missions in the T-28 were unique. A trainer configured with bomb and missile racks and a gun pod, the T-28 was used only in Laos. Flights were led by USAF Commando pilots or the few Laos pilots with U.S. training. Wingmen were straight off the farm, had never driven anything more complicated than a bicycle, if that. They received 75 hours of flight time, most in the T-28, and were off to war!

In accordance with the unique ground rules in Southeast Asia, we would lead a flight of four from Udorn, unarmed, land in Vientiane and be armed, serviced, and briefed. When possible, an English-speaking Laotian pilot would be in the flight or airborne with the forward air controller. Most of the time there was a glitch, and we had to be damn sure that we had crystal-clear hand and aircraft signals.

On my first mission briefing, I emphasized the signal for "Leave the formation and return to base," which really meant, "Get the hell outta here before ya bust my rear!" I was informed that the condensed training program had not included navigation; the wingmen were trained to bomb on Willy Pete (white phosphorus smoke markers) or on the leader's hits, and had to be led to and from the target.

I was tempted to ask what happened if lead was shot down, but decided I wouldn't like the answer, so I carried on. I found that there were inadequacies in my first briefing: the flight was to follow me at five-second intervals, 35° attack angle, drop the bomb, and strafe.

Something made me look back on the attack. The Tigers were in close trail, figuring they were going to drop on my release. Things were perfect for my bomb to eliminate Number Two, his bomb to do the same on Number Three, with the results that Ole lead (me) would be the only survivor, and Four's bomb would be the only effective one.

There followed the damnedest rat race, me trying to get enough spacing to bomb, my Laotian Tigers determined to show the Yankee that they couldn't be shaken. Finally, we bombed the target, plus or minus five miles, flew back to Vientiane, disarmed and serviced, and then back to Udorn.

I flew 21 combat missions in the T-28 and lots more around the area — wonderful airplane. I gained respect for the Laotian fighter pilots and I think that they finally accepted me.

The Royal Family of Thailand are all of that — *royal*! I saw the reverence in which they are held by the people and had several opportunities to observe them, including the Annual Military Ball hosted by the King and Queen.

Also, there was an incident when the aircraft carrying the Queen and Queen Mother was forced to land at Udorn, en route to Bangkok, because of weather. My boss was away, so I hurriedly had his air-conditioned trailer prepared for the visitors. Dinner was brought over from our officers mess, and served by Thai waitresses. In a few hours, the weather cleared and the royal party departed, after the most gracious of thanks. The American Consul was still making plans and then cancelling them when we let him off the hook!

I commanded a flood relief effort to Cheng Mai in northern Bangkok, and was honored by Her Majesty presenting me with the Medal of the Thai Red Cross at an audience in Bangkok.

The Awards and Decorations policies during Vietnam were established as if the USA had never fought a war:

1. Any flight in South Vietnam — transport, administrative, or training — was credited as a combat mission! People were rewarded 50 to 100 Air Medals, 10 to 20 Distinguished Flying Crosses, and never fired a shot. This was curtailed later, but in future conflicts it is hoped that there will be no awards until the threats are evaluated. In the Royal Air Force, and other services, awards are for valor only. At last count, a USAF type can slap on 24 to 26 ribbons, and never even be scared!

2. The KC-135 tankers refueled fighters and recce (reconnaissance) aircraft over Thailand or the Gulf of Tonkin, with no enemy ground fire or fighters, and logged "combat" time from takeoff to landing. B-52s did the same. They were over enemy territory, and lost some, but the hazard did not exist from takeoff to landing!

3. Combat pay was given to non-combat types solely because they were there, and it was amazing how out-of-country transport business increased on the last and first days of each month!

And I would like to say again that somewhere, soon, historians will recognize the injustice and devote volumes to the bravery, dedication, and unselfishness of the gallant armed forces of the Republic of Vietnam,

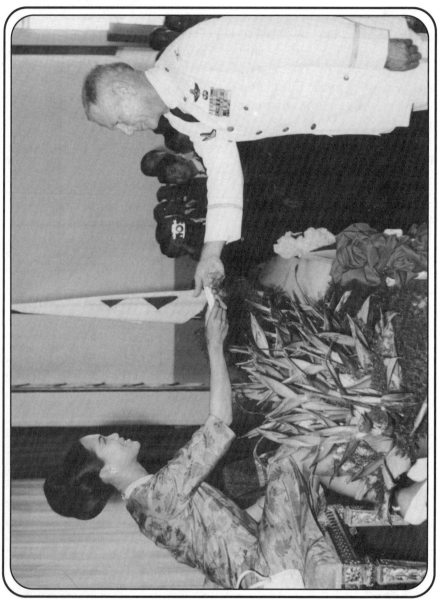

The Queen of Thailand presenting Jack Hayes with the Royal Thai Order of the Red Cross for work directing flood relief of Cheng Mai in 1967.

CHIEF OF STAFF, SUPREME COMMAND
MINISTRY OF DEFENCE
BANGKOK, THAILAND

3 July 1967

Colonel Jack W. Hayes
Tactical Fighter Wing
Langley Air Force Base, Virginia
U.S.A.

Dear Colonel Hayes:

On behalf of your many Thai friends, including myself, let me say that your tour in Thailand passed too quickly. We appreciate your interest in our country and its culture, as well as your personal contribution to the Free World effort to defeat aggression in Southeast Asia.

We hope you will remember Thailand and the Thai Armed Forces officers with whom you become acquainted, and that your successful military career will continue for many years. Someday, our paths will cross again, and I look forward to seeing you again.

Sincerely,

DAWEE CHULLASAPYA
Air Chief Marshal, RTAF

just as if they fought the long war alone — which they really did, you know!

I acknowledge the checks and balances of our executive and legislative branches in our democratic system, but they should be involved in approving war plans, declaring war, and getting the hell out of the way so that the military can fight the war!

When a president proudly states, "They cain't bomb a craphouse over there, lessen I tell 'em they kin," you have found the best way to lose!

A prime principle of war is the denying of supplies and equipment to the enemy by destroying the source and/or cutting (interdicting) all lines of supply. Operating west of Hanoi or exiting over the Gulf of Tonkin, countless stacks of freight and every type of freighter from every country in the world could be seen. And none had any camouflage or gun protection. So we wasted airplanes and men on the Ho Chi Minh Trail.

And what brought the Vietnamese to the Paris "Peace" Talks? The mining of harbors and bombing of Hanoi. And our Feather Merchant Whiz Kids in Washington acted like they had been the ones to discover gunpowder!

Then, of all the stupidity, the first chance to win the war is thrown away with the peace treaty, when everyone knows that it's just a piece of paper to the Vietnamese. And with the treaty came the greatest humiliation in American history.

Sometime, one of the "Peaceniks" is going to gloat over the outcome of the "war" in my hearing, and I'll be over the edge! And that goes for the apologists, without the guts to stand up for their country!

Chapter 16

Tactical Air Command
to Retirement

I RETURNED TO THE ZI in May 1966. Margee and the sons met me at Travis AFB after stopping at Reno to pick up the car I had ordered from Bangkok. The boys had sweet-talked Margee, and thus me, into a Pontiac GTO, and caused Margee Lou anxiety and shortness of breath scorching up the roads to Travis. I had a hunch they had become acquainted with guardians of highway safety, but got only silence and far-away looks when I asked about frequency and amount of fines. I still don't know.

The Secretary of Defense at the time, Robert McNamara — when he wasn't personally assisting the president in day-by-day conduct of the war (and people wonder why we lost!) — dabbled in things which the military didn't think were any

I was assigned duty as Director of Fighter Operations responsible for training and Operations of all tactical fighter units.

of his damned business! For example, he directed that the amount of duty-free booze allowed to GIs returning from overseas duty be decreased from whatever it was to one quart per soldier.

Always "by the book," I listed six bottles of a gin known as the Holy Water of Gins, hoping that Customs would consider that a fair amount to bring home, and look no further. Like in certain gift-wrapped items, bottles were labeled, "Medicinal: treatment of certain spiro-coccus of Southeast Asia." And, bottles of "Purified Water."

My contacts with the Customs Service have often, and mainly, been unpleasant, but I met a gentleman! He stopped me from opening my luggage, looked over the declaration form, and said, "You Air Force guys can't even count." He crossed out the "six," inked in "one," gave me a wink, and said, "Welcome home, Colonel." A warm, warm, feeling and a memory to last forever.

The family reunion was slightly dampened when I heard about the nights in Reno. The lads weren't allowed in the gambling rooms, yet could sit in the lobby with slot machines all around, dine with the booze flowing, and attend a stage show complete with drunks, dirty jokes, and topless babes! The Sin Cities sure have trouble when they try to demonstrate morality.

We then took a leisurely trip to Virginia visiting friends and relatives, stopped by the Air Force Academy and the Golden Dome of Notre Dame, but none of it rubbed off. No regrets, but I do admit to an oft-recurring dream: Margee Lou and I in the Notre Dame stadium, the Fighting Irish playing someone like Southern Methodist, maybe, and the announcer says, "Quarterback Hayes, Left halfback Hayes, Right halfback Hayes," or any combination. But life couldn't be better with the three fine gentlemen and their families that we have.

I was assigned duty as Director of Fighter Operations responsible for training and Operations of all tactical fighter units. The exception was the 4th TAC Fighter Wing flying F-4 Phantoms at Seymour Johnson AFB, North Carolina. They had been designated as "Test" because the fighter folks were trying to convince the SAC bomber weenies that the organization in World War II and Korea really did work and that maybe imposition of the SAC philosophy would screw up a great fighting force.

The Directorate consisted of 16 of the finest officers it has been my privilege to know — and not all fighter pilots! Even a navigator was accepted and made a part of the team — a rare accomplishment. They reminded me of the Command Post guys; they bitterly resented relegation to the role of staff officer, but by God, if that was what they had to do, they would be the best frapping staff officers in TAC! And they were.

My strong right arm was Chief Master Sergeant Richards, the highest enlisted rank. We reported in at the same time, and I was so impressed that I made him executive officer, a major's slot, and he did better than most majors could have. I heard that the other Directorate executives were perturbed by a non-com being in their august group, until the two-star Operations boss mentioned that it would please him greatly if all the Directorate administrations were up to the standard of the fighter folks!

We were responsible for planning, organizing, and directing fly-bys and aerial reviews, leading me to a first encounter with the splintering of responsibility and authority in all the Headquarters elements — separate domains and chains of command for weather, communications, Intelligence, and even the damned Postal Service!

To focus on communications: I was charged with an airlift demonstration of the short takeoff and landing capabilities of the C-130 Hercules transport. Among other things, aircraft were to land, demonstrate the back-up, and go again before the next clod crunched down. I sensed that there would be a problem when the tower chief questioned my need and/or authority to enter those hallowed grounds. Access was granted only when I quoted from the Articles of War and the Manual of Courts-Martial, and this was just the beginning!

My control team was very icily informed that radio communications were a responsibility of the Communications Service and any instructions to the units participating would be transmitted by the tower chief, if he deemed such directions valid, necessary, and in line with what he was going to say anyway.

I promptly convened a meeting with the tower chief and explained that I would control the demonstration through my team and that he was welcome to hang around but really wasn't needed.

Then came the greatest challenge to authority in my career. I was informed that he was entrusted with sole responsibility for tower operation by the chief of staff of the USAF, the commander of USAF communications, and the Almighty, in that order. And I could bug off!

I calmly explained that we were at decision time: 1. I could knock him on his keister and take over the microphone, wherein he could prefer charges against me for court-martial; 2. I would give a direct order that I was running the control tower and would have him under arrest for court-martial; 3. Since 1 and 2 involved someone getting in trouble, just give me the frapping mike and get the hell out — which finally happened, after the direct order.

But he was a real hard loser. I could see him on the next level down, pacing and frothing, and he undoubtedly made a phone call because appearing on the scene was a captain with the mission of re-asserting the authority of Communications Command.

It wasn't much of an encounter. He approached me and said, "Colonel?" To which I responded, "Captain, don't you understand the proper procedure in addressing an officer senior to you?"

He obviously didn't, so ensued a cryptic and pointed lecture on military courtesy, customs of the service, and ended with, "Who in the Gawd damned hell are you and what the hell do you want?"

By this time, he couldn't answer any questions, so he saluted and we could hear him chewing out the former tower chief for having bothered him. The demonstration went off with no problems, I'm proud to say, and we were entrusted with more high-level demos, including President Dwight D. Eisenhower's funeral.

I T-Birded to all the fighter bases (with a "seeing-eye" captain or major from the Directorate in the back seat to keep me from hurting myself and to check the pulse at the base working level), and found it reunion time — lots of old friends. No problems that weren't well in hand, with all the fighter expertise from top to bottom!

Later, the SAC element running the Air Force realized that there was an untapped source of general officer promotions in Tactical Air Command, and assigned fair-haired boys to Command and staff positions, Stateside and non-combat areas, of course. This really screwed up the fighter business, and I don't know if things are any better now. General officers donned the fighter pilot label and then claimed combat missions and flying time equating to 15 to 20 hours per sortie, or more!

The primary mission of TAC was training combat replacement pilots, and tactical fighter wings were converted to that function, one or more wings per each type of aircraft. It was evident that a critical shortage of fighter pilots was developing. The entire force was completing combat tours and manning tactical fighter wings. The chief of staff directed that there would be no second tours, except for volunteers, until every Air Force pilot had completed a tour in Vietnam — not necessarily combat.

There were numerous volunteers for second tours, but commanders were allowed to designate individuals as "critical," which was accepted by most. But stories abound of the angles used by jocks who "Just had to get back to the war!"

One of the best had to do with a character who was famous for wiping out the glass in the Air Force Academy Dining Hall during a graduation high-speed pass. The cadets loved it, and called themselves "The *Glass* of '65" — if that was the year. All that saved a court-martial was that the Operations order had directed a pass at Mach .94, and someone forgot to compute density altitude and other variables, resulting in a true airspeed of Mach .99 and a beautiful shock wave! He was soon on his way to his first combat tour in the F-105 Thunderchief.

He finished his tour in the Thud and lots of folks hadn't, since they were operating in the highest-risk area — around Hanoi and wading through surface-to-air missiles, flak, and MiGs. He wanted to extend his tour, but at the time it wasn't allowed. So he was sent back to the ZI and was assigned to a Southern base as instructor pilot in the F-4 Phantom.

The Tiger had no sooner started his new duties when the first of many "Request for second combat tour as a volunteer" was received for action. These were all returned with: "Officer's duty assignment has been designated as 'Critical,' in accordance with Air Force Regulations and request is disapproved."

Because officer trainees in the fighter training units were mostly without fighter experience, training problems developed — *i.e.*, weapons systems requiring 15 to 20 hours for fighter pilot proficiency took at least 70 hours to attain *minimum* proficiency for the multi-engine and bomber types.

Our hero recognized two ways that he could exploit this situation: 1. Scare the bejeezus out of the trainee(s) until a request was submitted for training in something (*anything*), not a fighter; 2. Recommend them all for disqualification, and he would then be recognized as lacking in instructor pilot abilities and would be back to the wars!

This approach was abandoned when authorities let it be known that instructional ability was an essential element in pilot performance — *ergo*, inadequacy in that field would result in loss of flying status.

His final act of desperation was to lead a flight of four Phantoms, requesting that the tower tell the world they were going to "see something." Here comes the flight, on initial approach for peel-off and land, echeloned right, but lead is *inverted*, which he maintained through his turn to the final approach, including lowering gear and flaps. He rolled upright at about 500 feet, and touchdown!

I don't know what happened to him, and I don't want to!

The contingency plans of Tactical Air Command called for augmenting the overseas commands with fighter, reconnaissance, and airlift forces in the event of limited of general war. The latter was somewhat moot, since the nukes would eliminate the overseas bases, to say nothing of U.S. TAC forces!

The boss felt that I should take a team to the European Theater and evaluate the support capabilities of bases that would receive TAC elements. I figured that he should know since he had commanded U.S. Air Forces in Europe before taking over TAC, but I didn't mention that.

The findings were no surprise. At the latitude that was the transfer-of-command point, from Stateside to European or Pacific commands, you better by God know who you were working for *now*, forget the regulations you had been under, and never make the mistake of saying "We used to do it this way," wherever you came from. Not only would there be a need to get your foot out of your mouth, but to extract someone else's foot from your rear!

Following normal courtesy, we started with the senior European commands and, with no courtesy, were shunted off to the lowest echelon, division as I recall. Not to be confused with Army division, in the Air Force the division commands two or three wings and doesn't really know what the hell they'll be doing when "The balloon goes up" — a quaint description for the outbreak of war.

Laid on for us were cocktail parties, dinners, and sightseeing tours, a sure sign that our hosts didn't have the foggiest notion of the status of TAC deployment bases. They finally whipped up a briefing, delivered by one of those golden-tongued boys who make a career of selling horse manure and making it taste like honey!

Unimpressed, I snuck out to a couple of bases that were in the TAC plans and it was like visiting old Eighth Air Force bases in England; the facilities were outdated and in disarray. It was a paper exercise, last priority.

USS *Pueblo* Crisis — An Exercise in Futility

In January 1968, the 83-man crew of the USS *Pueblo* was taken hostage by the North Koreans after the ship was captured in the Sea of Japan. The crew was released in December. It was a crisis that should not have been, and the U.S. Navy crew did what they could — suffered indignities and abuse from the North Koreans, and, even worse, were ignored by their countrymen when finally released. During captivity, despite poor physical condition, they posed for North Korean publicity pictures with hands arranged in the Western sign for "Copulate you," or half of the "V" for victory sign!

Their captors couldn't miss the standard hand positions, and when queried the crew explained that this was an American Indian sign for "good luck." (There are different versions as to the explanation, but it worked; the pictures were distributed internationally, and the world had a good laugh.)

The story is that there would have been no crisis and capture had Fifth Air Force staff procedures outlined actions to be taken in various contingency plans. The crisis arose after duty hours and on a weekend, duty officers were unfamiliar with the code name "*Pueblo*," and messages were left in "Incoming" until a Navy liaison officer found them on Sunday.

By then, the *Pueblo* had been boarded and was steaming for North Korea. Had action been taken on receipt of the first message, fighters could have been scrambled from South Korea and Japan in daylight, and there would have been one less vessel in the North Korean Navy — or at least safe return of the *Pueblo* to friendly waters.

Contingency plans existed for every possibility in Asia — general war, limited war, earthquakes, tidal waves, a shortage of rice, even an uncontrollable outbreak of social disease! But, as usual, the president called an emergency meeting of anyone who could possibly share the blame if the *Pueblo* situation turned dark brown, which it already was!

Alert duty officers on the battle staffs would be expected to bring up all plans that might be involved as soon as the *Pueblo* situation appeared, and maybe the air staff did. They sure weren't available to the Air Force chief, and when numbers questions were fired at him, some "boy in blue" fed him figures off the top of his head!

For some reason, figures that are presented at these panic meetings become engraved in gold, right or wrong, and the Service Chiefs are stuck with them. Any deficiency or excess from the magic number is addressed with, "Why have these figures changed?" or "Don't you know what the hell yer talking about?"

So, the contingency plans are waffled up to meet the magic numbers, with disregard of types of forces or equipment in the plan. Just make the numbers match. That's a helluva way to fight a war!

The magic number that came out of the "Panic Meeting" was unbelievable. The 4th Tactical Fighter Wing, which was mentioned earlier as being on test status to justify the age-old fighter organization, could have deployed with integral forces, some augmentation of logistic support aircraft, and additional aerial tankers in Guam.

A very normal deployment of forces turned bad, or as we used to say, "Able Sugar" (the initial letters standing for "Ape Shit!"). A Seventh Air Force F-4 Squadron from Vietnam was ordered to report to 4th TAC Fighter Wing for duty at Kunsan, South Korea, and airmen from the U.S. were assigned to the 4th for temporary duty. Transports, tankers, even air defense fighters were assigned to South Korea, and an Advance Headquarters, Fifth Air Force, was set up in Seoul.

Our leader could proudly say, "Movement of forces under way" — exactly the number of planes and people mistakenly advanced at the big meeting! Violating every rule of organization, management, and operations. But the numbers were right!

I was in the TAC Command Post helping with the deployment plans when it came out that the Ninth Air Force commander was between wing commanders at the "Fightin' 4th" — the former having left, the new one not back from overseas, and a well-experienced wing CO was felt necessary for the move, and maybe a shooting war.

The Ninth Air Force commander asked if I would volunteer to take the 4th Tactical Fighter Wing to Korea and do whatever had to be done, like "shoot 'em up," until the new commander arrived — who was Chuck Yeager, by the way. I was *asked* because I had only been back from Vietnam six months, and overseas duty can't be ordered before a year of ZI duty.

I convened a family meeting at our off-base quarters and can still picture Margee Lou and the lads as I outlined the problem — I couldn't be ordered to go, but felt I should. A brief huddle, and "We know you won't be happy if you miss this. Go get 'em Tiger!" (The question may arise: off-base quarters? By then, I was the highest-ranking colonel since Custer. I may explain this later, or maybe not.)

An F-4 arrived Friday evening with a seeing-eye Captain, Tony Cushenberry, who I got to know well during the Korean "Do." He had had a short time in pro football, chewed tobacco, and was a mean SOB — my kind of guy! And he was married to one of the sweetest, loveliest, and most demure ladies I ever met. Something else we had in common!

We loaded my gear in the belly-pod and we were off to Seymour Johnson AFB, me and my 16 hours in the F-4! I didn't fool anyone, especially Tony and the great major who helped me stumble across the Pacific, but they were very kind.

The advance party was held until I arrived and assumed command, which I thought was nice. Couldn't give much guidance since, as in all contingency plans, there was no information around on Kunsan Air Base or any other South Korean base. Like in the European Theater, the only way to find out the facilities and requirements of augmentation bases was to hike your rear over there and see for yourself.

So, besides having no indications as to base facilities, the ADVON, (advanced echelon, the team that was sent prior to moving the entire force) party leader had to tell Fifth Air Force, Fifth Air Force ADVON, and base personnel that he had no idea of numbers to expect — organizations, airplanes, people, or equipment. Where he could have presented a neat package of 4th Tactical Fighter Wing (Test) assets and requirements, all he knew was that the concept had been broken down and a mish-mash was on the way. All because of the "magic numbers" from the initial emergency meeting.

I saw the ADVON off, and held a short staff meeting just so they'd know who I was. Then I got the processing and shots, dinner, and snuck out to a Phantom for a little bootleg cockpit time. The 16 hours of flight training had been a while earlier, and I didn't understand all I knew about the F-4, then.

I forgot that the base would be on Alert posture, barely short of general war, and damned near got blown away before I talked (begged) the sentry into telling his bosses about the problem. He really told them — flashing lights, sirens, and I was spread-eagled on the cold ramp. The

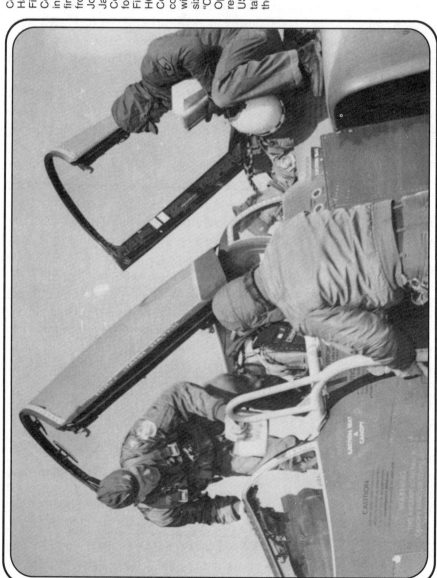

Colonel Jack W. Hayes, 4th Tactical Fighter Wing Commander, arrives in Korea with the first F-4D Phantom from Seymour Johnson AFB, on January 31, 1968. Colonel Hayes, former Chief of Fighter Operations, HQ Tactical Air Command, commanded the wing during the first six weeks of "Combat Fox" Operations in response to the USS *Pueblo* being taken hostage by the North Koreans.

Command Post *had* passed on the news that I was the new commander, and the sergeant of the guard pieced things together from the ID in my wallet, which he extricated from my back pocket with his foot on my neck.

I spent Saturday meeting people and learning about the deployment plans, one squadron per day. I was to fly with the first squadron, which was commanded by one of the Air Force's finest, Lieutenant Colonel Damewood ("Dagwood"), a member of aerobatic teams, Sierra Hotel fighter jock, and one I consider a great friend. Dag led his squadron and I flew element lead — not too well, until I felt better in the Phantom.

The number of meetings and conferences were few; there had been enough dry runs on preparation for emergency deployment. Besides, I wanted to give the married ones undisturbed time with families and the bachelors time to do whatever bachelors do before temporary duty, which I seem to have forgotten.

Sunday morning, at launch time, I had to strap the F-4 on well ahead of start-engine time to refresh my memory on gadgets and things like how to start. So the TAC commander, General Gabriel Disosway, had to come to my airplane for final words of guidance. He wished me good luck, and I raised a chuckle with, "General, tell our Navy friends that we'll find their goddamn boat."

It was ten hours and 45 minutes to Hickham AFB in Hawaii, requiring six refuelings — three over the U.S., and three over the Pacific. My "seeing-eye" major took the first two, giving me the chance to get the feel back, and I did the rest all the way to Korea. There were two different tanker forces, both KC-135s, with the first rendezvous shortly after takeoff for three refuelings, and the second over the Pacific for the last three.

The refueling planning over water is interesting. The first two are calculated to ensure enough fuel to return to the West Coast if refueling cannot be accomplished for mechanical reasons. The third is at a point where return is still possible, but to ensure reaching Hawaii there is maximum onload, meaning that the fighter is trying to keep from stalling off the boom while taking on the last few swallows.

A whole chapter could be devoted to air-to-air refueling, but briefly, the problems involve mating up entirely different aircraft and finding compatible, or nearly so, airspeeds, altitudes, and weight configurations. En route cruise is normally in the 30,000+ altitude, but the KC-135 had to descend to 25,000 for refueling and could only maintain 310 knots airspeed, not critical unless maximum onloads were involved. Then, the fighter angle-of-attack was such that maximum power was required to hang on the boom.

We found a system in the F-4 where one throttle was eased into first stage afterburner and the other was used to hold position. Even the first stage burner put out lots of flame, and we emphasized this at joint briefings. One night, not this particular trip, a spare tanker had been substituted and the pilot didn't know what to expect. I was approaching "stall or drop-off," so I slipped one go-knob (throttle) into afterburner and that was a real spectacular sight!

Thinking I was blowing up, or about to, the boomer called, "Emergency breakaway," etc. He retracted the boom while the tanker jock went to maximum power and climb, leaving me with a very lonely feeling. I finally talked them into coming back by including "shoot you down" threats, and we made it to our destination.

But back to our trip over the Pacific. I had noticed on Saturday that I was making an inordinate number of stops, even for a 48-year-old, at the men's john. I swore the duty quack to silence, laid on a sample from the "waterworks," and was informed that I had a bladder infection, which could be cured in a short time with miracle drugs.

This was nice to hear, but it didn't address the problem of disposing of the excess fluids in flight, a problem that would have been nonexistent in "our" airplanes, since Air Force contracts called for "relief tubes." I never figured out why this was not standard equipment in Navy/Marine fighters. Perhaps because of their short missions, enforced dehydration, large bladders, and/or shrunken male organs with minimal liquid flow capacity. I like the last reason!

I solved the problem with a quart plastic water bottle, one each, as the manual says. Relief times were planned just prior to refueling, but there were a bunch more, like every 20 minutes. I learned to smuggle the bottle off at the stops; I didn't want to hand the warm container to the VIP greeter!

It was smooth as silk to Hawaii, except for a small problem on landing. Old Dag, our squadron lead, was without airspeed for the approach, so we sent his wingman and mine in first, and the Dag flew my wing for landing

— my first since initial transition! And I was sweating getting down on my own. I had bunches of help from the back seat, and made it.

Dag and I were escorted to the office of Commander, Pacific Air Forces — a SAC man all the way — and we were from the ZI! (See my previous comments regarding overseas commands and their own little worlds.) I could tell that The Man was aware of my transgressions in SAC, but knew that he was stuck with me. He asked if our crews (I hate the word "crews" in fighters) were all combat ready, when we were on our way to what could be a real ass-kicking contest!

After being assured of our combat status, he dismissed us — no "Good luck," no "Go get 'em," or anything. Dag and I didn't need it, but I wondered how the troops would have felt. When we saluted and about-faced, I realized that the fitting for my flying suit had been too hasty, since I was dragging part of the legs behind my heels, screwing up my about-face to a less-than-precise military position and verifying his low regard of this "SAC reject." But that was an accolade to me!

We had barely enough eating and sleeping time before having to report to briefing for the Hawaii to Guam trip. Tanker crews were on the left of the aisle, fighter guys on the right. I was talking with my troops when there came a real high level "Attention!" I was in the position with all the rest. Sonofabitch if there didn't come strolling down the aisle a real rookie bird colonel who was a major when I was in SAC!

He was the "Task Force Commander" since he was riding in the lead aerial gas station. Before he had a chance to grant the "At ease" to his minions, I was over to the detachment commander — a TAC man for Christ's sake — who was responsible for flight planning and briefing. Eyeball to eyeball, I informed him that it would be wise if, in the future, he would check seniority and not have a colonel with 17 years in grade "popping to" for a snotty-nosed junior birdman. Guffaws from the fighter side, even grins from the tankers, and I ignored the SAC weenie!

The trip to Guam was in the "Buddy configuration": flights of four fighters were assigned to each tanker, taking off directly behind and formatting on the tanker until after the fourth refueling, then smoke on in to Guam.

As an example of civilian/congressional control of the military, we were briefed for maximum climb as soon as we became airborne, then an immediate right turn toward the Pacific — for *noise abatement*, if you can believe it. This was no problem for us, but it was sickening to watch the tankers, with maximum load, drop a wing and stagger into a turn. The loss of an engine would have dropped them into the area they were protecting from the "bad old noise!"

Besides the climb, we were to come out of afterburners when airborne. I have a hunch everyone did what Dag's flight did — stayed in afterburner, on the deck until he was over water, then racked around to catch the tanker. That was our way of saying "F___ you" to the Hawaii rich folks for the tanker lads!

But then came the transmissions: "Fighter lead, did you understand the instructions about afterburner and max climb?"

Dag responded, "Say again?" Tower repeated the message.

Dag said, "Red Three [*meaning me*] did you copy?" Naturally me, Number Two, and Number Four failed to copy. The interrogation could only last so long because we had to contact en route control.

There was no follow-up by the tower. It is a truism that those en route to, or engaged in, combat are granted lots of privileges by the non-warriors, and, as far as anyone knew, we would probably be shooting and getting shot at.

We had some sticky weather en route, and Dag and I had to take our elements into close formation on opposite tanker wingtips. It was so bad that I could only see the wingtip and outboard engine; you had to hang onto that, it was your life's blood. We were quite "puckery" changing positions, to refueling, and back to the wing. But the conditions eased up and we flew into Anderson AFB, Guam, in the clear.

Then it was eat, sleep, eat, brief, and take off again for Kunsan, Republic of Korea, with one refuel. The weather was beautiful, and we were at our new home ready to kick ass and find the Navy's boat!

Dagwood thought it would be nice if the wing CO taxied in first — or was it my idea? Anyway, I led the first elements of 4th Fighter to the parking areas and a meeting with the three-star Fifth Air Force CO and bunches of colonels.

It could have been embarrassing because when I stepped off the ladder I noticed that I had failed to zip up after my last "personal de-fueling," and cameras were recording the historical moment. There was one shot as I stepped out of the cockpit where my checklist covered the private area, and all the pictures on the ramp were above waist level. Lucked out again!

Then came the introduction to "Alice in Wonderland!" The Fifth Air

Force commander took me to my new Headquarters, and my ADVON really ADVON'd — they had offices and quarters cleaned out for wing staff and left no doubt who would be running the show!

But then the "wonderland" was exposed when I was instructed on how the show would be run. I knew that Air Force functions had splintered and ignored command lines, but this was ridiculous. The base commander — who I quickly informed was responsible for support only, and to forget the base CO part — was to operate under some clown at Fifth Air Force ADVON, who would approve any orders I directed regarding base functions.

Also, the communications officer would respond to directives in that area only if approved by *that* clown at ADVON. All kinds of little staff officers were dying to clarify my *modus operandi*, and they were shocked when I respectfully informed the Fifth CG that I had not signed Assumption of Command General Orders and requested air transport to my home station, allowing him to designate a wing commander.

I didn't do this because I thought I was so essential, but because there would be a first-class intra-Air Force donnybrook. But the theme changed and the rule became: orders from the 4th Fighter Wing CO (me) would be complied with, and Fifth Air Force staff would be notified *after the fact*. This was one of my greatest Air Force accomplishments, but lots of ass-kicking was still required (there's always someone who doesn't get the word).

After a quick tour of the base, I knew that I had been dropped into the brown stuff — again. Quarters were only enough for the small house-keeping staff, but I was informed that Air Force engineers would be setting up tent cities for quarters, supply, and technical offices. The workers were late showing up but the logistics dumped more tents, cots, and blankets on us than we could store. So we just tied tarps across the stuff and to hell with it!

This was January, with freezing winds and many feet of snow. We were using the bowling alley and warehouses as quarters and put mess hall on 24-hour shifts, with augmentation from 4th Fighter support folks. When the engineers arrived, they produced — as always — and we finally had adequate quarters and work areas. But we still had functions like Field Maintenance spread out.

People had to come first, but I had the "Pearl Harbor shakes" when I saw the parking facilities for the F-4 Phantoms. There was no dispersal plan, or revetments, and aircraft were lined wingtip to wingtip on the closed runway, on parking ramps, and taxiways. We still hadn't learned!

We couldn't sit and hope that the MiG pilots would have severe vision problems, poor sighting systems, and guns that always jammed, so I worked with Fifth Air Force ADVON and developed a dispersal plan. In every F-4 there was a map with headings to a base of dispersal and enough fuel to get there. A crew was assigned to each aircraft continually, and the code name for launch was "Flush."

The jocks felt that "Flush" was lacking in clarity and often substituted "Shit and Git," which made sense, but I stuck with "Flush," to show my couthness. I ran three surprise exercises with excellent response times, supposing adequate warning, and scared the hell out of the natives. They had lots of company on the one we pulled at three a.m., but it didn't shake the fighter guys, and there wasn't even a scratched wingtip!

At the initial briefing the question was raised, "What if we're airborne when the base is attacked?"

I answered, "If the attack is over and the field is unusable, go to the dispersal base. If conditions allow, land at home base. If the attack is under way when you arrive, you tell me what you do."

They came up with a beautiful response: "*Kick ass!*"

We were shown reconnaissance pictures of the *Pueblo* at dock and the living area nearby housing the crew prisoners. So what did we do? Flew escort and cover for Air Force C-130s converted to "Snoopy Birds" and cruising off the east coast of North Korea, monitoring radio traffic and radar activity. We were over international seas, watching the MiGs, visually and on our radar, who were climbing above our altitude and paralleling our course. Shades of the Korean War.

More engineers arrived and set up tent cities at two other Republic of Korea Air Force bases so we could disperse two of the squadrons, and spread out the two squadrons remaining at Kunsan. It was a useless and expensive operation, the danger existed when we first arrived and we would have been under mass attack with the first sign of aggression on our part. But when it became obvious that the U.S. was really "candy ass," why should they attack? That loss of face was tough for us to take.

I mentioned that the Commander, Pacific Air Forces, was SAC to the core and there was an "incident" on his visit to Kunsan. I was driving him and the Fifth Air Force three-star around the base — how's that for career

Colonel Jack Hayes (right) awaiting the change of command ceremony at the 4th Fighter Wing, Korea, March 23, 1968.

progression? — when the Fifth gent asked, "How many more people are required for this *new* Fighter Wing organization?" (My emphasis.)

The PACAF leader replied, "Four hundred to five hundred more, depending on the weapons system." (We call them fighters.)

I had to respond to the gauntlet with "Sir, I have a briefing I can give you which demonstrates the results of the 4th Fighter Wing test — namely, no increase in manning, and in some areas reduction."

The commander snapped back, "Hayes, if I want any comments from you I'll let you know. Otherwise, you drive this car where you're told and keep yer mouth shut."

I did for a while, but then I *had* to say, "Sir, does that mean you don't want to hear my briefing?"

I heard some gurgling noises from the rear, and in the mirror saw the Fifth general trying to keep the other one from doing bad things to me while shouting, "Go to his airplane, Hayes, *go to his airplane!*"

At the foot of the boarding ladder, ever the epitome of military courtesy, I saluted and said (graciously, I thought), "Genrul, ya'll come back and see us reel soon, ya heah?"

This seemed to delay the boarding process a bit, but the Fifth general finally got him on, and went to his airplane, without even saying "So long." I saw him later, and nothing was mentioned.

It has always been keen for commanders of combat units in a combat/near combat area to pretty much give the officers who were leading the actual combat free rein. The attitude was, "Hey, these are the guys gonna be fightin' so let 'em go." Of course, there was an additional motive for them to let us do as we pleased: "If they can him, *I* might get assigned to take his place!"

Just as an example, I met the commander, Republic of Korea Air Force, early on, and we hit it off real good. They were still flying F-86s and vintage choppers, and he asked me if I could arrange flights in the F-4 for two senior civilian officials. I told him "No sweat," and we did. Air Force regulations required reams of paper before an American civilian could fly in an Air Force jet — and no way for a foreign national — so why even ask?

Two of our finest gave them the maximum takeoff and climb, where you reach 40,000 feet real soon, look over your shoulder and the field is directly under you! There was, however, some concern when one of the VIPs wanted to show he understood ejection procedures by pulling the "go handles." So it wasn't hard to believe that the ROK government soon bought the F-4. And the ROK Air Force boss gave me a farewell party you wouldn't believe!

While waiting for Chuck Yeager to take over my command, we had several *good* farewell parties for me. When Chuck arrived, I met him at the line, in front of my Phantom, with the same seeing-eye major in back. We held a brief change of command ceremony, I introduced Chuck to key staff (wondering where the hell the squadron COs were), and we were off.

We made a couple of rolls off the deck, naturally, then off for Seoul and the grind home. We were smoking along at 400+ knots when my mentor in the back said, "Boss, I think you should throttle back and circle, there

Colonel Charles E. Yeager (left) assumes command of the 4th Tactical Fighter Wing upon his arrival at Kunsan Air Base, March 23, 1968. Colonel Jack W. Hayes returned to HQ Tactical Air Command to resume his duties as Chief of Fighter Operations.

are some troops who want to say 'so long.'" Doing as I was told, here came my four fighter squadron commanders as escort to Seoul, two on each wing through the approach. After I landed, they did a fly-by in the "Missing Man" formation. What can top that?

Then it was home again, I hoped for the last time before the Air Force tour was over. I had a few days off, then back to being Director of Fighter Operations. I didn't have much to tell the TAC commander, since we had been documenting the whole show and reported all with reams of paper. But I did feel that he should know about the repartee between me and the Commander, PACAF. The TAC commander, who was about to retire, told me I gave him one of the best laughs of his career. He certainly gave me some of my best memories!

We had a retirement ceremony for the outgoing commander. The new commander, General William Momyer, had spent his career in TAC. He was a World War II fighter ace, and had commanded the Seventh Air Force in Vietnam well enough to get his fourth star. He recognized me from Southeast Asia, but still kept me on as Director of Fighter Ops!

The Fightin' 4th redeployed after six months in South Korea, and no action. I got to Seymour Johnson AFB, North Carolina, to welcome the first squadron back, the one I had deployed with, but couldn't get back after that. I wanted to tell them "Good Show," but I know it wasn't missed. The only welcome those fighter jocks had in mind involved perfume and silk sheets — and, oh yeah, the kids!

Chuck Yeager finally got his star and went elsewhere, leaving a SAC type as commander of the 4th (another example of the Air Force using TAC slots to promote SAC fair-haired boys). The 4th had been home a short time when the new commander sent a message to COMTAC requesting waiver of the training requirements for the previous six months.

General Momyer called me and said that he understood that the 4th had been training, when not escorting the Snoopy Birds, which was right. We had full-time use of bombing and gunnery ranges, upgraded most of the backseaters, and kept the jocks busy to counter the frustrations of not kicking ass after a long trip. I explained this to the boss, closing with the remark that a *real* wing CO would have known this. He concurred, and directed me to educate that person on the ways of fighter pilots.

This was another one of my joyful career moments. It seems that this guy, let's say his name was Schmaltz, had been on the latest promotion list to general, but had not stuck the stars on yet. He appended "Brigadier General Designate" to the signature block after "Colonel, USAF" — sorta like sprinkling on holy water.

So my conversation with him went like this: "Schmaltz, this is Colonel Hayes, Director of Fighter Ops at TAC." I've been told that there is a nasty tone to my voice when perturbed, which I was.

I could almost hear his heels click with the response, "Yes Sir, Colonel Hayes. I have heard about the great job you. . . ."

"Lay off the B.S., Schmaltz, and just listen while I educate you! Fighter pilots know only one phrase, and attitude — 'Can Do' — and it seems that you were never taught this when you were deemed qualified to command a fighter wing."

I continued, adding more obscene — and probably insubordinate — language, and I damn near had him in close order drill in his office! The conversation terminated with his, "Thank you, Sir, for your help." Ecstasy, *sheer* ecstasy!

Once the 4th was back in the clutches of Air Force HQ, there transpired the biggest travesty in history. Folks had been "frozen" while in test status, so the Air Force changed that and scattered people around like buckshot — mainly to the sorriest assignments available, like it was their fault they had been in the 4th. They even sent some back to Korea, including Dagwood, even though I called in all the favors I could think of trying to change the orders. So, people who had been away from families for six months had to leave again for another 14, and settle families off base! All in the name of personnel management.

I was trying to forget a great experience that had turned dark brown, when the final straw dropped. It didn't break my back, but raised my ticked-off status to the highest ever. A Department of the Air Force letter, months old, with about 18 endorsements, had gone from the Pentagon Puzzle Palace through all the commands to Kunsan. The Republic of Korea retraced its return voyage, and the missive finally found me at TAC HQ.

Briefly, the Fightin' 4th had been in Kunsan couple of weeks when my sergeant major reported to me that the base Post Office had posted a notice that nothing had changed as far as they were concerned, and that the four-and-a-half day week, with one-and-a-half hour lunch periods, would remain in effect.

I asked the sergeant major if he would be so kind as to pass on a message to the technical sergeant Postmaster: "The Post Office would *immediately* assume a seven-day work week and that he would lose one stripe for every Gawd damned five-minute delay in compliance!"

Soon, there came a tip from a friend that the Air Force had directed adherence to the four-and-a-half day work week, and a message was en route so stating. So I had the sergeant major rustle up eight or so of the meanest chief or senior master sergeants, and had them seated around my office when the Postmaster requested a moment of my time.

To paint the picture: these were top people, all with over 20 years of service, and not too happy to be over there just sitting. So the degree of meanness was at a very high level.

In marched the smug mail shuffler. "Sir, I have a message from the Chief of Air Force Postal Services, stating. . . ."

But I interrupted him with, "Son, I wouldn't tell us about what you have in your hand. The gentlemen you see around you," giving him enough time to check out the meanies, "have reminded me that the mail service has not improved and, since my orders have been ignored, feel that it is time for direct and harsh physical retribution against those responsible for this sorry state."

This worthy had probably picked his career as one sure to be remote from combat, and now he was about to get the bejeezus kicked out of him! Obviously, a reply was not expected, nor would be accepted, from him.

So, I continued. "What's gonna happen now is, these gentlemen will accompany you while signs are changed to reflect the new Post Office operating hours, and assist you in answering questions from your subordinates, if they don't have the message."

I did weaken enough to direct augmentation of the Post Office by detailing junior airmen in the manual labor aspects of toting mail sacks. I was informed by the aforementioned "Postmaster" that *only* properly trained and certified specialists would be allowed to cope with mail sorting! The idiot still hadn't learned!

Anyway, the letter and 18 endorsements which launched me on this diatribe was originated by a slick-chested Pentagon captain demanding to know why a fighter wing commander, in a potential combat environment, had ignored his directive regarding Postal Service operations! The obvious question is why 18 Command Headquarters dignified the correspondence by passing it on. The way of the society of paper-shufflers, I guess!

But the whole thing had a real nice ending. General Momyer accepted my proposed 19th indorsement, "Noted," and sent it back to the Concrete Complex. That's the last we heard of it!

Next came the hot breath on the neck for Tactical Air Command when the commander of the Pacific Air Forces was named Air Force Chief of Staff. Sure enough, it wasn't long before the Air Force Inspector General, who just happened to have functioned as headhunter for SAC, conducted random inspections of TAC units to evaluate effectiveness and performance under SAC criteria.

It was no surprise when a voluminous report was received, detailing the inadequacies and wanton ways of Tactical Air Command, but the TAC commander couldn't believe that the Command had sunk to such depths. I was directed to form a team (I seemed to do a lot of that in my last Service days!) to visit the bases that had been inspected, and verify or dispute the report findings, evaluate corrective action taken, and recommend Command actions for the future.

As I may have mentioned, when the SAC folks brought "The Truth" to TAC, just prior to the Cuban Missile Crisis in October 1962, the theme was STANDARDIZATION. Every fighter, reconnaissance, or transport base was to be identical to every one of the same mission. Especially in the fighter racket, attempting to form all in the same mold violated every premise, personality, and attitude of a distinctly individual way of life.

The "Peace is Our Profession" types overlooked the fact that during the SAC ascendance, most of the bases were new and had been constructed to SAC uniform and specific outlines, whereas the fighter units inherited pre- or early World War II bases, some Training Command rejects, or commercial fields abandoned for new facilities. Standardize? Besides the problems, *why*?

Anyway, off I went with my team in our private transport airplane, the nasty report broken down by functions and assigned to guys who might know something about what was said.

I immediately encountered a problem. The new commander was strictly "straight arrow" and I was informed, just after wheels-up, that drinks would not be served, and furthermore, alcohol was not allowed on board!

The more senior of us were ensconced in the VIP section and had, naturally, packed enough personal spirits to carry us through any crises up to general war. So I instructed the chief steward that it would be unthinkable to impose on his staff for individual orders of soft drinks and ice and that he could, therefore, transfer those assets to our area and his folks could relax during the trip. And I instructed the junior officers in the main cabin that they would be available for consultation with us ranker(?) types and would report to the VIP section, as requested, with glass in hand.

There were some signs of mutiny from the crew members, and I couldn't blame them when some of our team were falling down a lot and experiencing airsickness. The dissension was quelled at our first stop, a gung ho fighter base, when I explained the problem. The married crew members were regaled with stories of parties and eyewitness accounts of dalliances — stories that would be passed on to marital partners, even before our return.

The single airmen were not threatened and were even invited to the NCO Club, where they were subdued by nasty looks and enjoined by the more senior crew members to just be quiet! So that problem passed!

But back to the purpose of the inspection follow-up team. The methods and conclusions of the Inspector General were laughable, to say the least, and totally without substance!

There must be some explanation of any IG report, which I'll try and make short: only deficiencies, shortcomings, and screw-ups are addressed. Good things, never! Normally, the unit commander addresses each item wherein he was found wanting, explains in detail corrective action taken, and promises to sin no more. The *mea culpa*. This report goes through higher commands where comments are made regarding previous comments.

Because this inspection was carried out under criteria unknown to Tactical Air Command, the Air Force Chief of Staff endorsed it, "For your information and corrective action." My team's job was to verify and evaluate discrepancies and recommend any Command action deemed necessary.

It was obvious from the start that we were facing a first-class "hatchet" job. Remembering that only discrepancies and deficiencies were to be noted, we found such things as: "Fighter pilots did not don G suits until at the flight line," "External power units were started prior to pilot pre-flight," and lots more.

Nothing says when you are supposed to put the G suit on, nor is there a stipulated time for starting power units, although the SAC mind would expect it. Besides, the G suit is tight and puts pressure on the "jewels," so it's normally the last equipment donned, and the crew chief usually wants the power unit warmed up for pre-flight.

I briefed the commander on our findings and he couldn't believe it, either. I had prepared a Command message to all units telling them what kind of horse manure to expect and to stand by the shovels. The boss signed, but gagged some when he read his letter to the chief of staff which I had prepared. Guess he sent one in saying, "Noted," which was best, I suppose.

He thanked me as I left and I got a laugh when I said, "Sir, I am probably the only officer in history to inspect the Inspector who pulled the rug out from under him!"

It was just a little while until retirement, and I stayed in the "balls out" mode running fighter Ops. But I still went to the Personnel Center at Randolph Field now and then to give the yea or nay to pilots outside the fraternity wanting to go to Vietnam as fighter pilots. I also helped with fighter base problems, and ran the annual Fighter Conference at Nellis Air Patch.

Regarding the latter, I had always planned to invite U.S. Navy fighter guys to the fighter blasts, but was always shot down, for some unknown reason. And some of us attended their conferences at North Island and Miramar.

Despite my many caustic criticisms of Air Force life, as may have been noticed, I have only the deepest gratitude for the way TAC handled us "Old Soldiers" as we approached the Rubicon, finding respectable assignments instead of "Special Assistant to the Whoever" — in my case delaying reorganization of the directorate, separating training, and operations until my retirement.

After the many years absent from my family, it was sheer luxury to take part in the boys' activities (especially sports), which Margee had been managing on her own, in addition to housekeeping and working. The lads weren't always pleased to have me there, especially when I was tossed out of a track meet for complaining about some elbow work in the mile relay and was almost handed my head by the football coach regarding more playing time for the boys.

My official retirement date was February 1, 1970. *The* high point of my career was my retirement party, which exceeded anything I could have imagined. There was a formal "Dining out," which included the ladies, and

A plaque presented to Jack Hayes at his retirement party in 1970; on the left is a Cavalry spur, on the right is the spur worn in the F-104 Starfighter.

followed the strict format derived from the Royal Air Force tradition. I couldn't possibly express my grateful feelings to my "Troops" — I just hope they understand.

Most humbling was the fact that many came from so far away. Harry and Pat Hodgetts from college (a frat brother) — I'm godfather to their oldest — all the way from San Diego. Tony Levier, Chief Test Pilot for Lockheed Aviation in the days of the P-38 Lightning of World War II and the F-104 Starfighter. Tony was not only a "Sierra Hotel" fighter pilot, but a gentleman and friend. Margee's brother, John Roby, and wife Frances came from Seattle. And because the 4th Fighter Wing had been scattered to the winds, we only had a couple of Tigers, including Tony and his wife, the hospital commander, and Mike Griffin, the great Irishman from Bangkok. I know it's a mistake to acknowledge people, because you'll miss some and hate yourself forever!

I gave a short — for me — thank you speech, acknowledging Margee Lou as the "Woman Behind the Man." I had to go out doing something different, so I reached the podium and announced, "Any fighter pilot what cain't jitterbug is a queer!" You should have seen the fracas. I forgot that the head tables were elevated and damn near collapsed the whole arrangement!

I didn't say goodbye and thanks to so many guests — hope they understand that there was a problem finding my head the next morning.

Onward and upward? How could anything be more "on" and "up" than all this?

Chapter 17

Civilian Life

$\mathcal{I}$ PUT OUT SEVERAL BUCKS to a "professional placement agency" for a resume and sent out many copies before donning the mufti. The biggest deflation yet came when I didn't even get acknowledgment in most cases. Two or three said, in effect, "It appears that the only positions for which you are qualified are at the vice-president/executive levels, and we got plenty of them and guys lined up!"

I guess I should have made the personal approach, but I really felt guilt doing such on government time. Always the simple, naive, even virginal type. So, it being obvious that the Hayes way of life was going to descend to a level far below that of Air Force life, I turned to the classifieds.

I couldn't get interested in

I couldn't pin down what was happening to me, it was like trying to pick up mercury off a table . . . .

lawn work or ditch digging, especially "Male companion to share apartment. Must be tender in emotions, loving, and artistic!" I wanted to reply in person, just to really shake up he (?) of tenderness, love, and artistry! But Margee wouldn't let me.

At last: "Multi-apartment manager needed. Skilled in personal relations, planning, management, and business acumen." Who better qualified than the Ole Tiger?

At my interview with the owner, I had my first contact with the civilian attitude toward military service retirees: "You're getting retirement pay so it is obvious that you should work for around one-half what the job pays." I agreed to the pittance offered, probably because my self-esteem was by then at the lowest.

At the apartment office the next a.m., we had a sorta "Change of Command" ceremony, except that the previous manager was absent, having been deep-sixed sometime previous. The maintenance personnel were fine, but I got the tight-lipped, thoroughly turned-off treatment from the assistant manager, who had expected to fill the vacancy.

I couldn't pin down what was happening to me, it was like trying to pick up mercury off a table — I just knew that I had a problem. I felt like the German soldier in World War II who encountered an African-American GI armed with a straight razor with which he swiped at the enemy. Said the German, "Ha, ya missed me." And the Yank replied, "Yeah? Le's hear ya whistle 'Lili Marlene.'" Maybe not a good analogy unless you've cut yourself with a razor; you finally realize that you're getting sliced up, but it's too late!

I should pass over those days, but I think the experiences may be of interest to others who have made the trip back to civilian life. And I acknowledge that many are eminently successful, who even became millionaires, which tells you something about my abilities.

My return to civilian life after 30 years in the military was a shocker. I was determined to meet the challenge and put in seven-day weeks and long days, but finally gave notice after a few months. I felt good the way it ended: a drunken tenant came by the office and announced his intentions to commit mayhem on me. Seems I had been bothering him about rent payments. I left him napping on the grass — not one of my more worthy pugilistic endeavors, of which there were few.

A nice lady was doing good things to my knuckles when the downed gladiator returned to the arena with a wingman, just as drunk as he was, and not much bigger. It took a little longer and I bruised some more knuckles, but they gave up before I did — but still hadn't paid the rent. I returned to the office, phoned in my two weeks' separation notice, and carried a billy club around for the last days, but had no more encounters.

With approaching fall 1970, I was still among the out of work, and was so desperate that I found myself watching transports in and out of Langley. Now that's desperate!

Stephen decided that football scholarships were more plentiful in the West, while Patrick wanted to graduate from Hampton High. So, with our usual priorities, Stephen and I were off to Seattle to live with John and Frances, Margee Lou's brother and sister-in-law. I was earning my keep and some tobacco/booze money helping John move to new warehouses and offices. I went to Steve's football games and didn't get in many fights, hardly.

Margee and Pat stayed behind while she was selling the house, and joined us after Christmas to start house-hunting, again, while Pat stayed with Air Force friends in Virginia.

Then it was back to Virginia for Pat's graduation and one of my finer accomplishments. He had never been the pushy type, so I wanted to be sure that this was an epic day. I went up and down the bleachers telling the audience that "This Patrick Hayes is all alone and let's make him feel good when his name is called." You should have heard the roar when his name was called! One of my finest moments, and his, too, he tells me.

Back in Seattle, Margee's brother John was checking around for a flying job for this old Tiger. His banker came up with a commuter airline that was maybe interested in hiring a co-pilot, at minimum — *real* minimum — wages. I found out later that their interest had nothing to do with my qualifications, but the possibility of my brother-in-law investing some of his mega-bucks in what turned out to be a losing cause.

I was hired as a "Co-Jo" — copilot — and approached the new career with abysmal lack of preparation and knowledge. Now I know that I should have attended civilian flight schools and learned about the new way of aviating. I even reported for the first flight without a current medical and, by the way, with no time in the BE-99. I got the medical, but still made the first trip as a rookie — carrying passengers, yet!

Even with my civil aviation innocence, I had misgivings about some of the operations — flying with a questionable engine (you only had two!), summertime loads off the maximum limit charts, ignoring the MEL (Minimum Equipment Lists), which said, "Don't go if some of these things ain't working," and more.

As my flying time increased I was granted "Left seat privilege," meaning that I could fly from the captain's seat as long as there was a captain in the right seat to guide my faltering steps. I passed the FAA written exam (the second time), for Air Transport Pilot Rating, which was required for captain position.

I noticed on the flight schedules some "training flights" with two or three pilots and an instructor, and wondered why I wasn't included. Being a fighter pilot, I wasn't concerned, having the "I can fly this airplane and the Gawd damned box it came in" attitude. I found out later that my days were numbered ever since my bro-in-law cold-shouldered the investment invitation, the only attraction I had to the company brass. (Ole John didn't make all his bucks on bad deals!)

I probably should have bailed out when I discovered early that the president and chief pilot were former navigators, and I'll let that statement stand for whatever interpretation it suggests. But I blundered on.

My first FAA check ride for the ATP rating was ghastly — marginal, in that I made the rating, but I was not granted the BE-99 Type Rating required to fly as captain. A recheck was scheduled for 90 days.

I figured that there would be training flights scheduled to overcome my inadequacies, but there was no mention, and I wasn't about to plead (proud but not very bright). The night prior to my recheck, we landed at Walla Walla, Washington, for an overnight — me and Captain Ron Berry, about whom there will be more later.

I mentioned that I would turn in early since I had to deadhead to Spokane the next morning for my "last chance." Ron asked how many training flights I had flown since the bad one and when I replied "nil," he exploded. Off we went at midnight, and he tried to teach me in two hours what should have been covered in 10 to 20. My check flight results were as expected, the most humiliating day in a life with some low points, but none because of shortcomings in ability. Until this!

I figured I'd be looking out that right window for as long as employed — undoubtedly for a short time — and had decided that airline work wasn't for me, anyway. A brilliant conclusion.

Termination of employment occurred fairly soon, not because I had been found wanting, but for *union* activities! *Me!* Unions had been sniffing around, and the president allowed that it would be peachy if the pilots formed a company union. Yes, sir; we had a pilot meeting at my house, approved a draft contract, and elected Ron Berry as president.

A few days later Ron, another captain, and I got "Yer fired" letters waiting at Seattle. They both had families and I suggested they appeal, announcing that I was "outta there." They were rehired, and I was onward and upward!

I have to tell more about Captain Ron Berry, who picked me up off the canvas and started me on a new civilian flying career, for no reason except that's the kind of guy he is!

He is one of the rare breed with natural talent and love of competition who excels at everything they do. I only observed his flying in the commuter airline and when he instructed me getting FAA Instructor's tickets, but he was red hot, one of the best! Had I been able to get him into aerobatics, he would have been a top competitor and/or airshow pilot.

Ron gave me the instruction qualifying me for the Flight Instructor, single and multi-engine airplane, Instrument Flight Instructor, and I'm sure he got me on with Queen City Aviation at Boeing field where he was instructing part-time — when not flying the airline, building a home, and raising a family!

With my keen hindsight, I realized that this was the way I should have started my venture into civilian flying. There would have been no reason to join the different world of airline flying, but if I had, I would have done a hell of a lot better!

Since I had instructed most of my "blue suit" time, I was looking forward to the same in civilian life, and it provided some of my most rewarding and satisfying aviating days. There was remarkable similarity to SAC days; almost as much rigid uniformity and standardization, as well as check flights.

I worked my way up to Chief Flight Instructor and Air Taxi Chief Pilot, mainly because the young troops in those jobs built up enough flying time to move on to corporate and airline careers. My progression, by the way, encountered considerable opposition from some FAA gents.

Working with the Federal Aviation Administration inspectors and supervisors, I made some good friends, a couple of bitter enemies, and neutrality from the rest. (In my life, it seems that I generally elicited one of two extremes of opinion, the highest regard or the lowest, and I can only hope that the majority were of the former!)

I sensed a problem early on when I made my first visit to the FAA to take the written exam for Air Transport Pilot. The application called for a breakdown of flying time — day, night, instrument, dual, solo, *ad infinitum.* I showed the inspector my Air Force logbook with 10,000 plus hours, and the "simp" told me to break down the time by the above categories. Just before I told him what he could do with his application, his boss yelled, "What the hell's a matta wit you?" and I was over another hurdle.

Some of my most pleasant memories came from teaching and giving check rides on the "how to's" of aviating, from teens to the middle-aged. It was impossible to be bored in the face of rapture and delight displayed by the flying newcomers. We had the highest percentage of course completions, successful flight checks, and those continuing on to the higher ratings. And, numbers hired by airlines. We were "Sierra Hotel!"

My first conflict with the FAA came from a mid-level chief with a low regard for military pilots in general, and me in particular. He made inane decisions that were engraved in gold and impervious to logical argument. His claim to fame, extolled at great length, was some time as a civilian instructor in the North American T-6 Advanced Trainer. It's possible that the conflict arose when I allowed that, "I knew lot's a little girls who were qualified in all the bombers 'n fighters en ferried 'em all around. More contribution to the war effort than strappin' a T-6 to yer rear!"

I spent many hours trying to get his approval for the various flight and ground training courses, which had already been approved by the administrator, but he made me retype every course outline! And then he wouldn't even schedule me for flight check as Chief Flight Instructor or Chief Pilot, Commuter Air Operation.

All was saved, for a while, when a friend gave me both flight checks while "Mushhead" was on vacation — a break that he sorely needed and deserved, I'm sure. There was nothing he could do when he returned since the paperwork was approved and forwarded. Anyway, he had orders for reassignment (to a higher position, of course), and was busy covering his tracks.

Then, more trouble. We got an inspector with a reputation as a hatchet man, and I had to hurl the gauntlet at his feet. He had been chief pilot at one of the general aviation companies and had been notorious for unlawful (or at least shady) carrying-ons. So he joined the FAA!

It wasn't long before the guy was nosing around, a lot more than I thought necessary; he didn't like the paperwork, our folks, me, the offices, my classrooms, me, *et al.* The problem was obvious, but I wasn't about to bail out.

Then students returned, with a terse note stating that the recommendation was improper and would have to be submitted correctly before a check flight could be administered. So it had to be completely redone, when all it really needed was a written correction. After a few, I approached his seniors and got the run-around. We got *real* careful, but it didn't help much.

Next, he came for a no-notice observation of a six months' proficiency check for an air taxi pilot, who was one of my sharpest lads. It was a beautiful flight, but "Peter Pilot" handed me two pages of things the kid did wrong and said he'd be back to recheck. We were in the second floor classroom and I told him that if he didn't get out I'd throw him out the nearest window — without opening it!

Finally, he flunked my student on an Air Transport Rating flight check because he followed a procedure that would be dangerous in one type of airplane, but had *nothing* to do with the one he was flying! So I took the problem back to the higher echelons and they did take him off our company, but we met again later.

After a while, I found that the straight-and-level flight instructing ("Now do one to the right," etc.), and thousands of takeoffs and landings began to pall. I could say that I looped and rolled the Cessna single-engines, the double-breasted ones, and the Beech Baron, which belonged to the company owner, but I won't. And I have no idea why there was a high malfunction rate in the gyro instruments of those airplanes!

Next came a new chapter and rescue from ennui with a visit from a flying cadet roommate and great friend named Cliff Patton, an example of the saying, "Only the good die young." He owned a Bellanca Decathlon aerobatic two-seater and it took one flight for me to be seduced.

With the help of my friendly banker, some loans on life insurance policies, and Margee Lou's understanding, I bought a factory Decathlon and
brought it to Boeing Field in February 1973. It had the basic paint on it,
white, and the Thunderbird paint scheme was added at Boeing.

I felt that the paint job reflected my Air Force pride, but I understand
that there was some resentment from some current and former Thunderbird pilots. But I really didn't care, since I had flown on three aerobatic
teams in three different fighters, including the Mustang.

Redemption came at my first performance at Paine Field, Washington,
and the Thunderbirds were there. After the first show, the Air Force
ground crew asked if I would taxi to the Thunderbird parking area. They
had pulled Number One out of the five-ship "V" and hauled *78ML* into
position. (The "78ML" stood for Margee Lou and her birthday, July 8th.)

I noticed an absence of officers on the scene, but luxuriated in the attention of the non-coms. Several pictures were taken and I later received
copies, annotated with "The Littlest Thunderbird," and was informed that
the pic would be in the Thunderbird Hall of Fame at Nellis AFB. I don't
believe that happened, but I will always appreciate the courtesies of the
Thunderbird ground crews.

I flew the Paine Field show my second year of civil aerobatics, but I had
a real thriller the first year. I was invited to perform at the dedication of the
new airport at Ketchikan, Alaska, through the auspices of a student from
there. I was the only performer and had a ball.

I leaped off from Boeing with the Queen City manager — who accompanied me to witness the dedication — in the back. He was a non-pilot,
portly, and with the baggage we were well over maximum weight. I know
that he experienced regrets when he saw the terrain under us for most of
the trip.

We had seven hours of flying, with stops at Vancouver and Port Hardy,
Canada, before landing at Ketchikan. We were offered typical Alaskan
hospitality: the deal called for en route expenses, three days there, and a
performer's fee, but after the three days I only paid for the hotel room.
Most of the drink and meal tabs seemed to disappear.

Dedication/airshow day had low ceilings with unlimited visibility and
the FAA monitor asked what I needed for a low show. Being my first civil
do, I hadn't planned for such, but I answered "One thousand feet," with no
idea of the maneuvers that could be done safely at that altitude.

His reply was, "I'll give you fifteen hundred. Less than that, the show's off, or you can fly back and forth with no aerobatics." He turned out to be a good troop.

On the first pass I did an aileron and barrel roll off the deck, I pulled up vertically for a hammerhead turn around and was into the soup at 900 feet. I have no idea what the maneuver was, except that it was spooky, but I did end up going the other way, which was the idea.

Mickey was on the microphone and told me that the FAA fella wanted to know the height of the clouds. Without thinking and with my inherent honesty, I replied, "Nine hundred feet."

The FAA monitor asked, "What did he say?"

Mickey saved the day with quick thinking: "Fifteen hundred feet."

The FAA good guy replied, "That's what I thought he said!"

I spent the next 30 minutes in and out of clouds and had no idea how close the maneuvers were to what they were supposed to be! I'm told that the spectators had a great time betting on where I'd come tumbling out of the clouds, and in what gyrations. (In case the statute of limitations doesn't apply, I was never over or toward the crowd.)

I stayed another week giving aerobatic rides and instruction, 20 hours worth, which paid mighty handsomely. I did the servicing, but had to pay for a tire and plug change. The airplane was outfitted for instrument flight, but the primary instruments went bananas and I didn't want to pay the local rates for repair. Anyway, I *thought* I could fly home in visual conditions.

Another farewell party and I was off for Seattle. Since the reporting weather stations are few and far between in Alaska and Canada, and what forecasts they had were not too shiny, I decided to make a short hop to Prince Rupert for the latest weather "poop."

The "weather guesser" at Prince Rupert allowed that I could *probably* stay visual by flying down the coastline and over water, but "Ya can never tell." About 35 minutes out of Prince Rupert, I saw that it was a "never can tell" day and scampered back, where they suggested I stay the night because it would probably be better in the morning.

I bummed a ride to a local motel, which happened to include a bar as an attraction. It was early in the evening, but I figured that someplace nearby it was bound to be after 5:00, the "witching hour," so I conducted myself accordingly. I made some Canadian friends — due, I think, to the rounds I bought rather than my sparkling personality.

Out of Prince Rupert the next morning, I was surrounded by "No sweats" and glowing forecasts, which soon turned dark brown, and I was getting mighty low on the water. But I pressed on, for two reasons: the first was "Get-home-itis" (which has done in many jocks); the second was because of a phone call just before takeoff. It seems that during the previous night's gaiety I reneged on a bet I had lost — something about who could slide the farthest across the dance floor on their stomach, and stop closest to a spot. I believe it's called "precision landing."

I vaguely recalled the contest, but had no idea of the wager, or who won, for that matter. Before I could request clarification, the caller stated that he didn't want to delay my departure and that I could leave the money with the weather folks. And, by the way, if the debt wasn't settled, he would gladly visit Boeing Field and "pull yer haid out thru yer rear end," I believe the phrase was. Thus, my motivation to press on!

The difficulty in flying down the coastline is that there isn't just one — coastline, that is. I was constantly meeting open water spaces and wasn't sure whether it was an inlet or a change in coast direction. So I had to hold a general heading and hope that land would reappear, which it kept doing, for a while.

I was down to 20 or 30 feet over the water and slowed down so I could turn around before the clouds and water met, which I could see was about to happen, and the engine was overheating due to the slow speed.

Besides all those things, I was approaching the point where I wouldn't have enough gas for the return to Prince Rupert. So I made a skidding turn, to keep from dragging the wingtip, and headed back from whence I had come, and it was praying time! Zero everything, so I had to keep skidding. A 30-foot ceiling is better than none — not much, but better.

The panic level was at Mach 1+ with maximum "pucker factor," when I stumbled across a sand beach — shallow crescent shape, short (800 feet when I paced it off), tall trees at both ends, and with Hayes luck, the tide was out! I had been wondering what there would be left of me and my airplane when I ditched, and then I came across what looked as good as La Guardia International!

I couldn't figure out the wind, but felt it would be best to land north since the tree line angle from the beach was less. I found out when I got my seaplane rating that wind can be determined from the way the water acts, but that didn't help this situation at all.

It would not have been possible to stop if I approached over the trees, so I came in, left turn, belly up to the tree line, wing just off the water, and low, *low* airspeed. Then I kicked it level, cut throttle, skipped a couple of times, and stopped with a little beach to spare.

I had transmitted on "emergency" frequency and did the same on the transponder, but I knew it was "no joy" because of the scarcity of radar/radio stations and my low altitude. I unstrapped the emergency transponder/transmitter and found the battery healthy, but I soon realized that I was off airways and the chances of someone aviating in that klag were weak to none.

The tide was coming in, and I knew I had to get the bird as far as possible out of the salt water. The high water line stopped a few feet short of the trees, which were fairly sparse for the first ten feet or so. I reckoned that I could push the nose between the trees and stack logs under the tail until the airplane was in a level position and, hopefully, out of the water.

I knew I was stuck with squatter's rights for three tide changes, with a night in the cockpit. I was picturing all kinds of savage beasts drooling and waiting for dark — at least bears and mountain lions, which are bad enough, and I shut my imagination off there. The night would be chilly, but I had enough clothes in my bag to bundle up, and for comfort I could curl up in the small baggage space. I moved cautiously, and seldom, so as not to disturb the log pile under the tail. I refused to darken the picture with concerns about mosquitos, food, and water, but they did come to mind.

But soon, over the horizon and out of the murk, came the Cavalry, in the form of a small fishing boat. Mac and his wife, both Canadians, had been close enough to hear my engine, recognized an emergency, and got to the beach as I was skidding to a halt. Mac dropped anchor close in (the water was deep near the shoreline, and I would have had to swim after ditching, provided I still had the requisite parts functioning).

Mac called me a couple of times, but I guess my eardrums were still numb from fright, so he came chugging in with his outboard. I explained my plan for over-nighting, to which Mac replied, "You can't stay all night here." I had no desire to find out why, certain the reasons would be one hell of a lot worse than the bears, lions, and mosquitos, which I figured were pretty bad.

He suggested that he get the current weather and forecast between "Hayes Beach" and Port Hardy on his ship's radio. Not only was this a great idea, but his gloomy statement and the rising tide convinced me that I'd better get out of there soon. *78 Margee Lou* had sunk into the sand, so

I asked Mac if he had small jacks on board, and damned if he didn't. I later realized, with cold chills, that it would have been impossible to follow my plans for the night with the water up to my navel and "Margee Lou's" prop, and no chance for the morrow!

With Mac and his jacks came the news that if I could get by the next spit of land, about five miles down the road, I could *probably* — I hate that word! — make it to Port Hardy. With the jacks, we got the airplane turned around and the wheels up on some boards we found in driftwood.

I gave Mac my deepest thanks, got his address, strapped in, and cranked up. Takeoff would be running up to full power, holding the brakes, releasing, and "over to you, God!"

I was just starting run-up when Mac came over and beat on the window. When I opened it, Mac asked, "What happens if you don't get off?"

The answer was obvious, but I appreciated Mac's concern.

We accelerated fairly well on the sand, to the tree line where I dragged her off and turned right, wingtip barely off the sand/water, with the "stall warning" horn blasting. By the trees, I took a turn to the south under a 20-30 foot ceiling. The weather got better and we staggered into Port Hardy. I called Queen City, and they had champagne waiting at Boeing Field.

It was after working hours when I finally reached home, so the help had a glass and took off. Margee Lou — my wife, not the airplane — and I had a few and took the rest home. I had several bottles of booze delivered to Mac, by means of which I shall not divulge, with my humble thanks. You just don't find guys like that anymore! And he told me, off hand, that they had been on the way home to a wedding when they made a slight detour!

I continued teaching flying at Queen City Aviation, instructing from the first to the highest ratings, and was Chief Flight Instructor for all. This gave me great satisfaction, mainly because of the wide variation in students — teenagers to middle aged, all enraptured with the joys and new world of the flying fraternity. There can be no greater joy (with your clothes on!) than being part of a first solo. Any pilot, no matter age or experience, can recall in the most minute detail his solo, and the instructor's memories in granting that moment to the "embryo" are just as vivid.

One of my greatest experiences in civil aviation was getting to know a little ole blonde Tigress by the name of Joann Osterud — one of the greatest aerobatic, and overall pilots, to smoke around the skies. Joann was the first lady pilot hired by Alaska Airlines, and now flies for United. She performs some 30 airshows a year, including the big ones.

Jack Hayes taking off before the "missing man" formation honoring the pilot who was killed during her first show.

The "missing man" formation, in honor of the pilot who was killed during a show.

We met during my first years in the show business and she instructed for me at Queen City, part time, since flight instructor pay was equivalent to that in the Siberian salt mines. For budget reasons, Alaska furloughed a bunch and she came back full time.

She had the highest student pass rate around, and I couldn't satisfy all the requests for her as a teacher, even though she was known as *tough!* She flew with me on practice flights for Chief Pilot and Chief Flight Instructor FAA checks, which I came back from all sopping wet and talking gibberish, but the FAA ones were really pieces of cake. "That's the reason you practice," I told myself.

We also practiced together for airshows. We each had copies of the other's routine and observed. Joann took notes, but I was so impressed the first time I saw her that I could only come up with "gosh" and "gee whiz" for a critique. For this I was chastised: "How can I improve without criticism? Anyone can 'ooh' and 'ahh!'" I did better after that.

For her critique of me, she unrolled three pages of legal-size paper and proceeded to wreak havoc on my blood count and self-esteem. I did improve; there was no way that I would face *that* again!

Our student enrollments — and, most important, pass rates — were among the top in the Northwest and we had people coming from Alaska and surrounding states for training. Most satisfying to me, which I mention with my typical humility, was the number of lady pilots in our program. At one time we had nine of them as instructors and/or students. They had a large montage made for me, captioned "Jack's Angels" — a most prized possession.

On the very dismal side, there was a heartbreaking tragedy involving one of the ladies, who was one of the greatest. She had earned all of the ratings and was instructing for me. An exceptional aerobatic pilot, she bought my first Decathlon when I acquired a later model, and we worked out formation airshow routines with me flying wing. Then we broke up for single routines.

On her first show, we flew formation and singles, and I returned to Seattle for another presentation while she stayed for a singles act. I had set her altimeter where the lowest altitude would be 1,000 feet above ground, but she crashed and was killed.

I flew commercial back to get this great friend and took her body back to New Jersey for the funeral. I was heartbroken and had some real low days and nights, but honestly, I can't accept the blame for poor judgment.

Joann had 150 hours less flying time when she flew her first show than the pilot who had died. Some of the locals heaped ashes on my head for various wrongs in the matter, but you gotta accept the dangers.

I stayed with Queen City a little longer before going to another outfit on Boeing Field, initially as flight instructor and then Chief Flight Instructor. I tried to restrict my flying to student progress checks and aerobatic instruction. My airplane was on lease-back to the company, which meant that I was paid for use of the airplane as well as instructional fees — very important in keeping my banker happy.

I made a different pitch promoting aerobatic flying, "Flying Safety Through Aerobatics," which meant control of any aircraft through unusual, extreme attitudes. This approach was enhanced considerably by several fatal accidents caused by small aircraft flying into jet engine wake turbulence — one of which happened on the approach to Boeing Field.

Entering the turbulence, a vortex of several hundred miles per hour, resulted in violent rolling or pitch-up and the mechanical reaction of opposing the induced movement caused the aircraft to end up inverted or vertical. These foreign and extreme environments led to a vertical dive or violent spin.

The students were shown the ease of recovery by continuing the roll to upright or pulling through the vertical and rolling out of the inverted. By the time things are back to normal, you are out of the vortices and can proceed on your merry way, although it's probable that most fly-folks will want to land ASAP and either kiss the ground or go to church.

So many pilots, most approaching middle age, came in for the "orientation" with these definite words: "Get this straight, I only want to learn recovery from unusual positions, none of this barnstorming, airshow stuff!" I had real satisfaction from the majority who completed the short course and had to ask, "Uh, Jack, what are these barrel, aileron, slow rolls, and loops?" From there we went to the basic and advanced aerobatics, and some even to the outside/inverted maneuvers.

One of the Seattle TV stations heard about the "safety" approach to aerobatics and wanted to make a clip about it. Their contact man said that they pictured aerobatic/airshow types as "Red hot, dashing daredevils and men of adventure." I hastened to establish myself as one of them, but more versatile!

We had a ball making the show: I flew 3 hours and 45 minutes for 12 minutes on TV. One of our chopper pilots, Mark Hanson, did a brilliant job flying the cameramen in a Jet Ranger, and the shots were hard to believe. The FAA cooperated; their chief of safety said he agreed with my approach and cited an example where a pilot in California with aerobatic training saved a multi-engine aircraft when it was flipped upside down.

I forgot an important item in mentioning my new employer. Every flight school or charter outfit had an FAA inspector assigned primary responsibility, and ours was the gent to whom I had previously sworn all kinds of bad things to his physical being. Because I needed the job, I wrote him a groveling, humble pie letter, which worked out, but it was a long time before I could keep food down!

After a year or so, the company went "belly up," and I was back on the pavement, or ramp, or runway, whatever. And so it was humble pie time again, until I was accepted by Jim Galvin's Flight Service. Jim was one of the finest gentlemen, pilots, and friends. I taught aerobatics only; it seems I was suspect with the junior brass and never really felt on the team without Jim around. But the chance to meet Jim Galvin made it all worthwhile!

A drawing by employees of Jim Galvin's Flight Service.

Jack and Margee Lou Hayes in front of the first *78 ML*, a Bellanca Decathlon aerobatic trainer.

The second Bellanca Decathlon trainer, *278 ML*.

I finally taught more courses, and had one great blast! A request came for a formation flight of two Cessna 150s, two-place trainers, for a TV station to advertise that they would have not one, but *two* airplanes on "traffic watch." The chief charter pilot wondered why it hadn't come to him and when I explained that it involved close formation, damned if he didn't want to try! That would have been an epic show!

Me and the other pilot, a nice lad as Number One, were out of Boeing at 3:00 in the a.m., night formation, for Tacoma Industrial airpatch across the Sound. We were briefed: over the runway with me in trail, lead descends and I go to right wing as we go to the deck.

First of all, I was almost wiped off in the trees when the lead started down too soon, which I clarified; then on every pass the head honcho was yelling, "Closer and lower!" We were almost dragging the wheels, which took care of the "lower," and I called lead with, "Next time this guy says 'closer,' look out yer right window." This he did, once, and I thought he was going to bail out!

When we were on the ground, someone asked him what he saw when he looked out, and he replied, "His wingtip almost rubbing my window!"

Again, we flew almost three hours for a 15-second blurb! The TV folks sure got their money's worth out of Jack!

The airshow days, from 1974 to 1982, let me play fighter pilot again; there were 20 different locations, and I flew three, four, and five years at many. I flew four shows at Paine Field, Washington. We had a magnificent time until they brought someone new in to run the program. I spent five years at Nanaimo, British Columbia, some of the happiest. Roger Ball, his lovely wife, Barb, and their sweet daughter were friends you hope for, and the other locals were a pleasure. One show was held with the "Bath-tub Races," and you have to see it to believe it! The loggers come down from the mountains and house trailers are brought in to serve as auxiliary jails!

I flew five years at Corvallis, Oregon, until they went commercial, but my heart attack had come along by then, anyway. The other Canadian shows I flew were Abbotsford and Vanderhoof. One show, at Vancouver, Washington, was a gathering of antique and home-built aircraft. Performers fly for free, and I don't know why I got so generous in my routine except it was a great bunch of people for whom I almost spread myself and *278 ML* all over the countryside.

I performed the usual inside/outside tricks in my typical airshow maneuvers, but I started and concluded with crowd "gaspers." These were practiced countless times and under all possible atmospheric conditions, but some of the fraternity felt that they were dangerous and that I had only marginal control.

To end the show at Vancouver, I came down the runway, or crowd line, on the deck and at the airspeed red line; sharp pullup to vertical, with some airspeed left, hard left and full forward stick, with simultaneous full right rudder.

I was looking for a *lomcevak* — a maneuver whose name actually means "headache" in Czech and consists of a cartwheel to an inverted spin to a normal spin — but I didn't always get it. And the Decathlon aircraft wasn't supposed to be capable of it. What I got was, at least, a nasty, inverted, outside snap roll, which I'm told was quite a sight from the ground and was something to see from the cockpit!

We were soon in a power-on spin, and the throttle was chopped to idle, for a regular spin. When I could pick out the rocks and weeds on the ground, I recovered from the spin and made inverted or normal recovery, depending on the altitude. I'm told there were lots of gasps and folks on their feet, which made me very happy, being the real ham.

My usual crowd gasper at the beginning of the show was to take off, let the airspeed build, nose up, and roll inverted. I had full control, but when inverted would let the nose drop sharply, which made it look like Ole Jack was about to bust his rear! Some performers felt that I was out of control and after Joann saw it a couple of times, she said she wished I would take the roll out of the act.

On that fateful day in Vancouver, I was in the takeoff slot when some weenie in an amphibian buzzed the runway, which was officially closed. This type of airplane leaves bunches of turbulence with all the garbage he has hanging out, so I told show control that I'd hold for a minute for the air to smooth out.

But I still got a real jolt as I lifted off, and even though I let more speed build up, it wasn't enough. At the vertical, there was a *real* bump and the left wingtip touched the ground! With momentum into the roll, I continued to inverted, climbed, back to upright and in for a landing.

The FAA cleared me for a one-time flight back to Boeing Field, and I borrowed a Decathlon from a nice guy for the Sunday show. He insisted on "no roll on takeoff," but he had nothing to worry about!

In March 1982, five days after the formation-flying for the TV commercial, I joined the ranks of those with heart glitches! I was 63 years old, flying three to five hours a day, instructing and flying check flights for everything from private pilot ratings to multi-engine transport ratings. And, bunches of aerobatics. Sometimes I worked six- and seven-day weeks, still managing three racquetball sessions per week. My flight surgeon couldn't believe the news, which tells you something about him!

A couple of nights before my "flame-out," I felt some heartburn, laid on the Alka Seltzer, which seemed to work until the third night, when it was obvious that I was having a "biggie."

Ever the thoughtful husband, I drove myself to the nearest hospital. That was the closest I ever came to losing Margee, and she had been given more than enough provocation! She learned of the situation when the call came after midnight saying, "Your husband is in intensive care here with a heart attack."

A couple of weeks under TLC, back home with only 25 percent heart damage, I loafed until the "wall-climbing" syndrome arrived. I never got the FAA to renew my Medical Certificate, for reasons which I will not address here, but have maintained my Instructor's Certificate.

I had the privilege of teaching a good friend, Marion Spath, through commercial, instrument, flight, and instrument flight and instructor tickets — a retired school teacher who would have made a fine fighter pilot!

Then came one of the highlights in a flying career with bunches of them, and a real memory reviver. Joann Osterud asked if I would give her dual and certify her as qualified in a P-51 Mustang. It seems that either the few pilots acceptable to the owner weren't available or refused to give dual in a fighter with nothing but an intercom in the rear seat!

I accepted immediately, which may tell you something about me, but actually it was a matter of my high regard for Joann's unmatched pilot ability, which was more than justified in her 26 hours of dual instruction, after which I soloed her. I would have let her go solo after four flights, but she had to be satisfied, not me.

On about the eighth flight we had partial engine failure at 500 feet on

Jack Hayes, flying a Decathlon in the "*lomcevak*" maneuver.

Airshow pilot Joann Osterud, of Oxnard, California, and her Ultimate 10-300S stunt plane.

Joe Reeves, Washington, UT

takeoff ("partial" meaning three-fourths!). She handled it beautifully, despite my high-pitched gibberish from the rear. She flew four airshows, flawlessly, until the Mustang was put on the market.

I'll never forget the nice spring day we taxied out for the first flight. Pilots, students, mechanics, *et al.*, ran out of buildings at the unmistakable Mustang sound, and there was mass shock at the sight of long, blonde hair streaming from the front seat. The easily read lips were saying, "It's a girl!"

Joann Osterud is now a first officer for United Airlines, but even more importantly, in 1989 she set a new *world record* for consecutive outside, or inverted, loops — 208 of them! In the summer of 1991, she eclipsed the former time and distance inverted flight records by flying upside down for 658 miles in four hours, 38 minutes, and ten seconds. And on July 4th, 1994, Joann set a record for the first inverted double-ribbon cut over water at Commencement Bay off Tacoma, Washington. Talk about a Tiger!

For what it's worth — I've said it all in what goes before this — I'm humbly thankful for the experiences, events, and especially the people, making up this life. I've had a hell of a good time!

Index

by Lori L. Daniel